Jessie's Grove

Jessie's Grove

ONE HUNDRED YEARS

in the

SAN JOAQUIN VALLEY

WANDA WOOCK

[redacted]

ISBN 0-9759964-0-1
Photographs on the cover, pages 13 and 170—by Lewis Kemper
Printed in Singapore

VERA, THE GRAND LADY WHO LIVED TO BE 102 YEARS OLD, WAS A SECOND GENERATION NATIVE OF THE TOWN OF LODI. VERA CARED ABOUT THE PAST AND SAVED THE DOCUMENTS FROM THE HOME WHERE SHE WAS BORN, AND FROM THE SPENKER HOME WHERE HER MOTHER JESSIE WAS BORN. WITHOUT VERA, THIS BOOK WOULD NOT EXIST.

I dedicate this book to my beloved aunt, Vera B. Perrin.

Acknowledgments

THERE ARE MANY PEOPLE who helped me with this book. Their patience, knowledge, and perseverance were inspirational to me. Needless to say, the book would have been impossible without their help. They all have my deepest thanks. I will introduce a few of these people to the reader, and briefly describe their contributions to my book.

Gabriele Libhart and her mother, Charlotte Eisenmann, spent endless hours translating the 113 German letters Jessie had saved from 1894 to 1952.

Steve Von Berg, a high school teacher of United States history, worked many hours carefully checking time sequences, and adding to the historical framework with details to some of the major events in the book.

Maynard Smith, shared stories and pictures about his great-grandfather Jacob Brack, the man who played such an important role in early Central Valley history.

Sandy Smith and Behjat Kerdegari from the Lodi Library, patient and resourceful, were a wonderful help in the long hours of research.

Oscar Bacon, with the Heidrick Agricultural History Center in Woodland, identified many harvester pictures and took me on several personal tours of his outstanding museum. For some pictures he did extensive time-consuming research. His recommendations for reference material proved excellent.

Kyle Williams Wyatt, with the Sacramento Railroad Museum, answered many questions over the phone for me. He quickly came up with the explanation for the "clickety clack" sound Anna always referred to when telling her story of riding the transcontinental railroad.

Anders Christensen, director of Woodbridge Irrigation District, gave me factual information, encouragement, and resources to use.

Leonard Thompson, a prominent local farmer, provided many facts about the Woodbridge Vineyard Association's history. He also made valuable additions to the story of the Lodi grape industry.

Pastor Robert Fickenscher, provided a copy of the dramatic letter from his uncle on the San Francisco earthquake of 1906. His uncle, a Lutheran minister, had mailed copies to ministers in other Lutheran churches including Jessie's church in Lodi.

Janet Babbitt, legal assistant to Richard Konig, provided expert critiquing and put together the family tree.

Betty Ann and Chuck Spenker, owners of Spenker Winery, provided information of their family history and the harvesting crew picture in the second chapter. Betty Ann identified the men.

Don Peirano contributed the World War I painting from his art collection.

Sue Warmouth, my friend, spent many hours typing and providing technical computer assistance.

My responsive readers who checked for errors and offered helpful suggestions: Del Woock—my brother, Brenda Morgan—aspiring author and daughter, Betty Macomb—museum docent at San Joaquin Historical Society and retired history teacher, Delta College, Del Macomb—retired history instructor, Delta College, Marilyn Cook—docent at San Joaquin Historical Society, and Annie Smith—curator of collections and exhibits and on the staff of San Joaquin County Historical Society.

The supportive professionals who wrote the comments on the back cover:
Christie Kennedy Weybret—journalist and author of "Lodi A Vintage Valley Town.
Mark Chandler—Executive Director of Lodi—Woodbridge Winegrape Commission.
Airi Kulpa—retired professional journalist and honored community leader of Santa Clara, listed in the Second Edition of the International Directory of Distinguished Leadership.
Ralph Wetmore—retired educational leader in the Lodi Community.

Al Bechthold, my husband, never tired of talking about the book over the years of its creation. His interest in the Civil War and railroad history has led him to read countless books over the past twenty years. This background has added to the book, along with his vivid memories of the Great Depression and his knowledge of farming. He not only has been patient and supportive, but also a valuable resource person.

Thank you everyone!

Contents

Introduction

THE YEARS FROM 1852 THROUGH 1952 brought dramatic challenges and achievements to the United States: a devastating civil war settled, two world wars fought and won, a severe depression overcome, and achievements of science and technology that amazed the entire world. It was a period of time that created challenges unique in history—both for complexities of change and extreme contrasts. Four people in my family lived during those years, and their history has been preserved and recorded. Through their true stories you can imagine what it was like to live way back then—especially as a farmer, or a woman, or a young man who wanted to do anything but farm. Joseph and Anna Spenker, and their children—Jessie and Otto, experienced those years in the Lodi and Stockton area of the San Joaquin Valley.

Come—read through these pages and meet:

JOSEPH SPENKER, the original pioneer who died before I was born, but his strong image made a lasting impact on everyone who knew him. Even today, when I walk on his ranch among the oak trees he so deeply loved, I feel his presence.

ANNA SCHLIEMANN SPENKER, the little old lady who sat in her rocking chair and knitted yard after yard of delicate lace. Anna, looking at me through her tiny wire glasses, would keep me entranced with story after story as she rocked back and forth. She would describe in vivid detail her experiences in those long ago days—creating a living picture as she led me to see what it was like to live way back then. With any pause, her fingers would resume their busy occupation of creating the beautiful lace.

OTTO SPENKER, their son, I remember but I did not know him. I did not get acquainted with Otto until I read his journals, letter after letter he had written, and dusted off treasures he had saved. Otto was a prolific writer, the primary communicator in this story. Otto—the dreamer, the inventor, the artist, the tender-hearted God-fearing man, always tried to find a better way to accomplish daily tasks. The vast majority of photographs in this book are from his camera. Through his writings and photographs, Otto left behind a rich legacy.

JESSIE SPENKER BECKMAN, their daughter, strong in character like her father Joseph. I knew her the best of the four and deeply loved her. Her strength, intelligence, and courage to tackle any project has been an inspiration to me all my life.

The details of this book were gleaned from the family diaries, letters, photographs, legal papers, receipts, sheet music, and postcards that Jessie's daughter Vera saved over the course of the 102 years of her life. Writing down many of the stories she heard as she grew up, Vera was the beginning historian—I have been the gatherer and coordinator. In writing this history, I have retained the social and racial slurs found in documents to give an honest portrayal of the attitudes of that period of time. I briefly described the unique period of history these four people were living through, to give the reader a factual framework. I have attempted to recreate the early stories as Anna told them to the family. The later periods of time relied on the wealth of Otto's writings and Jessie's records, collections and written comments. In doing so, I acknowledge I have put my inflection on the history—whether by what I chose to write about, or what I chose to leave out.

I invite you to read these pages and step back into time—step into the lives of these four people and the wide world in which they lived. I invite you to imagine what it was like to live

Way

Back

Then

in the San Joaquin Valley.

JOSEPH SPENKER

CHAPTER ONE

Immigrants and Pioneers

AMERICA, THE LAND OF OPPORTUNITY, created dreams for countless people throughout the world in the nineteenth century. Opportunities seemed endless: thousands of miles of country to explore, virgin ground to plant, freedom from political upheavals, dictatorships, and gold lying in the streambeds of California. The stories were repeated again and again among people living in Europe.

During the 1840s, 1850s, and 1860s, Europe was in turmoil. Liberal revolutions were sweeping the continent in response to the conditions produced by the industrial revolution. The disunified, feudal states that were to make up present-day Germany, experienced the chaos that swept the continent. Political upheavals that most people could not understand caused thousands to leave the country of their ancestors.

JOSEPH SPENKER

In the small village of Dargun, near the Baltic Sea, Joseph Spenker heard stories of the New World when he and his three brothers would meet with other farmers living in this northern tip of Germany. They heard about the vast open spaces, land you could homestead, rich soil to plant. The stories provoked vivid dreams in the four young men who were farming the same land their grandfather had farmed before them. The land was tired and too small to support all of them, and the tight community constrained them. The future looked bleak, and the political chaos of the time intensified their anxiety. Joseph made a decision—he would leave Germany and start a new life in the United States.

Joseph booked passage on a ship leaving from Hamburg harbor. Fifteen years later, a young woman named Anna Schliemann would embark from the same German harbor. The lives that these two California pioneers made individually and together in the San Joaquin Valley, were part of the transformation of California from the boom times of the Gold Rush to a stable, agriculture-based society that in its turn helped change the face of nineteenth-century America.

The city of New York was a dramatic change to the young man from rural Germany. Working on his father's farm all the eighteen years of his life, had given him no opportunity to travel and see the country of his birth. Now he was in a huge foreign city teeming with activity. People were rushing everywhere and speaking languages he had never heard before. In the chaos of the city, Joseph met a few German immigrants who helped him find lodging. Hearing the familiar language eased him through the first nervous days of starting life in a new country. After a short time Joseph began traveling this new country where he intended to make his home. He explored the Eastern states for a few years, trying to decide where to settle. He would work for a while to replenish his meager money supply, but nowhere appeared to fit his needs and dreams. There was always work to be had for a capable young man experienced in farming, but Joseph dreamed of owning his own land—so he kept searching.

One of Joseph's goals was to speak, read and write fluently the language of his newly adopted country. Joseph had therefore settled in Stephenson County, Illinois, for two years to attend school and to work as many hours as possible. Stephenson County was also a desirable place to settle for a time because it was one of the starting points for the trip to California, and Joseph had finally decided that would be his destination. Everyone was talking about California and the gold just waiting to be picked up, riches beyond imagination could be found! It would be difficult to remain in school for two years, but he had made his decision.

In the early spring of 1859, wagon trains started forming in the county. People gathered from all directions with wagons bulging with their possessions. Some looked like they couldn't hold one more item, let alone the people that owned the possessions. It was evident most of the people would have to walk all the way to California. The wagons pulled in and camped together, allowing the people to get to know each other before the long, hard trip.

It surprised Joseph to see so few horses. "Horses eat too much," one man told him. "They eat too much and you have to carry their food because they won't eat the prairie grass. Mules will eat the wild grasses and do fine, but those cantankerous critters are a curse to handle. I wouldn't have one on a bet." Oxen were the overwhelming animal of choice to pull the wagons because they were patient and strong, gentle and durable, and not inclined to run away. They also did very well just eating the prairie grasses. Their only problem was they were slow—they moved along at about two miles per hour. People who wanted to get to California faster could try mules, but most people didn't want to put up with the frustration and the risk. It seemed best to stay with the slow, calm, dependable oxen.

Joseph watched several trains venture out in the early spring, and in April, when a new one started to form, he decided to join the group. Joseph knew he didn't have enough money for a wagon and team, but he could buy a horse. He found a wagon that wasn't completely loaded and paid the owner to haul his few possessions and his horse feed. The horse would be useful in California and a valuable asset.

On April 15, 1859, eighteen wagons moved out—making for an impressive sight for the townspeople who cheered and waved them on. It was a beautiful day, a perfect start for this grand adventure. Joseph was now twenty three years old and on his way to California.

The wagon train took 154 unforgettable days to arrive in California—days that seemed endless. At times, they felt like they were barely moving, and at two miles per hour, that would be close to the truth. They moved so slowly that often as they were packing to leave their campsite in the morning, they could see where they would camp that night.

Joseph told only a few stories about the trip, and those often included the fear they had of the Indians. A wagon train that had left earlier in the year had been attacked by Indians and all the people had been killed. Joseph said they were always looking into the distance for Indians, and once in a while they would see one or two. One day they saw a group of Indians mounted on their horses on a bluff they were passing, silently watching them for miles and miles. Joseph said everyone held their breath, said their prayers, and quietly kept moving on.

Finally, they arrived in California. People from the wagon train were exhausted, excited, worried, and mainly impatient to get on with the life they had been dreaming about for years. Joseph had no doubt in his mind what he was going to do or the direction he would head in this unexplored state. He was going to look for gold!

Joseph arrived in Murphy's Camp, California, on September 16, 1859. He immediately became swept up in all the excitement and the stories that gold was everywhere—instant riches were to be had for anyone who cared to look. Men bragged about who had found the largest nugget, the richest claim. "Hurry, hurry, get in on it fast before it vanishes" was the general mood of the day.

Joseph looked around and rode his horse to different areas of the mining fields. Finally, he started talking to one man.

"This is a great claim" he told Joseph. " I could make a fortune here, but I just heard my wife is sick back east, and I'm going to have to leave. You want to buy my claim?"

"What do you want for the claim?" Joseph asked.

"I'm not sure, but it's worth a lot of money!"

"I don't have a lot of money."

"Well, how about trading me your horse for the claim?"

"O.K.," said Joseph, " It's a deal." With that declaration, Joseph became a gold miner. He worked the claim day after day, trying not to notice some of the miners laughing at him. Finally, one man came up to Joseph, patted him on the back, and said, "Son, you've been taken in. This claim is worthless—it has never produced anything."

Welcome to the gold fields! Joseph knew he was ten years too late for the "easy pickings" he had heard so much about when gold was first discovered, but there was a strong opinion that any day there could be another rich strike because gold was proven to be in the area. Men continued to dig for gold in the foothills of California for decades after the initial discovery in 1848 at Sutter's Mill. When the Transcontinental Railroad needed a labor force in the 1860s, the Chinese proved to be the most reliable source of labor. Other workers would work on the Railroad just long enough to get the needed money to go and look for gold one more time.

In the fall of the year 1859, Joseph had not found one flake of the elusive metal, and his money was running out. He decided to swallow his pride, leave the claim and the fields, and go to Stockton, where he hoped to find work. Stockton was the place where he thought his future could be established. He wanted to get back into farming as soon as possible and had heard the ground around the Stockton area was rich and fertile. Stockton also had a deepwater port where produce could be shipped to San Francisco. Joseph started walking to Stockton with the grand total of $1.27 to his name.

After a while, a wagon came by heading in his direction. The driver asked, "Where are you going, young man?"

"Stockton," Joseph replied.

"That's a mighty far piece to walk. You got a dollar?"

"That's about all I got."

"Well then, climb on board." Joseph gratefully joined the man in the wagon.[1]

Joseph arrived in Stockton with twenty-seven cents in his pocket. The amount of money was small, but his dreams, energy, plans, and experience gained were immense. He eagerly looked forward to his future, but first he had to get a job and earn some money.

Joseph got a job the next day at a ranch on the north edge of Stockton, a place referred to as the "Yolland Ranch," and worked as many hours as the owner would allow. His starting pay was twenty dollars a month, which included his room and board, but the extra hours he put in helped increase his monthly check. He saved every cent with the determination to develop an idea that was burning in his mind. He would haul supplies up to the gold

[1] Joseph's early years in California were recorded in: An Illustrated History of San Joaquin county, California (Chicago: Lewis Publishing Co., 1890) p. 411.

fields. He had seen how scarce food, shovels, lanterns, gunpowder, and other needed items were, and if they were available at all, they sold for exorbitant prices. Joseph quickly realized how a profit could be made by buying in Stockton and selling in the camps.

As soon as Joseph had enough money to buy the supplies to make one load, he rented a wagon, borrowed four horses from the farmer he worked for, and took off for the gold fields on the weekend, leaving before dawn. The trip took him most of the day, but it was worth every minute of the travel time. He sold everything he had at a fine profit within hours of his arrival at the mining camps, and returned home the next day.

Joseph repeated this process again and again, working all week and hauling supplies to the camps on the weekends. Soon he could afford his own wagon and horses. The next step was the purchase of an additional wagon and four more horses. He then hired a man to drive one of the wagons while he drove the other. It was a golden opportunity, and soon Joseph was making more money than even he had dreamed possible.

Joseph did not lose sight of his main reason for coming to America—he wanted to own land. Within four years of arriving in California, he bought the 385-acre Yolland Ranch where he worked. He added to these acres whenever the opportunity arose and he had enough funds to secure the land.

Land would often be offered for sale on the steps of the courthouse. Bids would be taken, and the winner immediately handed over gold coins closing the deal. With gold coins taken out of his pocket, Joseph bought many acres of land. In this manner he acquired the piece of ground across from the Yolland Ranch, 160 acres, and named it the Adobe Ranch. There was a small, modest home on this ranch where he established his residence

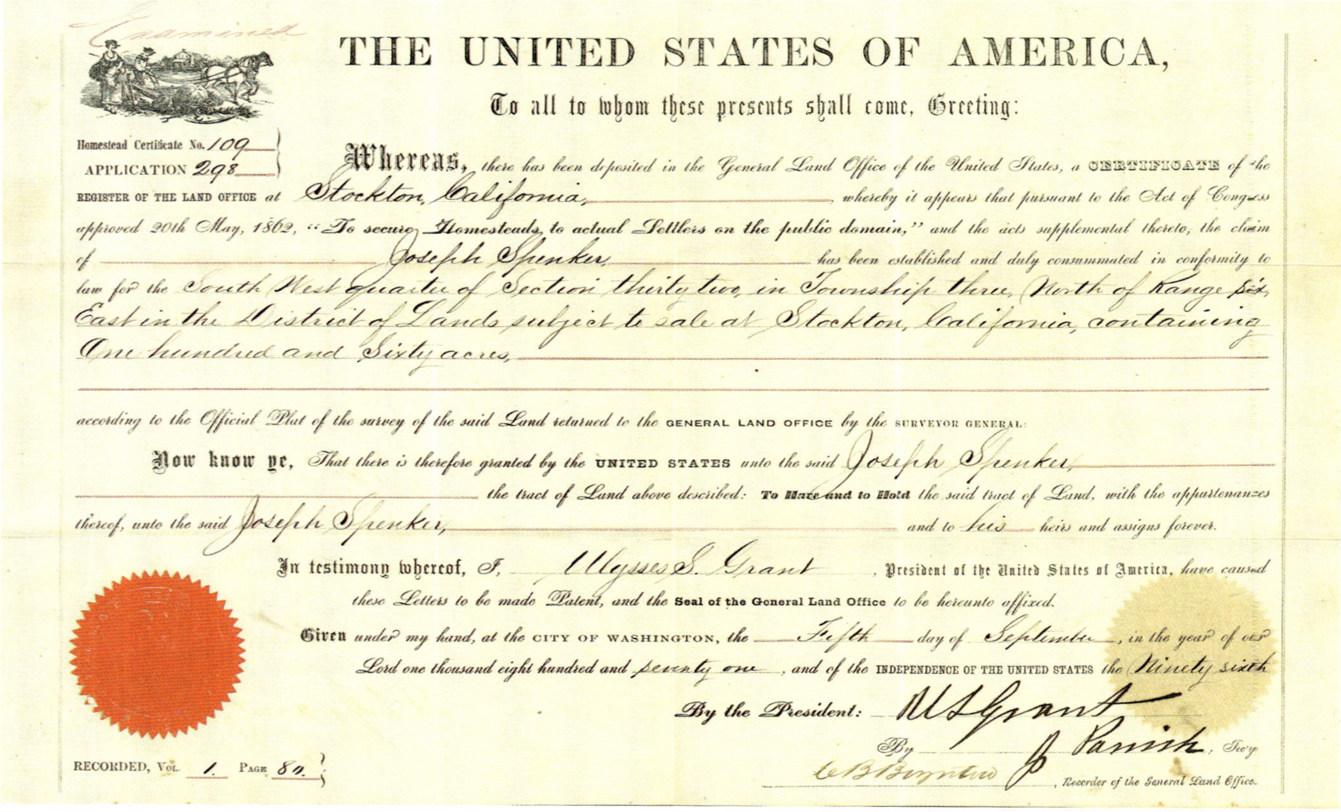

Examined

THE UNITED STATES OF AMERICA,

To all to whom these presents shall come, Greeting:

Homestead Certificate No. 109
APPLICATION 298

Whereas, there has been deposited in the General Land Office of the United States, a CERTIFICATE of the REGISTER OF THE LAND OFFICE at Stockton, California, whereby it appears that pursuant to the Act of Congress approved 20th May, 1862, "To secure Homesteads to actual Settlers on the public domain," and the acts supplemental thereto, the claim of Joseph Spenker, has been established and duly consummated in conformity to law for the South West Quarter of Section thirty two, in Township three, North of Range six, East in the District of Lands subject to sale at Stockton, California, containing One hundred and Sixty acres,

according to the Official Plat of the survey of the said Land returned to the GENERAL LAND OFFICE by the SURVEYOR GENERAL:

Now know ye, That there is therefore granted by the UNITED STATES unto the said Joseph Spenker, the tract of Land above described: To Have and to Hold the said tract of Land, with the appurtenances thereof, unto the said Joseph Spenker, and to his heirs and assigns forever.

In testimony whereof, I, Ulysses S. Grant, President of the United States of America, have caused these Letters to be made Patent, and the Seal of the General Land Office to be hereunto affixed.

Given under my hand, at the CITY OF WASHINGTON, the Fifth day of September, in the year of our Lord one thousand eight hundred and seventy one, and of the INDEPENDENCE OF THE UNITED STATES the Ninety sixth

By the President: U S Grant

By J Parrish, Secy

C B Boynton, Recorder of the General Land Office.

RECORDED, Vol. 1 Page 80

THIS WAS ONE OF THE MANY DEEDS JOSEPH ACCUMULATED IN HIS EARLY YEARS IN CALIFORNIA. JOSEPH NAMED THIS GROUND, WHICH WAS ACROSS FROM THE YOLLAND RANCH, "THE ADOBE."

A few years later, Joseph purchased another section of land farther to the north, near the small town of Woodbridge. The land had hundreds of oak trees, and although it would be work to clear some of them for planting, with the trees growing so abundantly, he knew the quality of the soil would be excellent. He later told how he had walked into the main grove and knew instantly it was his intended destination in California. He said the majestic trees towered over his head, reaching for the sky with strong limbs that were the color of damp earth. It was early spring, and the limbs ended in complex patterns of delicate branches—black lace against the clear blue sky. Here and there, a hint of pale green was showing, so slight it almost wasn't visible. As he stood in the grove, a hawk soared away from a nest in one of the trees. Soon it would be returning home, and Joseph knew that he had found his home.

The San Joaquin Valley Joseph had heard so much about was living up to his highest expectations. He had acquired over a thousand acres by 1869, and was getting the ground ready to plant a crop on which he knew he could make money—wheat. Joseph's future looked exciting, and now he was invited to a wedding where he would meet someone who had arrived in California from Germany by a similar, and yet different route.

GOING TO A WEDDING

ANNA SCHLIEMAN

ANNA

IN HAMBURG, GERMANY, in the cold winter of 1867, a young woman struggled to survive the dramatic turn her life had taken. She was Anna Schliemann, twenty one years old and in the prime of her life, but her heart was heavy with despair.

Anna had grown up in a close, loving family in Elmshorn, Germany. They had been poor, but the small family had been together. She had worked with her mother and sister, doing extra washing for other families to stretch her father's small wages. She also had started sewing as another way to help her family. When her father had become ill and could no longer work, however, their lives had become desperate. Months passed, and finally the suffering of her father was over.

A few days after the funeral, Anna's mother explained the plan for her future. She would be placed with the Scramsberry family in Hamburg, to work as an indentured servant until the money she earned was sufficient to pay off the debt incurred by her father's illness.

Indentured servitude was very common in this period, and in earlier years as well. When a sizable debt had been established and there was no foreseeable way to pay that debt, a child or adult could be placed in someone's home for a specified number of years to cover the debt. Many people who wanted to come to America, but could not afford the passage, signed indenture papers. When they arrived in America, people needing workers would pay for their voyage, and essentially they would become that person's slave for five to seven years. At times, false accusations would be made so the person had to work more years to pay off the so-called debt.

Anna said she didn't know the amount of her mother's debt, but she knew it was a large sum, and working every day from before dawn to late at night was all she could do. Her life seemed without hope. One day followed another, all the same, and for how many years? Anna, a consummate story teller, described those sad days in later years to younger generations.

"Every day I would get up before dawn, go down the stairs and gather wood for the kitchen stove from the large pile in the backyard, being careful not to slip on the ice as I had on my first day. The cold logs froze my hands and arms to the bone. I jammed the logs into their place in the stove, lit the fire, and watched the small flame grow and grow. Soon the cook arrived, and I started another day of endless work.

Two days a month, Mrs. Scramsberry allowed me time off from my work to visit my mother in Elmshorn, twenty miles away. I was so grateful to get away from the demands of those people. At times they made me feel like they owned me, and I guess they did. I would walk into Hamburg, and a close friend would take me in his carriage to Elmshorn. He would return for me the next day and give me a ride back to Hamburg in time for another month of endless work.

When I walked into Hamburg, I always went by the penitentiary. I felt drawn to the cold, dark stone walls and the tower, with its small, barred windows. My heart reached out to the people trapped inside. "I'm also trapped," I thought, "and for how long?"

One day when I walked by, looking up as I always did, I saw a hand extend through the bars and wave to me. Shocked, all I could do was give a small wave in return and in my heart wish him God's blessings. This happened again the next month. I could not see a face, only an outstretched hand. The following month, when I walked by, he held something in his hand and threw the object out toward me. I gasped—What was it? It landed in some shrubs at the base of

THE NAME INSIDE THE COVER OF THE BOOK

the tower. When I found it, I discovered it to be a small book. On the inside cover of the book was a name written in beautiful script.

I waved toward the window and continued on to my friend's house with the little book carefully tucked in my pocket. It was a prayer book to lead you away from the Devil to God. Some time later, I learned the man had been executed for murder. I treasured the book and still have it to this day.

A year passed—a year of endless days, weeks, months with every day the same. Then one day in 1869, my uncle Andrew Hansen paid a surprise visit. He said, "Anna—I'm going to America, and I want you to come with me. Your cousins Julia and Mata are coming, too."

"She can't go. It'll be years before she pays off her indentureship. She has to stay here and work!" declared Mrs. Scramsberry in an angry voice.

"We're all set to go, and I want her to come with us now!" With that declaration, Uncle Andrew pulled gold pieces from his pocket and stacked them impressively on the table. "This should change your mind. Anna, get your things."

I couldn't believe what I heard. America, freedom, a new life! My heart raced as I flew up the stairs. I pulled my small wooden trunk away from the wall and threw into it all my possessions and clothes.

Soon I was in the carriage with Uncle Andrew, clipping along the cobblestone streets of Hamburg, with my little trunk carefully tied to the back.

"Anna, we'll go by your mother's place so we can tell her goodbye, and then we'll go and pick up your cousins."

When I saw my mother, I started to cry—I knew I would never see her again. I held her close, gave her a kiss, and ran out the door. We climbed back into the carriage, Uncle Andrew put the horses into a trot, and put his arm around my shoulders. Without saying a word we continued on to pick up my two cousins. Within a few hours, we were all approaching the Hamburg harbor, where one of the biggest ships I had ever seen was tied to the dock. The ship was big, and the harbor was huge! There were ships and boats of all sizes moving in the water, and people were everywhere—all seeming to be in a frantic hurry. We were told Hamburg harbor, in 1869, was considered one of the world's leading ports.

Uncle Andrew unloaded our trunks on the dock and left Julia, Mata and me guarding them while he went off to sell the horse and carriage. Soon he returned, and we all descended down the stairs into the cold, dark, deep body of the ship where we had a designated space for the voyage across the Atlantic. It was so small! The tiny area was surrounded by people we couldn't even talk to—they all spoke languages I never heard before. Everyone seemed to be a potential enemy. We were fearful and trusted no one but each other. My heart was filled with dread thinking of the long, endless days to come in this tiny space with these strange people so close to us.

We went back up on deck just in time to see the ship cast off from the dock. It gradually moved away from land as it was pulled out to the center of the harbor by a small rowboat. Soon the ship was moving under its own power. Some of the sails had been raised, and they caught enough of the gentle breeze to move us slowly along the sixty-nine miles of the Elbe to the open sea. I was thrilled with this part of the trip. We were going through the beautiful country of my birth. I knew I would never see it again, and I tried to imprint the impressions on my mind to treasure forever."

ANDREW HANSEN, THE COURAGEOUS MAN WHO TOOK THREE YOUNG WOMEN HALFWAY AROUND THE WORLD IN 1869.

ANDREW HANSEN

AMERICA! THEY WERE ALL ACTUALLY ON THEIR WAY TO AMERICA in this wonderful year of 1869. Andrew Hansen and his wife had dreamed of this day for years. When his wife died in 1865, Andrew continued the dream for the sake of his nieces. Life was hard in Germany, and opportunities were limited, especially for young women. Andrew wanted to get the girls to the United States where they could have a chance at a better life.

One of Andrew's nieces, Julia, was promised in marriage to a man named "Little Joe" Spenker, who lived in Stockton, California. The marriage had been arranged for the two young people, but getting Julia to California was almost impossible since the United States was embroiled in a Civil War. Finally the war was over and Andrew seized the first opportunity to finalize the trek. Julia's sister Mata would also accompany them to California. Anna, the daughter of Hansen's younger sister, Marie, had increased the urgency of the trip when she was placed out as an indentured servant. Marie had tearfully pleaded with him to include Anna in his plans. He readily agreed—no niece of his would be a slave for anyone!

Andrew knew several families who were settled in California that could help Mata and Anna, and he contacted them. Being responsible for three young ladies increased the need for care, and so Andrew made detailed plans. The boat trip to New York would be difficult, but the necessary first step.

When Anna talked about her trip across the Atlantic, she would just shudder and say, *"Oh Julia and I were so sick! We had to stay in a dark, crowded room, deep down inside the ship for days and days! All I can remember is being sick!"* Based on comparable ships that left from the same harbor with New York their destination, the voyage probably took from sixteen to twenty-eight days.

Crossing the Atlantic had been just the beginning of Andrew Hansen's problem. That part of his carefully elaborated plan had been relatively easy. How to get his group to California required the most planning of all. He originally had thought to cross the country by covered wagon, but as years went by, another alternative developed. The Americans were building a railroad from New York to San Francisco. In 1861, however, the Civil War started and the railroad was put in a secondary role. Waiting for the completion of this wonderful achievement would delay their departure, but he felt it was well worth the wait.

Finally, in 1865, when the war came to an end and peace was once more restored, America exploded with creative ideas and new inventions, as if to make up for time so tragically lost. President Lincoln, anxious to help the country heal and reunite placed major emphasis on the completion of the Transcontinental Railroad. *"The railroad was the longest ribbon of iron ever built by man. It was a stupendous achievement."*[2] Andrew Hansen and his three nieces would be passengers on the amazing railroad a few short weeks after the final spike was driven at Promontory, Utah in 1869.

Andrew, Julia, Mata, and Anna arrived in New York in the late summer of 1869. They went directly into the city to secure lodging as close to the train terminal as possible. It was time for the three young girls to recuperate after the hard voyage. Ellis Island, the gathering point for future immigrants, did not open until 1892, twenty-three years later.

---

[2] Steven Ambrose, Nothing Like It in the World, (New York: Simon and Schuster) p. 385.

New York was a city expanding so fast it could not catch up with itself. People were everywhere, and many were nationalities the girls had never seen before. Everyone seemed to speak a different language, and German was seldom heard. People were coming from all over the world to this young country that was performing so many miracles. The building of the railroad they were soon to be traveling on was a feat of unsurpassed technology and courage noted throughout the world. Frontiers were attainable for the mere price of a train ticket. The devastating Civil War was over, and peace was sure to bring prosperity and opportunity as available nowhere else. Aspirations were high, and people were excited.

New York in 1869, however, was a city they were more than ready to leave after the first short walk down one of the busy streets. Many of the streets were simple dirt roads, dry and dusty, while others were paved with cobblestones, which riddled the streets with deep cracks where refuse collected and rotted. Wagons and carriages rushed along all day and deep into the night. The manure from the horses required to pull these vehicles added greatly to the smell and filth of the streets. There also were accumulations of household garbage, dead animals lay here and there, and the "water closets" added a special and unsavory dimension to the city of New York. Yes, they wanted to be on their way as quickly as possible.

Andrew bought the train tickets for their journey. They would go to Omaha, Nebraska, where they would await their transfer to the Union Pacific Railroad. He regretted he could not purchase the first-class tickets that included a Pullman sleeping car, but the staggering price of $150 each was more than he could afford. He purchased the "emigrant" class for $70 each.[3] These tickets would get them all the way from New York to Stockton, California. He was told they would have to provide their own food for the journey and was advised to take a bedroll for each passenger. Andrew reasoned it would be best to buy the needed items in Omaha, where they would have a two-day wait before boarding the Union Pacific. In a short time, vendors would be selling food to needy travelers at the necessary stops for the train's fuel and water. Andrew and his group, traveling a few weeks after the railroad's completion, would not have that advantage.

They were on their way. The trip to Omaha excited everyone, mainly because it was the first time any of them had been on a train. Before they could believe it, they were in Omaha and looking for lodging.

Omaha was another rapidly growing city. People were pouring into the city to seek work, sell supplies, or provide needed services for the railroad. After the end of the Civil War, the railroad became the center of everyone's attention and imagination. Buy a ticket and be in California the next week—unbelievable! You didn't need a horse or wagon, or months of grueling, slow travel, you just sat in a seat and watched the scenery go by.

After two days of gathering as much food as they thought they could carry and the necessary blankets, they boarded the Union Pacific for the first part of the journey across the continent to Promontory Summit in Utah. Anna recalled the railroad trip with many stories in later years.

"After Uncle Andrew checked our trunks, we four approached the big, long car in a line of other people waiting to board. We were assigned a car and proceeded into it to find some seats. Fortunately, we found two benches together, so we stuffed our blankets and food under the little benches, sat down, and looked around. The ceiling was low and flat, but the windows were large. After awhile the train started moving and we watched out the windows day after day. The country we were going through was huge—mile after mile of wide open spaces that seemed to go on forever. I watched it endlessly, and all I had to do was turn my head and look out the window."

---

[3] Steven Ambrose, Nothing Like It In The World, (New York: Simon and Schuster) p. 369.

Ten years later, in 1879, Robert Louis Stevenson was also looking out the window of an emigrant train as he rode across the plains of Nebraska. He wrote:

"To one hurrying through by steam there was a certain exhilaration in this spacious vacancy, this greatness of the air, this discovery of the whole arch of heaven, this straight, unbroken, prison-line of the horizon. Yet one could not but reflect upon the weariness of those who passed by there in old days, at the foot's pace of oxen, painfully urging their teams, and with no landmark but that unattainable evening sun for which they steered, and which daily fled them by equal stride."[4]

Joseph had made his crossing "at the foot's pace of oxen." Whereas in 1859, the trip had taken him 154 days, Anna would make the same passage in seven days.

Anna describes the train's accommodations:

"We were comfortable, but the little, narrow, hard benches did cause a few aches and pains. The hardest problem was sleeping at night. When you wanted to go to bed, they gave you a board to put on the seats and we put our bedding on the board. We were lucky we were so short, some tall people had a terrible time, and many slept sitting up. It was very uncomfortable, but I didn't complain—I was so happy to be traveling on the ground instead of on the water in a big ship!

In our car there was a small wood-burning stove at one end and a "convenience" at the other end. The "convenience", in a little closet like room, consisted of a stool surrounding a hole through which you could see the tracks race by. It was very frightening, but necessary. When the train would stop for coal or water every thirty to forty miles, we could get out, walk around a bit, and breathe in the fresh air. There also was water available at these stops so we could splash water on our hands and faces. A few men even took off their shirts and rinsed off in the cold water. As we proceeded on the trip, more people did this, and some mothers tried to rinse their children off. Seven days without a bath and wearing the same clothes added to the difficulty of the trip."

Whenever Anna referred to the train ride, she always included the phrase "clickety clack." This was a sound she heard throughout the trip. She explained it by saying the tracks were so newly laid down, they assumed they weren't all bolted to the ties. The real explanation of the sound was caused by the rail joints. In the United States, the joints are staggered, so the "clickety clack" sound occurs twice as often as in some other countries where the joints are directly across from each other.[5]

They finally arrived at Promontory Summit, where they would leave the Union Pacific and board the Central Pacific, which would take them on to Sacramento, California. Promontory Summit remained the terminus point for the railroads until the Central Pacific negotiated with the Union Pacific to purchase the tracks into Ogden.

"For a few months Promontory Summit was the last "Hell on Wheels." Boxcars on a siding provided living quarters for railroad employees. A row of tents faced the railroad across a dirt street. The tents served as hotels, lunch counters, saloons, gambling dens, a few shops, and as nests for the "soiled doves." There was plenty of whiskey, but precious little water. The railroads had to haul it on their cars in barrels from springs thirty to fifty miles distant."[6]

---

[4] Robert Louis Stevenson, "The Plains of Nebraska" in *The Travels and Essays of Robert Louis Stevenson, the Amateur Emigrant,* Charles Scribner's Sons. New York, 1905, p. 125.
[5] Sacramento Railroad Museum
[6] Stephen Ambrose, Nothing Like It in the World. p. 372.

Andrew had been warned about this town and quickly walked the three girls to the waiting Central Pacific train. When they were seated, he returned to the street to pick up the food for the rest of the trip.

The train pulled out, and now, instead of a coal-burning engine, they were being pulled by a wood-burning engine. They had heard this engine had been made on the East Coast, taken apart, put into crates, and shipped around the tip of South America to San Francisco, then transferred to a barge and taken up the Sacramento River to a dock in Sacramento where the engine was put back together again. That trip took five months.

They rode along going "clickety clack" mile after mile, making the necessary stops for water and now for the new source of energy—wood. Anna couldn't believe so much wood existed. They would pull into a stop, and she would see hundreds of cords of wood stacked in readiness for the train. They learned it took from twelve to sixteen cords of wood to go 140 miles,[7] and whenever they went through a forested area, they could see evidence of the engine's insatiable appetite. Often as far as they could see there would be nothing but tree stumps. They also saw windmills, banks of windmills, whirling away to bring up the water for the train. The engine consumed copious amounts of both wood and water.

Anna describes the Central Pacific train:

"The Central Pacific car was beautiful. The windows were even larger, and the ceiling was so high. It even had little windows above us that would catch the air and bring it down to us. Of course, it often brought the smoke and soot down upon us from the engines, but it was such an improvement over the other car we had been riding on. The benches were comfortable and planned so they would slide together at night, so you didn't need that terrible bed-board. We were very happy with the Central Pacific Railroad."

[7] Sacramento Railroad Museum

THE CENTRAL PACIFIC TRAIN—PALISADES, NEVADA —PHOTOGRAPH FROM SACRAMENTO RAILROAD MUSEUM

They were nearing the end of their long journey. After passing through mile after mile of desert, the train started climbing over the high Sierra mountain range to the summit, at an elevation of 7017 feet. This was the most spectacular and dramatic part of the entire trip. They went into tunnels, one of them was 1659 feet long. This amazing achievement had been carved out with liquid nitroglycerin when the preferred and safer black powder didn't do the job. The nitroglycerin did a better and faster job than black powder, but was extremely dangerous. Many people lost their lives building the Road. Alfred Nobel perfected dynamite in 1866, but it was not used or tested by the Central Pacific.[8]

Anna continues her description of the trip through the Sierra Mountains.

"We got to a place called "Cape Horn," and the train stopped so we could get out and see the amazing sight. It terrified me! The train was on a track that had been cut out of the side of a steep mountain that was solid rock. It looked like we were hanging in midair. We couldn't see the mountain face underneath us, and the gorge was so deep, the river looked like a tiny stream. We looked up and the granite mountain was high above us. I will never forget that sight as long as I live."

[8] Steven Ambrose, Nothing Like it in the World. p. 200–201.

CAPE HORN WAS A DRAMATIC THREE MILE STRETCH ALONG THE STEEP GORGE OF THE NORTH FORK OF THE AMERICAN RIVER. THE SLOPE WAS AT AN ANGLE OF SEVENTY-FIVE DEGREES, AND THE RIVER WAS TWELVE HUNDRED TO TWENTY-TWO HUNDRED FEET BELOW THE LINE OF THE RAILROAD. AFTER MANY FAILED ATTEMPTS, THE CHINESE VOLUNTEERED AND CARVED THE LEDGE THE RAILROAD RESTED ON. THEY USED BLACK POWDER, A CHINESE INVENTION, WHILE BEING SUSPENDED OVER THE CLIFF IN REED BASKETS WHICH THEY HAD MADE FOR THE PURPOSE.

—PHOTOGRAPH FROM SACRAMENTO RAILROAD MUSEUM

POSTCARD FROM JESSIE'S COLLECTION

Anna continues:

"When we continued on, we went into some boarded-up tunnels where we couldn't see anything but tiny cracks of light between the boards. This seemed to go on forever."

Anna was traveling though the twenty-seven miles of snow sheds erected to keep avalanches from closing the railroad in the winter.

The train continued on its way, nearing the completion of its dramatic journey. Anna said she gripped her seat and held her breath until they were once more in an area where she could see solid ground stretching out from either side of the train. Ground and trees and sky once more made her relax as the train pulled into the Sacramento station. Soon they were moving along again, now traveling through the beautiful San Joaquin Valley. The next stop would be the small town of Mokelumne Station,[9] and then their final destination—Stockton! They had come an amazingly long, *long* way.

These stories of Anna's trip were told by her again and again as she sat knitting in her rocking chair. I remember hearing them, Vera wrote them down for future generations.

[9] Mokelumne station changed its name to Lodi in 1873.

THE WEDDING

ANDREW HANSEN AND HIS CHARGES arrived in Stockton in the fall of 1869. Julia Hansen was to be married to "Little Joe" Spenker early in the coming year, and Andrew had found a family in Linden, just outside of Stockton, who could employ Anna as a maid, and Mata would work for a family in Stockton. Julia's relatives and the two employers met the girls at the train station, and soon they were going their own separate ways to start new lives in California.

The Fairchild family welcomed Anna into their spacious home, on a ranch in Linden. There was always plenty of work to do, but Anna did it happily. She was treated as a person—someone who had individual rights. It was a dramatic contrast to the slave-labor status she experienced in Germany. Mrs. Fairchild, a gracious woman, instructed Anna in many aspects of her new work. Fortunately, she spoke German, but she encouraged Anna to speak English whenever possible.

In July of 1870, Julia was going to be married. On the trip, Anna asked Julia why her fiancé was called "Little Joe" Spenker, and Julia told her he had a cousin named Joseph Spenker who was very tall. To distinguish between the two young men, the name "Little Joe" developed.

The following story was the favorite of all the "Anna Tales."

"On the day of Julia's wedding, Mr. Fairchild loaned me a horse and I took off early in the morning, riding sidesaddle to Stockton. I got there in time to help with some of the preparations for the many guests.

Among the guests was a tall man with a dark beard. I was introduced to him. His name was Joseph Spenker. I laughed—now I knew why they called Julia's fiancé "Little Joe" Spenker. We talked a short time, and then I was called to help Julia. Throughout the wedding, I often caught Joseph watching me. When it was time for me to go home, Joseph walked outside with me and held my horse while I mounted. We looked into each other's eyes, and he said, 'I'll come for you tomorrow and we'll be married!' I was afraid to believe him, and I just laughed.

The next morning, I was busy doing the family washing at the Fairchild home when I noticed a two-horse wagon coming down the road. Everyone stopped working to look, because any traffic on the road was unusual enough to cause interest.

A man in the wagon stood up. It was Joseph Spenker! "I've come to get Anna," he announced.

"She can't come, she's doing the washing, and besides, her clothes are all mixed up in the laundry," said Mrs. Fairchild.

I looked at Mrs. Fairchild and said, I want to go with him! Mrs. Fairchild smiled at me and gave me a hug. Then I called down to Joseph "I'm coming!" I pulled my wet clothes out of the washing and handed them to Joseph. Then I went inside to pack my trunk. My heart was racing—this was hard to believe, but I did not have one doubt in my mind. This was my future, and matched my wildest dreams.

I quickly threw my belongings into the trunk and dragged it to the door. I thanked Mrs. Fairchild for all her kindnesses and promised to come back for a visit. Joseph put my trunk into the back of the wagon and helped me up onto the seat. We waved goodbye and proceeded down the road. Joseph turned to me and said, "Anna, we're going to Stockton to be married!" Off we went, and all my dreams started coming true."

Anna and Joseph were quietly married in a simple courthouse ceremony in Stockton on July 25, 1870. After having some formal wedding portraits taken, Joseph took his bride home to his modest dwelling on the Adobe Ranch.

THE WEDDING PORTRAIT TAKEN ON JULY 25, 1870

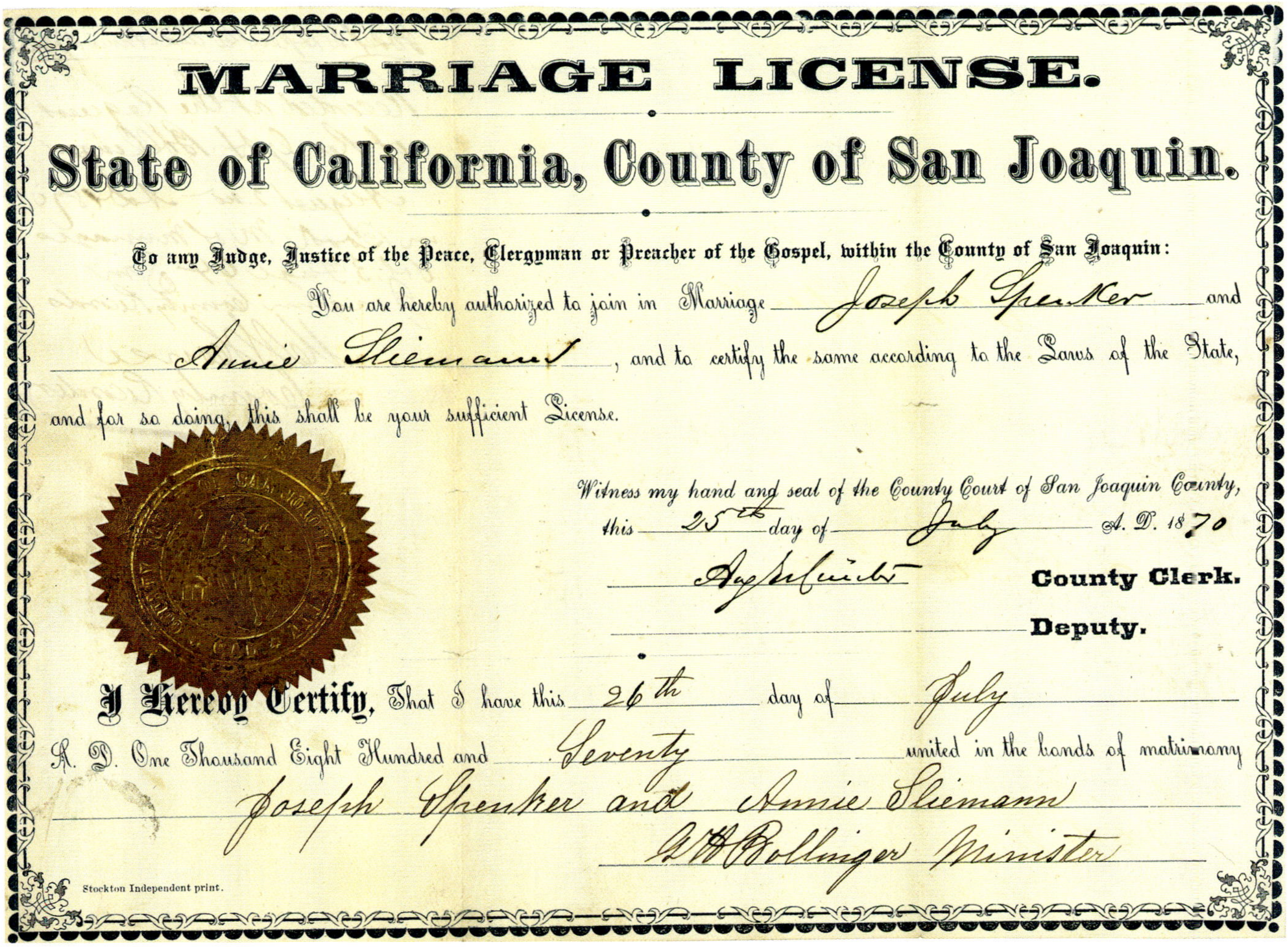

MARRIAGE LICENSE.

State of California, County of San Joaquin.

To any Judge, Justice of the Peace, Clergyman or Preacher of the Gospel, within the County of San Joaquin:

You are hereby authorized to join in Marriage Joseph Spenker and Annie Sliemann, and to certify the same according to the Laws of the State, and for so doing, this shall be your sufficient License.

Witness my hand and seal of the County Court of San Joaquin County, this 25th day of July A. D. 1870

[illegible] County Clerk.

Deputy.

I Hereby Certify, That I have this 26th day of July A. D. One Thousand Eight Hundred and Seventy united in the bonds of matrimony Joseph Spenker and Annie Sliemann

A H Bollinger Minister

Stockton Independent print.

JOSEPH AND ANNA'S MARRIAGE LICENSE

Anna cherished every minute of being in her own home. She was the one in charge of the cooking, washing, and baking. This was her space, her world, and she gloried in every moment of her day.

In November, Anna received a letter from Germany.

Kiebitzreihe Nov. 13, 1870

Beloved Anna!

Since we are far away from each other, I can't help to share some of my thoughts with you. It's been over one year already since you have left. I sometimes think of the last time we were together. How sad you were when your mother got ill, and you couldn't come. But after the rain, comes the sunshine. How happy and full of joy you were when your mother gave her consent for you to go with your uncle. Yes, dear Ann, it was your fate to go there, but not your parents and sisters. Otherwise, our dear God would not have allowed your mother to get so ill so fast. But for you it was the right time and you had to go, so that you would meet the husband our God had chosen for you. Because your sisters told me that you are already married. I didn't want to believe it when they told me. But they showed me the picture of you and your husband to convince me. I want to congratulate both of you a thousand times, and wish you all the luck and God's blessing, and hope you will live many wonderful years in peace and happiness.

(No signature)

He closed the letter with the following poem:

The beautiful day appeared to you
As bridegroom and beautiful bride,
And you may love each other forever
As a betrothed couple.
Live happy like hoards of angels,
And celebrate after fifty years
Your golden anniversary,
As happy and healthy as now.

Anna placed this letter with her most treasured possessions.

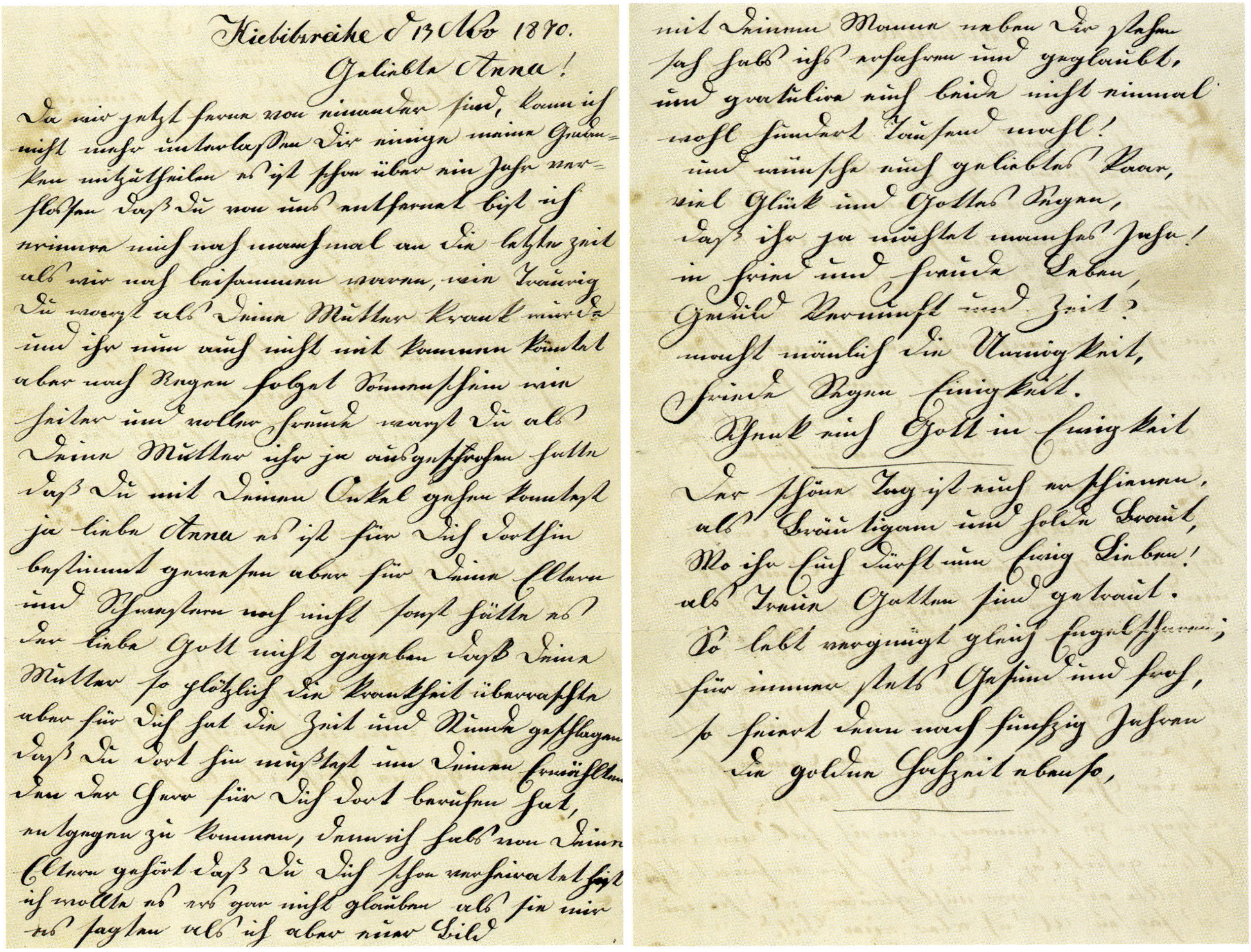

Kiebitzreihe d 13 Nov 1870.
Geliebte Anna!

Da wir jetzt ferne von einander sind, kann ich nicht mehr unterlassen Dir einige meiner Gedanken mitzutheilen es ist schon über ein Jahr verflossen daß Du von uns entfernt bist ich erinnere mich noch manchmal an die letzte Zeit als wir noch beisammen waren, wie traurig Du warst als Deine Mutter krank wurde und ihr nun auch nicht mit kommen konntet aber nach Regen folgt Sonnenschein wie heiter und voller Freude warst Du als Deine Mutter ihr ja ausgesprochen hatte daß Du mit Deinem Onkel gehen konntest ja liebe Anna es ist für Dich dorthin bestimmt gewesen aber für Deine Eltern und Geschwister noch nicht sonst hätte es der liebe Gott nicht gegeben daß Deine Mutter so plötzlich die Krankheit überraschte aber für Dich hat die Zeit und Stunde geschlagen daß Du dort hin mußtest um Deinem Erwählten den der Herr für Dich dort bereitet hat, entgegen zu kommen, denn ich habe von Deinen Eltern gehört daß Du Dich schon verheirathet hast ich wollte es erst gar nicht glauben als sie mir es sagten als ich aber eure Bild

mit Deinem Manne neben Dir stehen sah habe ich erfahren und geglaubt. und gratulire euch beide nicht einmal wohl hundert tausend mal!
und wünsche euch geliebtes Paar, viel Glück und Gottes Segen, daß ihr ja möchtet manches Jahr! in Friede und Freude Leben, Geduld Vernunft und Zeit? macht nämlich die Einigkeit, Friede Segen Einigkeit.
Schenk euch Gott in Ewigkeit

Der schöne Tag ist euch erschienen,
als Bräutigam und holde Braut,
Wo ihr euch dürft nun ewig lieben!
als treue Gatten sind getraut.
So lebt vergnügt gleich Engelschaaren;
für immer stets Gesund und froh,
so feiert denn nach fünfzig Jahren
die goldene Hochzeit ebenso,

THE "BELOVED ANNA" LETTER

TRANSLATED BY: GABRIELE LIBHART AND CHARLOTTE EISENMANN

On June 22, 1871, Anna bore a son they named Otto. A year later, Joseph moved his small family to the ranch he considered his prize—the Oak Grove Ranch, north of Stockton near the town of Woodbridge.

"Anna—This is where we'll stay, build our home, raise our family. This will be our place in the world. Anna, it's beautiful! There are wonderful majestic oak trees, a whole grove of them. And flowers—Oh Anna you'll love the flowers in the springtime! The house is small, like this one, but one day we will build a new home, one with extra bedrooms, a parlor, a real kitchen. It'll even have a basement. Anna, we'll build our future on this ranch. It will be a fine, productive ranch, the soil is some of the best around. We have more land to level and get ready for planting wheat, but the crop will be strong. This is all virgin soil, beautiful and rich. Anna—this ranch is my dream come true."

Anna always smiled with love when she repeated the words of the happy man she had married. Life was wonderful.

ANNA AND JOSEPH'S "LITTLE HOUSE THAT WAS ALL THEIR OWN" WHERE JESSIE WAS BORN

RANCH LIFE IN THE 1870s

LIFE IN THE 1870S provided some exhausting roles, especially for women living in the rural areas of the San Joaquin Valley. Living without the luxury of running water, and no source of energy except the wood burning in the stove, intensified the simplest house chores. Anna was a veteran of hard, endless work, but now she was married and on their own land. This fact certainly eased the burden.

Anna described her days on the ranch with many stories in later years.

"The ranch was all that Joseph had described to me. I loved the trees, the flowers, the little house that was all our own. I loved the endless acres where I could walk—when I had time. There were so many chores that I rose at dawn and worked until past sundown. There was always breakfast to cook for Joseph and the hired help. I gathered the eggs the night before to save a little time in the early hours. There was pork to fry, because the ranch had many hogs that were raised for market. These had been butchered, cut up, and sections placed in a large box with rock salt to keep them fresh. Potatoes and other vegetables were readily available and had been stored carefully in a cool barrel. I got the bread started the night before to save time in the morning rush. I churned butter every week and stored it in the cool earthen pit Joseph had dug when we first arrived on the ranch. This pit, kept nice and damp, could keep items cool for days. Coffee, salt, flour, and sugar were about the only items we had to buy. Any shortening needed, I had made before and could take out of the pit. This process was time consuming. I would take the kidney from a cow or sheep that had been slaughtered, cut off the surrounding hard fat into little pieces and then put them in a pan over the stove until it turned into liquid. When cooled, this provided the shortening I needed for baking and cooking. Breakfast was early, and thankfully, baby Otto usually slept through most of the preparations. Once the fire in the stove was ready for cooking, I had my hands full.

Otto was a wonderful baby. He was such a good baby—with me being so busy he had to be good. I always took Otto to any area where I worked, and he seemed to enjoy all the activity, especially when I went to the chicken house. I think he loved the sound of the chickens as much as I did. I felt their busy life matched my own, and they were always talking to each other. At times I wished I had someone to talk to, someone with whom I could share ideas and problems. Otto tried to listen to me, but his responses were only good for a laugh."

Anna did all her many chores happily, except for one—the family wash. She said she dreaded laundry day, almost always a Monday. For her, this was the most exhausting chore of the whole week, and of course baby Otto's diapers only made it worse. Joseph created a wash area outside to make it easier for her, but she had to work all day to complete the task. She had to haul countless buckets of water from the pump to the area, fill the large cauldron that was placed on a rack and build a fire under the rack. Then she would gather and sort the clothes, get the scrub board in position on a large bucket filled with water, place the diapers and other white clothes in the water over the fire, water she hoped was hot by now, add the soap, and start scrubbing the colored clothes on the board. She had heard that some women soaked the white clothes in lye and water and then rinsed them in scalding-hot water, but she had not perfected her wash day to that extent. Once the clothes were as clean as possible, she had to scoop them out of the hot water and put them on a board until they were cool enough to handle. When she had squeezed out most of the soapy water, she put them back into clean rinse water. After swishing them around, Anna scooped them back onto the board. Now she had to wring out each piece again. Because she had small hands, Anna said she found this to be the hardest job of all. The next step was hanging them up on the clothesline. Often, since she wasn't strong enough to wring out most of the water, they took a long time to dry.

Of course, this was only the first step of the laundry process. The dried clothes had to be taken down from the line, brought in and folded, and in special cases ironed. Anna used several irons of different sizes. She placed these irons on the cook stove to heat, often put a little beeswax on a towel to wipe the bottom of the irons, and started to work. She had one very small, pointed iron for lacy ruffles, but she seldom used it. Anna preferred knitted lace, which looked fine without ironing. When she found a rare few moments to sit down and relax, Anna would pick up the ever-present little shoe box by her rocking chair and take out her knitting. She would knit yard after yard of delicate, beautiful lace.

The time of the year Anna liked the most was the spring, when she could walk out into the oak grove and search for wildflowers. She would happily recall these walks throughout the years. *"The oak grove was so beautiful— the trees had a pale green glow, the grasses were green, and flowers were everywhere! I*

ANNA AND HER CHICKENS

saw some Johnny-Jump-Ups, some Buttercups, Cream Cups, Rattle Boxes and Nigger Heads. I also saw a few Poppies and some Jelly Flowers—it was truly a wonderful sight!"

In 1875, Anna gave birth to another child—Anna Jessie Marie Spenker. For the rest of her life she would be called Jessie.

As the years passed and the children grew, Otto started to work with Joseph. He was a strong, young man that learned quickly under Joseph's excellent leadership. Joseph always included him in the decision-making process, providing detailed explanations so Otto would understand and learn. Jessie helped Anna with many chores and could do things Anna could never do. Anna found horses very frightening, but Jessie loved the animals, and they seemed to love her. She never had to chase them—they would come right up to her and she could lead them to the barn to harness them to the cart. Jessie started taking the butter and eggs into town when she was twelve years old. Jessie was a confident young girl and appeared ready to tackle any task on the ranch. She eagerly ventured into unfamiliar projects and most often met with success. In later years, her independence and self-confidence would serve her and her family well.

THE NEW BABY ON THE RANCH—ANNA JESSIE MARIE SPENKER

DRILLING IN THE WHEAT ON THE SPENKER RANCH. THE SEED IS PLACED IN THE LONG BOX, CALLED A HOPPER, BEHIND THE HORSES. A GEAR IN THE BOX TURNS AND CAUSES THE SEED TO DROP INTO TUBES WHICH "DRILL" THE SEED INTO THE SOIL IN THE GROOVE CAUSED BY THE SHEAR BLADE THAT PROCEEDED THE DRILL. A SECOND ROW OF SHEAR BLADES ARE BEHIND THE DRILLS AND COVER THE SEED WITH SOIL.

THE LONG BED WAGON USED TO HAUL GRAIN SACKS. IT WAS BUILT LOW TO THE GROUND TO MAKE IT EASIER TO LOAD THE HEAVY SACKS.

CHAPTER TWO

Wheat in the Valley

STOCKTON, THE AREA WHERE JOSEPH HAD CHOSEN to settle, was ideally situated on the San Joaquin River with direct access to San Francisco's deep-water port and hence to the world. This valley town, which had been serving as a resource center for the unique needs of the gold miners, was about to play a major role in the story of California. Stockton became a center of commerce for the farming interests of the valley in the 1870s, and drew some of the most creative men in the state. Their ideas in the designing of harvesters and tractors would change farming throughout the world.

The years after the Gold Rush and completion of the Railroad, saw the San Joaquin Valley start to grow into its true destiny as one of the leading agricultural areas in the union. Rich fertile virgin land, much of it level, and water rushing down from the Sierra into rivers branching through the valleys, created the environment for a crop that would soon make history. That crop was wheat.

All the farmers were talking about wheat. All they had to do was plow the soil, drill in the seed, and wait—wait for it to grow and ripen. No other care was necessary. The water table was only two feet below the surface, and the roots quickly grew down to the nourishing moisture.

"From 1860 to 1880 the wheat market justified the almost exclusive devotion of California lands to wheat production. Throughout the greater portion of the county the farmers have never known a failure of crops. Without irrigation they have harvested from twenty to fifty bushels of wheat per acre."[1]

Everyone planted wheat. The valley lay covered in grain from the mountains to the marshes—a moving sea of grain stalks. You could almost call them money stalks, the price was so high. In 1880, San Joaquin County raised the largest wheat crop in the world, 3.4 million bushels. A high percentage of this came from the Lodi—Woodbridge area, a few miles to the north of Stockton, where Joseph's ranch was located. Joseph was proud to be helping make agricultural history.

The focus on wheat as a cash crop in the San Joaquin Valley in the last decades of the nineteenth century fostered the development of some of the century's most significant technology centered around the harvester. In the 1860s, some harvesters had been shipped around the horn to California. These harvesters relied on a complicated set of hard-to-maintain moving parts to transmit the power from one part of the harvester to another, and were extremely noisy. The noise of these gears, pinions, shafts, and countershafts banging together often

[1] History of San Joaquin County, 1890, p. 118.

terrified the horses harnessed in long trains to pull this monster. There were frequent cases of the horses bolting, running away in pure terror. Many operators were killed or injured, and many horses suffered a similar fate.

In the 1880s, most harvesters were ground-driven. Joseph's harvester, for example, was a ground-driven harvester. In these harvesters, operation of all the moving parts depended upon the turning of the six-foot-diameter wheels on each side. (one is seen behind Joseph). This resulted in "ground power." The horses created the ultimate source of power—causing the wheels to turn, which turned the gears, which threshed the wheat. Most farmers used from twenty-six to twenty-eight horses to pull the harvester—Otto increased the number to thirty. A long ladder extended out over the horses, called a "Jacob's Ladder." A man sat on the top of this ladder with a bag of rocks. If one of the horses didn't do his job, the man would throw a rock at him. From this precarious position, he also controlled the direction of travel via reins to the lead horses.

THE SPENKER HARVESTER. JOSEPH IS TO THE RIGHT OF THE LARGE SIX FOOT WHEEL, JESSIE IS ON THE HORSE.

JOSEPH'S HARVESTER VIEWED FROM THE BACK SIDE WHERE THE WHEAT IS PROCESSED

Wheat harvesting was starting. Since Joseph and Otto did the harvesting for many other farmers with their equipment, they were extremely busy. In his diaries, Otto described the trials and challenges of running the huge operation that wheat harvesting entailed.

"June 16—Harvesting is starting today. I got all to work smoothly and made two rounds on the oats west of the vineyard. We cut 81 sacks. The next day we took the machine apart and moved one and a half miles to the Hart Ranch. We set it up again—all in one and a half hours. We made one round and cut over 100 sacks.

June 24—Awoke at 3:30 and no more sleep till tonight. Mrs. Brown up at 2 am to get breakfast. Boys got up at 4:00 to harness teams and went into breakfast at 4:45. Everybody happy and plenty of fun. Started at 6:15 and ready to start cutting oats at Beckman's shortly after 8. Cut the field west of the house -about 500 sacks. A splendid days work!

June 29—Hitched in four more horses—30 pulling the harvester. The machine runs much better now. We finished the wheat at noon and started on the oats. They were slightly shrunk and light but went about 25 sacks to the acre. Beckman furnished 2 four horse sack buck teams and 3 men to carry off the filled sacks.

July 2—Fine weather, but worse days run of the season. Started about 8:30 expecting to make a good run. Straw carrier choked every half round all forenoon. Stayed out at noon and cut off straw carrier bottom about a foot which is the best thing that ever happened to the machine. Runs better than ever before. PM broke elevator and grain drag—quite a delay, but runs fine now. Took horses home for over Sunday.

July 16—Started earlier than usual, but lost a belt on the first round and much time also. Sent Gus back to look for it. He went back to the start while the belt was hanging on the machine.

The harvesting is going well for the most part. We move from one ranch to another. Last week the Hansh field was the worst I have ever cut—part of it was down and so many weeds! Then we moved to Hasens place and cut two rounds before dark—that field was fearfully rough."

FROM THE TOP OF THE HARVESTER

GRAIN SACKS LOADED IN THE LONG BED WAGON. THESE TWO PHOTOGRAPHS, AND MANY OTHERS IN THIS BOOK ARE FROM A GLASS NEGATIVE. CELLULOID FILM WAS AVAILABLE IN 1887, BUT OTTO CONTINUED TO PREFER THE GLASS NEGATIVE CAMERA FOR MANY MORE YEARS.

THE HARVESTING CREW. LEFT TO RIGHT: FRITZ SPENKER, BILL BLOHM, GUS DEGENER, MAX LEETZOW, ALBERT LANGE AND OTTO SPENKER.

—PHOTOGRAPH FROM COLLECTION OF BETTY ANN SPENKER

LOOKING OVER THE BACKS OF THIRTY HORSES. THE SEAT TO THE LEFT IS KNOWN AS THE JACOB'S LADDER. FROM THIS LOCATION A MAN CONTROLLED THE DIRECTION OF THE HARVESTER. THE SACK ON THE SEAT CONTAINS ROCKS HE WOULD THROW AT ANY HORSE THAT WASN'T DOING HIS JOB. THERE IS ANOTHER ROW OF HORSES UNDER THIS LADDER THAT DID NOT GET INTO THE PHOTOGRAPH.

To serve the needs of local farmers, a number of innovators in the Stockton area developed a series of remarkable harvesters almost fifty years before they came into use in other wheat producing areas in the United States. One of the first of these innovators was Benjamin Holt. When he and his brother Charles came to Stockton, surrounded by the major wheat fields in the San Joaquin Valley, they became aware of the increasing trade in harvesting machinery. Benjamin felt he could design a far more efficient and safer harvester. He had grown up working in his father's lumber and milling operation where belt driven pulleys were used. Adapting his knowledge of belts, he designed a link belt that could run quietly and efficiently, connecting all the functions of a combine. Advertised as a "quiet" harvester, they started production in 1886.

In 1890, the Holt Company of Stockton produced a steam engine tractor to help all the farmers. It was an amazing machine, but Joseph was not interested in trying such an "experimental" idea. Farmers nicknamed the tractor "Old Betsy." It was noted you couldn't get a horse anywhere near her. Henry Beckman was fascinated by the new idea and invested in the tractor, but Joseph decided to stay with horse power.

NOTICE THE BELT-DRIVEN PULLEYS ABOVE THE HEADS OF THE MEN. THIS SYSTEM CREATED A "QUIET" HARVESTER.

OLD BETSY WAS A SPLENDID MACHINE BUT YOU COULDN'T GET A HORSE ANYWHERE NEAR HER.

In 1895, the Holt Brothers acquired the Matteson Williamson Manufacturing Company, a Stockton maker of the Harvest "Prince" combined harvester. This was the harvester Joseph gave Otto on June 27, 1900. You can see by the receipt it cost $1,000. This company was bought out by the Holt Manufacturing Co. in 1895, and so the sales agreement was made out to the trustees for the creditors of the former company. By the year 1900 the Holt Brothers had produced 1,072 combines, more than all the competition added together.

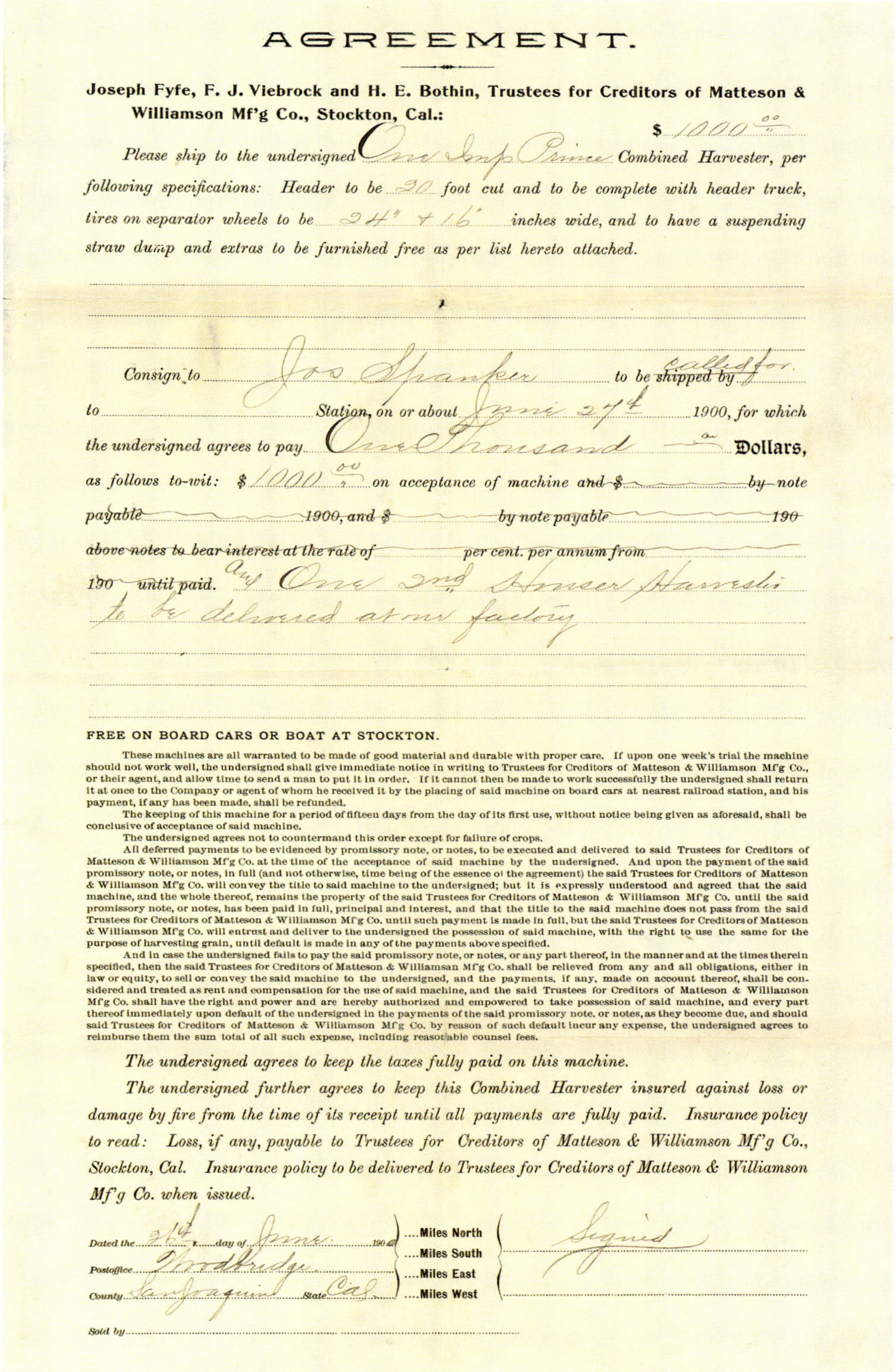

AGREEMENT.

Joseph Fyfe, F. J. Viebrock and H. E. Bothin, Trustees for Creditors of Matteson & Williamson Mf'g Co., Stockton, Cal.:

$ 1000.00

Please ship to the undersigned One Imp Prince *Combined Harvester, per following specifications: Header to be* 20 *foot cut and to be complete with header truck, tires on separator wheels to be* 24" + 16" *inches wide, and to have a suspending straw dump and extras to be furnished free as per list hereto attached.*

Consign to Jos Spanker *to be* ~~*shipped by*~~ called for

to .... *Station, on or about* June 27th *1900, for which the undersigned agrees to pay* One Thousand **Dollars,**

as follows to-wit: $1000.00 *on acceptance of machine* ~~*and $ by note payable 1900, and $ by note payable 190 above notes to bear interest at the rate of per cent. per annum from 190*~~ *until paid.* as One 2nd Houser Harvester to be delivered at our factory

FREE ON BOARD CARS OR BOAT AT STOCKTON.

These machines are all warranted to be made of good material and durable with proper care. If upon one week's trial the machine should not work well, the undersigned shall give immediate notice in writing to Trustees for Creditors of Matteson & Williamson Mf'g Co., or their agent, and allow time to send a man to put it in order. If it cannot then be made to work successfully the undersigned shall return it at once to the Company or agent of whom he received it by the placing of said machine on board cars at nearest railroad station, and his payment, if any has been made, shall be refunded.

The keeping of this machine for a period of fifteen days from the day of its first use, without notice being given as aforesaid, shall be conclusive of acceptance of said machine.

The undersigned agrees not to countermand this order except for failure of crops.

All deferred payments to be evidenced by promissory note, or notes, to be executed and delivered to said Trustees for Creditors of Matteson & Williamson Mf'g Co. at the time of the acceptance of said machine by the undersigned. And upon the payment of the said promissory note, or notes, in full (and not otherwise, time being of the essence of the agreement) the said Trustees for Creditors of Matteson & Williamson Mf'g Co. will convey the title to said machine to the undersigned; but it is expressly understood and agreed that the said machine, and the whole thereof, remains the property of the said Trustees for Creditors of Matteson & Williamson Mf'g Co. until the said promissory note, or notes, has been paid in full, principal and interest, and that the title to the said machine does not pass from the said Trustees for Creditors of Matteson & Williamson Mf'g Co. until such payment is made in full, but the said Trustees for Creditors of Matteson & Williamson Mf'g Co. will entrust and deliver to the undersigned the possession of said machine, with the right to use the same for the purpose of harvesting grain, until default is made in any of the payments above specified.

And in case the undersigned fails to pay the said promissory note, or notes, or any part thereof, in the manner and at the times therein specified, then the said Trustees for Creditors of Matteson & Williamsan Mf'g Co. shall be relieved from any and all obligations, either in law or equity, to sell or convey the said machine to the undersigned, and the payments, if any, made on account thereof, shall be considered and treated as rent and compensation for the use of said machine, and the said Trustees for Creditors of Matteson & Williamson Mf'g Co. shall have the right and power and are hereby authorized and empowered to take possession of said machine, and every part thereof immediately upon default of the undersigned in the payments of the said promissory note, or notes, as they become due, and should said Trustees for Creditors of Matteson & Williamson Mf'g Co. by reason of such default incur any expense, the undersigned agrees to reimburse them the sum total of all such expense, including reasonable counsel fees.

The undersigned agrees to keep the taxes fully paid on this machine.

The undersigned further agrees to keep this Combined Harvester insured against loss or damage by fire from the time of its receipt until all payments are fully paid. Insurance policy to read: Loss, if any, payable to Trustees for Creditors of Matteson & Williamson Mf'g Co., Stockton, Cal. Insurance policy to be delivered to Trustees for Creditors of Matteson & Williamson Mf'g Co. when issued.

Dated the 26 *day of* June *1900* ....Miles North ....Miles South ....Miles East ....Miles West

Postoffice Woodbridge

County San Joaquin *State* Cal.

Signed

Sold by ....

OTTO'S 29TH BIRTHDAY PRESENT. HE WAS NOW IN THE HARVESTING BUSINESS.

THE HAUSER AND HAINES COMPANY WAS ESTABLISHED IN 1889 IN STOCKTON. THIS WAS THEIR GROUND-DRIVEN HARVESTER PRODUCED AROUND 1900.

THE HOLT MANUFACTURING COMPANY ACQUIRED THE HAUSER-HAINES COMPANY IN 1901.

YOUNG JESSIE—1890

CHAPTER THREE

Coming of Age with the Twentieth Century

AS JESSIE AND OTTO GREW AND MATURED in the last decades of the nineteenth century, many aspects of ranch life in the San Joaquin Valley remained constant. At the same time, however, the world was changing. Jessie and Otto would participate in those changes and come of age with the advent of the twentieth century.

YOUNG JESSIE

Jessie grew up on a beautiful ranch with parents she adored, and a brother who was her best friend. Jessie, surrounded with love and beauty, had plenty of work to do—at times it seemed the work never stopped. She helped her mother with the cooking, often for as many as six hired hands in addition to the family. There were also cows to be milked, butter to be made, vegetables to be gathered from the garden that she helped to maintain, and of course, there was the washing. Jessie also helped with all the ranch animals. Her mother took care of the chickens, they seemed to be a favorite of hers. When some chickens were needed for dinner, however, it was up to Jessie to shoot them. This usually did not take too long, because Jessie was an excellent shot. She used a single-shot .22-caliber Winchester rifle.

Jessie found the animals to be one of the biggest joys of living on the ranch, especially the horses. Every evening she rode her favorite horse to round up the cows, and often she extended the ride for pure enjoyment. Some of her happiest times were spent with friends riding down to the Mokolumne River. Of course, the horses were essential on the ranch, and her father had as many as eighty horses at all times: they pulled the plows, the harvesters, the seeders, the Fresno scrapers, and of course, if you wanted to go anywhere, you needed a horse. Otto seemed to enjoy his bicycle, but that never appealed to Jessie. She had seen some women riding bicycles in town, but by the time they got their long skirts tied up they looked pretty silly. Jessie preferred a horse any day.

People living on ranches in the last decades of the nineteenth century had challenging roles to fill, but they did take time out for enjoyment, and Jessie recorded some of the happy diversions. From her diaries, it appears that one of the most meaningful enjoyments was associating with friends and relatives in the evenings, and especially on Sundays. If you went out visiting, someone from your household always stayed home so guests coming to your home could be properly greeted. This was a joy, and Jessie dutifully recorded who came to visit. Six guests would be an average number for a social Sunday afternoon—often more came to call.

Jessie had a favorite uncle Bill. She wrote: *"Went to Bills' again, had a great time. Bill danced to the music box. Mary and Millie played on the organ. On the way home we sang 'Annie Rooney'—Mama was at the gate and heard us singing."*

Jessie and Otto both attended high school in the small town of Woodbridge, a few miles from the ranch. This town had anticipated being one of the leading communities in the valley, but the train passed them by and went west to Mokelumne Station which later became Lodi. When the train station was established, some business owners literally picked up their stores and moved them to Lodi.

In 1882, the San Joaquin Valley College opened in Woodbridge with great expectations. It was believed this would make the whole community thrive. Otto attended the college in 1885, three years after it opened. Jessie entered the school in 1889, the year Otto graduated. They both felt fortunate in later years that they had this opportunity, because a decline in enrollment caused the school to close in 1897. Woodbridge lost another dream.

Besides her studies in college, Jessie took confirmation lessons once a week for introduction into

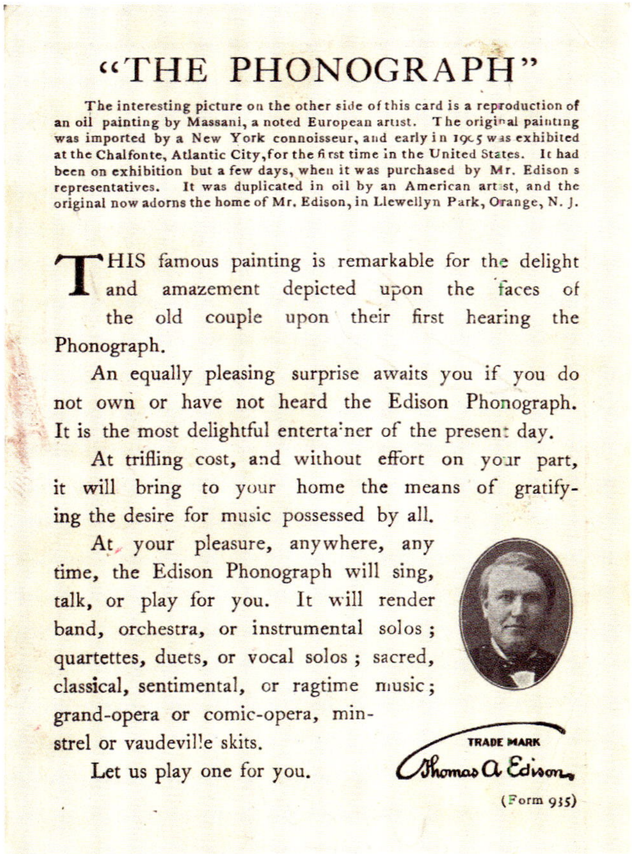

"THE PHONOGRAPH"

The interesting picture on the other side of this card is a reproduction of an oil painting by Massani, a noted European artist. The original painting was imported by a New York connoisseur, and early in 1905 was exhibited at the Chalfonte, Atlantic City, for the first time in the United States. It had been on exhibition but a few days, when it was purchased by Mr. Edison's representatives. It was duplicated in oil by an American artist, and the original now adorns the home of Mr. Edison, in Llewellyn Park, Orange, N. J.

THIS famous painting is remarkable for the delight and amazement depicted upon the faces of the old couple upon their first hearing the Phonograph.

An equally pleasing surprise awaits you if you do not own or have not heard the Edison Phonograph. It is the most delightful entertainer of the present day.

At trifling cost, and without effort on your part, it will bring to your home the means of gratifying the desire for music possessed by all.

At your pleasure, anywhere, any time, the Edison Phonograph will sing, talk, or play for you. It will render band, orchestra, or instrumental solos; quartettes, duets, or vocal solos; sacred, classical, sentimental, or ragtime music; grand-opera or comic-opera, minstrel or vaudeville skits.

Let us play one for you.

TRADE MARK

Thomas A. Edison

(Form 935)

the Lutheran Church. This was considered necessary to give young people a good foundation in their faith. Jessie was confirmed on May 31, 1890 at Henderson School, where services were held once a month. The other three Sundays required a trip to Stockton. Jessie describes her confirmation in her diary: *"A little baby was christened first, then singing, praying, the sermon, and lastly, we took the Lord's Supper. First we seven conferment's, next the brethren and then the sisters. When the people had gone out, we went to Rev. Block, bade him good-bye and he gave us some good advice. The most important being that we should never forget it."* Jessie revered Reverend Block and retained close communication with him for the rest of his life.

Jessie seemed to enjoy writing, but mainly letters to her friends. When Jessie wrote in her diary, which she did faithfully year after year throughout her life, she used an abbreviated style. She recorded factually daily events and activities with friends and her brother Otto, such as *"going to a circus in Lodi where we saw many curious beings and performances."* Later, after she got married, a new "Line a Day" style of diary came out and she thought it was wonderful. You wrote one line to cover each day, and then you went to the next page. When the new year started, you started again at the front of the book and wrote the new entry under what you had done last year on the same date. Eventually, you could look at one page for March 30 and see what you did on that date during the last five years. Of course, that left no room for descriptions or emotional statements. Thankfully, Otto never adopted that style—he often needed a whole page of a large journal to cover one day.

On August 26, 1890, Jessie wrote: *"Otto and I went to Stockton, past the asylum and on to the race track. There we saw the Stockton parade and saw the vaqueros ride colts. We saw a balloon ascension. At 2 p.m. we went to the Pavilion and heard a phonograph sing "A Curl from Baby's Head."*

These phonographs, designed by Thomas Edison, had been manufactured for sale to the public since 1889. Otto, always interested in mechanical things, thought it would be a wonderful invention to own.

THE EDISON PHONOGRAPH WAS A DRAMATIC INVENTION IN THE YEAR 1889

The town of Woodbridge had become a focal point for Jessie and her family. Usually someone made a trip to town every day just to check the mail, if for no other reason. On November 12, 1891, there was a great celebration in town for the completion of a local engineering achievement, the Woodbridge Dam. The town had been decorated beautifully for the event—they even fired cannons. Jessie took "edibles" to town for the occasion, as did all the other farmers. This event had been eagerly looked forward to with hopes the wood dam would stop the devastating floods that so often occurred. Everyone had a marvelous time.

There were other forms of entertainment available in 1892. On April 9, Jessie and Otto *"went to Woodbridge and watched a football game between the Stockton High School team and our College team. Several players were injured, there was a great crowd, the Stocktonians were victorious."*

On January 1, 1894 Jessie wrote: *"Woodbridge Cal. A very pleasant but rainy New Year. Men are on the adobe, Otto and Papa went down this p.m. I shot two chickens, which I intend to take to the feast tomorrow.*

January 2nd, 1894, I prepared the two chickens, one cake, a piece of butter, and a jar of pickled cucumbers for the feast of Woodbridge Grange No. 84. I was chaplain. We had a very good feast. I went with H. C. Beckman."

The Grange Hall in Woodbridge was the center of learning and social life for Jessie, Otto, and their friends. The Grange had been established in New York in 1873 by Oliver H. Kelley and quickly spread across the country—especially in the northern and western states. It was formed to give farmers a unified voice with which to express their opposition to unfair practices used against them by big corporations. Until the Grange was founded, independent farmers could not bargain from positions of economic strength or equal knowledge of business conditions with those who bought and shipped their produce. Consequently, rate discrimination was rampant against the small, independent farmers who were wholly dependent on the railroads and grain warehouses to get their crops to market. The Grange provided a forum where farmers could express their opinions, share their thoughts and concerns, and put their combined conclusions into resolutions petitioning for change. One of the Grange's greatest early victories was persuading the U.S. Supreme Court to declare constitutional the regulation of the prices that warehouses could charge. Small farmers would now be charged the same price as the large corporations.

From the very start, the founder, Oliver Kelley, wanted women to be included as full and equal partners. The Grange encouraged the women to participate in all public affairs, saying it was their duty and their right. Jessie felt this was the way all government agencies should be managed. She and Otto were very active members of the Woodbridge Grange. On March 31, 1894, Otto was elected vice president and Jessie became secretary.

As important as the Grange was for focusing the political interests for farmers and for disseminating information to them, its social function sometimes loomed larger—especially for young people. Jessie described an evening at the Grange Hall in Woodbridge. *"In the evening at the Grange meeting, the 5th and 6th degree were conferred on about 60 people. After conferring of the degrees we marched to the banquet hall in the Granger's Union building. H. C. Beckman and I marched together. We had a very good banquet After that we returned to the Masonic Hall where dancing was continued until a late hour. We went home at 1:30 A.M.—H.C. and I."*

JESSIE AND HENRY'S WEDDING PORTRAIT

Jessie was nineteen years old and in love. Henry was the only descendent of a prominent Lodi rancher, Christopher Beckman, another pioneering German immigrant. Christopher Beckman had come to the United States with his brother in 1848 and to California in 1853, where he settled on a ranch located near the southern end of Lodi. Christopher died on April 27, 1890, and now his twenty three year old son Henry was in charge of the beautiful ranch. This would be Jessie's home, because a wedding was being planned. The following is quoted from the *Lodi News Sentinel* in 1896.

"Wednesday May 20th, was the scene of a happy wedding at the home of Mr. and Mrs. Joseph Spenker the occasion being the marriage of their daughter Jessie, to Henry C. Beckman. A large tent had been erected near the house, and beautifully decorated by the willing hands of their many friends. A double arch of evergreen greens graced the entrance, and the walls were covered with a profusion of flowers. Early in the forenoon relatives and friends to the number of nearly a hundred assembled bringing with them many useful and costly presents.

At 12 o'clock the bridal party appeared, marching to the strain of Beethoven's Wedding March played by Miss Lillian Harshner, and took their place under a beautiful floral bell.

The groom was attended by his cousin Theo. Beckman and Miss Millie Spenker of Modesto acted as bridesmaid.

Rev. Block of the German Lutheran Church of Stockton performed the ceremony which made two happy hearts beat as one.

At the conclusion of the ceremony all repaired to the tent partitioned off as a dining room to partake of a beautiful and delicious wedding dinner. Toasts were responded to by Rev. Block, Philip Rohrbacher, William Hacke, L. C. McMurty, Geor. Emde, Frank and Theo. Beckman, and Henry Rohrbacher.

At 2:30 the newly wedded couple departed for Stockton amid showers of rice and good wishes from their friends to take the boat to the city. They will make a short tour of the coast, and on their return will reside on their beautiful farm near Lodi."

After her marriage, Jessie lived in the Beckman home with her husband Henry and his mother Marie. Jessie enjoyed this good woman and learned many things from her, such as how to cook some of Henry's favorite meals. Jessie was thankful that she was as comfortable with the German language as she was with English, because Marie spoke very little English. Often while they were doing the kitchen chores, Marie would tell Jessie stories about her home in Westphalia. She and Christopher had been sweethearts in Prussia, and he had promised to come back for her after he got established in California. In 1864, when she was twenty-five, Christopher came back across the ocean to take her to America. They were married in San Francisco.

She and her husband Christopher had returned to her homeland for a visit in 1873 with their three children. When Marie talked about this trip, tears would come to her eyes. While they were in Europe, both of her little girls—one age three and a half and the other age eight, had contracted influenza and died. Henry was thankfully spared. Marie said the pain would remain with her the rest of her life.

NIAGARA FALLS IN 1873. CHRISTOPHER BECKMAN IS ON THE LEFT. MARIE IS STANDING AND ? IS SEATED ON THE RIGHT.

JESSIE WAS HAPPY WITH HER NEW LIFE, SHE LOVED THE BEAUTIFUL RANCH AND ALL THE NEW ANIMALS TO GET ACQUAINTED WITH—

ESPECIALLY THE HORSES WHICH REMAINED HER FAVORITE. JESSIE IS WALKING OUT TO HELP MILK THE COWS.

Marie Beckman and Anna Spenker had been friends for many years. They enjoyed each other's company and often would share stories about their journeys to America. One would try to outdo the other amid peals of laughter. Marie always ended up with the top story, however, when she described her journey across the isthmus of Panama by pack mule in 1864. She said on the trip she vowed to herself never to straddle another critter in her life—and she kept her word. Marie would ride in a carriage or she would stay home.

Horses provided the principal means of transportation for people at this time. If they didn't ride the horse, the horse pulled their wagons or carriages. If it rained, they stayed home. They also had to plan plenty of time to arrive at their destination. Jessie wrote about a forty-mile trip to Modesto: *"We started at 4:30 a.m. and arrived at 3:00 p.m. We came close to two trains on the road and our horses remained calm."*

The age of horse power was about to change, as the nineteenth century drew to a close.

MARIE BECKMAN ARRIVING AT ANNA'S HOME. JOSEPH IS STANDING TO THE RIGHT.

THE MACHINE AGE AND THE VALLEY

THE END OF ONE CENTURY AND THE BEGINNING OF ANOTHER marked the dawning of the Machine Age, a time marked by an extreme optimism about the ability of new technological developments to improve the quality of life. This optimism was fueled by an outburst of successful inventions and innovations: the automobile, industrial mass production, the telephone, the moving picture show, widespread urban electrification, and the airplane, to mention a few. The men who developed these wonderful inventions, such as Henry Ford, Thomas Alva Edison, and the Wright brothers, soon became cultural icons and role models for many people, especially Otto.

The San Joaquin Valley had made significant contributions to technological progress during the last decades of the nineteenth century with the development of horse powered wheat harvesters. Then steam power and soon the advent of the gasoline engine drove the harvesters to further innovations. In the San Joaquin Valley, these led to the development of the tracked machine—the precursor of everything from the battle tank to the bulldozer.

A percentage of the area being farmed in central California was in the Sacramento-San Joaquin River Delta. This land, with its unique, rich soil, was directly west of Lodi and Stockton. Joseph Spenker had been intrigued with the idea of purchasing some of this land, but there were problems involved. The soil would grow almost anything, but when you brought horses and machinery onto it, the horses kept sinking into the soft earth. The only solution was to fit them with a version of a snowshoe. Getting the horse-drawn harvesters to stay on top of the land required them to be fitted with extra wide wheels.

The Holt Brothers purchased land in the river bottom of the San Joaquin Valley on Robert's Island, not far from Stockton. To farm this Delta soil, Holt developed steam tractors—some as wide as forty-six feet. This width made maneuvering them more difficult than managing the two or three dozen horses that the steam power had replaced, but the width kept the machine from sinking into the soft earth.

To facilitate farming this unique Delta land, Holt started developing a tractor that would conquer the problems of the Delta. He designed a track-based tractor that would use steam for its energy source. This idea had been experimented with in the past. Warren Miller, of Marysville, California, had patented a track-type steam tractor in 1858.[1] Because of a lack of financial backing, however, his idea remained on the drawing board. On November 24, 1904, forty-six years later, Holt tested his version of the steam crawler. Charles Clements, a photographer, was present and observed that it moved like a caterpillar. The name stuck. This machine started making history both on the farms and later in World War I and after.[2]

The next big change in the evolution of farm machinery was from the power of steam to the more dependable and easier power of gasoline engines. This change was quickly accomplished in 1906. The fairly easy process simply replaced the boilers with gasoline motors. The rapid innovations in agricultural technology accomplished in the Stockton region brought increases in productivity to farmers. Crops could be harvested faster and easier.

"By 1890, two men, with the aid of horse-powered machinery, could farm as many as 250 acres of wheat. By the end of the century, a farmer could plant and harvest two and a half times as much corn, seven times as much hay and nine times the oat harvest his grandfather had done. Between 1860 and 1900, annual sales of farm equipment rose from twenty-one million to over one hundred and ten million dollars. Because of all this equipment, ten of the eleven men needed to farm in the 1880's are free to do other work today."[3]

[1] Randy Lefffingwell, *CATERPILLAR Farm Crawlers and Bulldozers*, MBI Publishing Co., 1994, p. 30.
[2] Ibid, p. 34.
[3] Heidrick Ag History Center, Woodland, California

IN 1895, HOLT OF STOCKTON DEVELOPED A STEAM DRIVEN TRACTION HARVESTER. THE WIDE WHEELS ON THIS HARVESTER MADE FOR VERY DIFFICULT TURNING, BUT MADE PLANTING WHEAT ON THE SOFT RICH SOIL OF THE DELTA POSSIBLE. THESE HARVESTERS NECESSITATED A SMALLER STEAM ENGINE TRACTOR TO HAUL WATER OUT TO THE HARVESTER.

HENRY BECKMAN, JESSIE'S HUSBAND, WAS USING THE NEW GAS-POWERED TRACK-LAYING TRACTOR TO GET THE FIELDS READY FOR PLANTING. JOE BECKMAN, HIS SON, IS THE YOUNG MAN STANDING IN FRONT

DISK PLOW PULLED BY A GASOLINE POWERED TRACK LAYING TRACTOR. MAN WITH ARMS CROSSED IS HENRY BECKMAN. YOUNG BOY IS JOE BECKMAN.

HOLT STEAM TRACTION ENGINE. 1895. FIVE STOCKTON GANG PLOWS BUILT OF WOOD. PHOTOGRAPH FROM COLLECTION OF MAYNARD SMITH.

OTTO AND THE ERA OF INVENTIONS

OTTO GREW UP DURING THIS ERA OF INVENTIONS, when technological innovation transformed life both at home and in the nation as a whole. He found kindred spirits in the inventors who were changing the way people lived throughout the United States and the world, yet everyone expected him to follow in his father's footsteps and become a farmer.

In 1889, when Otto was eighteen years of age and had just graduated from San Joaquin Valley College in Woodbridge, he wrote: *"I will miss the intellectual discussions, the opportunities to explore my thoughts in words. I regret I did not train to become a teacher of higher learning—instead I will be a farmer. To encourage me, father said he would buy me a harvester for a graduation present when the improved model came out."*

The one aspect of farming that seemed to interest Otto was the equipment used to plant the fields and bring in the harvest. Otto wrote: *"New ideas—improvements in existing machinery, these are a very worthwhile use of my time and energy."*

A major improvement in the harvesting season came about by the development of Brack's Landing. Jacob Brack, a close friend of Joseph and Otto, had come to California in 1849 and had established himself on a ranch just west of Woodbridge. He was a major developer of the San Joaquin Valley, endowed with vision, creative powers, and industrious energy. When he bought land in the Delta, he started dredging a deep-water channel so produce could be shipped from his landing to San Francisco. This was located on Hog Slough, about six miles from the Spenker Ranch. Jessie and Otto enjoyed riding over to the slough to watch the dredger work. Prior to this achievement, the grain had to be hauled into Stockton and put into warehouses. It would take one man and a wagon an entire day to haul one load.

One part of farm life Otto did not seem to care for were the animals. Not only did he prefer riding a bicycle to riding a horse, he wrote many times in his diaries about how he hated working at the dairy: *"Personally, I would rather work at almost anything else than the dairy—the odor seems to stay with you for hours after you leave the barn."* But nothing compared with his feeling for hogs. He wrote:

"Rounding up hogs for market has to be the most frustrating job on the ranch. Just when you think you have them all together, they break away and you have to start all over again. I've heard hogs are very intelligent. You can see this by the way the sows make their nest—off by themselves in a protected area. They are excellent mothers and a joy to watch, until you try to round them up. It's like they figure out which way you want them to go and then they rip around and go the opposite direction. They certainly don't herd well! It can take us all day to get a group into market."

He also wrote: *"Father and I started for church but the horse was sick with a cold or distemper, so we turned around and came back after going a mile"* Otto felt horses were very undependable.

Otto's dislike for farm animals, however, didn't apply to dogs. Otto wrote: *"I found a little dog in the road coming back from the dairy. He was so frightened—but he eagerly came to me. I brought him home and gave him to mother. She has long wanted a dog, and this will help take her mind off her troubles. I think this little dog will make a happy addition to this ranch. Mother named the dog Shep."*

Otto was interested in all the changes his father was making on the ranch. He knew Joseph was one of the most capable farmers in the area, and he admired the way Joseph was eager to try new ideas, crops, and equipment. Otto felt there was one innovative avocation he could pursue that his father would greatly appreciate—the field of photography. Joseph always felt what he was doing was important and should be recorded, and in the past had hired professional photographers to photograph major equipment and events on the ranches. Otto happily took over this responsibility, feeling he could do as well as the professionals. Photography fascinated him, and he had many ideas he wanted to develop to improve the process.

He started experimenting with the camera in the early 1880s, and his interest continued the rest of his life. Otto had his own darkroom and processed most of his photographs to completion. Many were from glass negatives, and later, after 1896, he experimented with the new celluloid films. The vast majority of the photographs in this book are from the camera of Otto Spenker.

The Holden Drug Company in Stockton had an excellent camera department, and Otto used them as a good source of information and supplies. When the Cartridge Kodak came on the market, Otto bought one and enjoyed experimenting with its new features. It was hard for him to give up working with glass-plate photography, however, and many of his later pictures still used this process. His new camera came with a booklet describing the advantages of the new celluloid film. This booklet was printed in 1896.

EASTMAN KODAK COMPANY BOOKLET "THE CARTRIDGE KODAK", 1896, P.8

The Cartridge Kodak. 8

OUNCES VS. POUNDS.

I cannot say enough of the advantages of roll film, and especially of the film cartridges, over glass plates. In the first place, my camera is lighter than a glass plate instrument of the same capacity; and a film cartridge of twelve exposures weighs but 2½ ozs. while a dozen plates of equivalent size and half a dozen double plate holders to carry them in, weigh just three pounds, or nearly twenty times as much. It's no trouble to carry a half dozen film cartridges in one's pockets when out for a day's Kodaking. They contain material for seventy-two shots and weigh only fifteen ounces. An equivalent in glass plates and holders would tip the scales at eighteen pounds, weight enough to spoil any outing either afoot or awheel.

IN TWO MINUTES.

It's an easy matter to remove the cartridge after the film has been exposed and replace it with a new one. Being done in daylight, the operator does not become confused as he is likely to when working in a dark room. I can take out one cartridge and put in another ready for taking pictures in less than two minutes and never had any instructions other than those in the illustrated manual accompanying the instrument.

TAKING OUT THE EXPOSED ROLL.

THEY DON'T BREAK.

Film negatives don't break, a fact that recommends them to me very forcibly after my early sad experience. They can be sent by mail in an envelope; can be stored between the leaves of a book or kept in packages, a hundred of them taking up a space of only one-half inch by 4 x 5 inches.

OTTO EXPERIMENTED WITH HIS NEW CAMERA

"FEET"

SELF PORTRAIT

HAULING MILK TO TOWN

ACTION SHOT!

JOSEPH, ANITA, JOE, VERA, JESSIE. OH—FOR A FLASH!

SHEP

WHAT IS THAT MAN DOING?

THE PAN-AMERICAN EXPOSITION

IN 1901, OTTO HAD THE OPPORTUNITY of traveling east to Buffalo, New York, to visit the Pan-American Exposition. The exposition, which had been the scene of the assassination of President William McKinley on September 6, nevertheless continued to draw crowds to its exhibitions of technological marvels, especially those powered by the growing new energy source, electricity. Otto mailed all his letters to Jessie. She promised to share them with others and keep all of them for Otto so he could have a good record of this wonderful adventure.

THE PAN-AMERICAN EXPOSITION

The following are excerpts from some of those letters.

Salt Lake City:

"Arrived here last night at 8:20 over the Rio Grande Western from Ogden. This place is like Paradise beside the country between here and the Sierras.

Salt Lake is the most beautiful city it has been my pleasure to visit. The business part of the city reminds one of San Francisco. There are many 5 and 6 story buildings and many large wholesale houses. Nearly every building here is built of stone or brick including dwelling houses.

The streets are 100 feet wide from curb to curb, then a space about 8 or 10 feet wide planted to shade trees and then about 20 foot wide sidewalks. The center of the street is taken up by the poles to which are attached the trolley and lighting wires, a car track running on either side. At the street crossings the pole is slightly higher and carries an electric light on top.

Water is here everywhere in abundance—clear as crystal and pure as the snow. A stream of clear water flows along both sides of all principal streets and even in the business center of the city.

After a much needed nights sleep at the St. Elmo, I arose this morning at 6:30 and started out to see the sights. Not knowing where to go, nor caring much either, I started up Main St. going North. In about 10 minutes, I passed through the business district portion of town and came up against a stone wall about fifteen feet high enclosing a whole block. The entrance was guarded by a massive gate, I needed no one to tell me that I had discovered the great Mormon Temple. When we consider the circumstances under which the construction was begun, it seems almost a miracle that such a work could be accomplished—even more to think that any man could have the courage to undertake such a gigantic work. Whatever we may say against the religious doctrines of Brigham Young and his followers, we must take off our hat to him as a man who towers high above the ordinary mortal in business ability—who by industry and perseverance has made the desert blossom as the rose, and accomplished what to most men would be pleasant dreams of Castles in Spain.

At 8:30 pm I board my train and continue my journey over the Scenic Route of the World to Pueblo and Denver. Time is too short to get more than a glance at many things and places where I could pleasantly spend all the time I have for the entire trip."

Denver, Colorado Oct. 8th, 1901
Aboard R.D. @ Pac. Train

"We have now left Denver and are winding our way across the plains of eastern Colorado. The country is gently rolling with broad stretches of level land. As far as the eye can see is one continuous line of wire fence with an occasional cross fence and here and there a farmhouse standing out on the open plain. Occasionally a few Cottonwood trees can be seen growing in the bottom of a ravine or on the sides of a creek. These water courses are all dry at this season and from appearances I would judge that they never carry much water. The only vegetation seems to be a variety of long thin grass and a weed resembling our tier weed.

Nice looking cattle in small bunches can be seen at any time feeding on the dry grass. They seem to go in herds of from 25 to 50. Horses and mules seem to be a scarce article."

I have seen my first prairie dog. They are a cute looking animal somewhat resembling a yellow pup about a month old with a bob tail. Their little white mounds looking much like squirrel holes are here in abundance, sometimes in colonies covering an acre or more of ground. The holes are quite close together.

Next morning I find myself at Belleville about 3:30 am. Our car is cut out and we must wait one hour for another train. Never was the sound of a roosters voice so sweet as at this place—it's the first time I have heard a crow since leaving home. Cows are also calling out for the milkers. The moon is just rising over the eastern hills and the old lady in the smoking car is giving the break man fits for letting the fire go out. The car is heated by steam and she doesn't know that the engine is gone. Our sailor boy is in convulsions with laughter.

Our train is coming and we continue our journey eastward toward Kansas."

Thursday morning 5:30 Joliet

"We are getting nearer Chicago—only 40 more miles. Too foggy to see much. Have spent a comfortable night in the chair car. Crossed the Mississippi River at Rock Island at midnight.

We are now 20 miles from the big city—every few miles is a platform where can be seen from 50 to 100 milk cans awaiting transportation. They are painted every shade and color—I suppose to more easily distinguish them."

Toledo, Oct 13th, 1901

"The Lake Shore @ M.S. is a beautiful road to ride on; the train glides along as smoothly as if running on greased glass. We made a run of 81 miles in 108 minutes including 5 stops and about 2 miles run in the city limits of Toledo. The S.P. is the poorest excuse for railroad accommodations, both cars and road bed, I have found so far. A person who has been on no other road doesn't know what railroad comfort means. This house I am stopping at is one of the most tony in Toledo. It costs $2.00 a night, and the porter expects a tip besides. I am glad I got into it though: have learned a thing or two. It is now 10 o'clock and I must go to bed so I can get up early—if I can get up without having to tip the elevator boy. Otherwise I can climb the stairs."

Buffalo, Oct. 23, 1901 Pan-American Exposition 7:30 am

"I have now been out to the exposition two days and am just beginning to find out where to look for things; am lost most of the time, but that doesn't matter as it is all worth looking at. It would be impossible to see everything in a month, so I must do the best I can in the time at my disposal. A description of the fair is out of the question; even the best pictures only hint at the magnificent grandeur of this great work. The colors on the buildings are somewhat faded, but all the hues of the rainbow are still visible, and the illumination at night is simply grand. Over 200,000 incandescent lights shed a flood of light over the scene.

Everything is on a scale to stagger the imagination of ordinary mortals like we. I shall not attempt to describe anything in particular, will do that when I get back. The attendance is something immense as on account of the fine weather many people are taking a last look at it.

Souvenirs are on sale by the million and prices have been cut in half. Anything can be had down town cheaper than on the fair grounds. I am thinking of chartering a boxcar to bring my collection home, but I guess a Saratoga will have to do as I won't have money enough left to do any more.

Meals are pretty high here. Not only near the fair ground but in town too. As an example, at the Golden Buffalo Dairy Kitchen in Buffalo, you can get a meal of: fruit in season, cup of coffee or tea, rolls and butter, Lamb Chops or Club Steak, Potatoes fried or stewed for 45 Cents. They have a notice on the menu in large black letters: club meals served to one person only. The cheap places are dirty and give something to eat. The high priced ones seem to charge for their cleanliness as you don't get anymore to eat, only it's clean.

The best places I have found are the lunch counters. There you can get most anything at 5 cents a dish and it's generally pretty good too as they do lots of business and everything is fresh and hot."

New Orleans, Louisiana, Nov. 11th, 1901

"It is now 7:15 pm and my train does not go until 8:40 so I shall try to spend the time as best I can.

This has been the D____est[3] *day I have spent since leaving home. The thermometer has been about 85 all day and as I was togged out to stand zero and live to tell about it, you can imagine how comfortable I have been. This tropical warmth seems to be more penetrating than the same temperature in northern latitudes and its effects are easily felt. I am sitting on a bench in the S. & P. waiting room as I write. If it were not that I have two grips and an overcoat to guard, I would get out somewhere to cool off, but it is not wise to leave them to the public to take care of and I have better use for my money than to pay 25 cents to have them checked.*

By the way my tin, or rather shin plaster is getting down to such a pile that I can count it in a few seconds. I am quite away from being busted, however and still have a Canada quarter for luck. Have tried all day to pass it but they won't have it down here.

This is the queerest city in many respects one can expect to see in America. The first thing to attract my attention, and I could see it on the train in the dark, is the peculiar odor of the place. It may be called anything from a sewer in Chinatown to a fish stand or a slop barrel at close range.

This odor seems to pervade the entire city and everything you come in contact with. While it is not so marked in the district back from the river, still I could not get entirely away from it all day. It affected me to such an extent that I did not get any breakfast until about 12:30. I had, however, by that time managed to drink a glass of soda and eat some bananas, which are here sold quite extensively.

The odor is easily accounted for when you consider that the sewage runs in the gutter and all rubbish is dumped in the street to be carried away by this foul smelling filthy stream. What does not escape this way is loaded into carts and hauled through the streets at any time of day. This is especially true of the old French Quarter where the streets are only about 20 to 30 feet wide and as crooked as they are dirty. They look still narrower as every building has a porch extending to the curb, supported by posts on the outside. Many of the porches or in this case the sidewalks, are only 4 to 6

[3] "This has been the D_____est ...." is accurate. Otto never wrote a swear word.

feet wide. Where a car line runs on one of those streets, it scarcely leaves room for a car or team to pass.

The streets as a rule are in a miserable condition—macadamized streets being as scarce as horses. Nearly all the narrow streets and many of the sidewalks are made of stones about two feet square laid in diagonal patterns.

Four teaming mules are used almost exclusively, a few horses being employed at light work of the better class. Two wheeled vehicles seem to predominate and they are of every conceivable construction, most of them after a pattern no one would imagine who has not seen them. Imagine a vehicle carrying 6 bales of cotton, or a sprinkling wagon running on two wheels.

The better class of vehicles such as light carts, buggies, wagons and bikes are conspicuous for their absence. I haven't seen a buggy all day. Fortunately, the street car service is excellent and by this means you can reach nearly every part of the city.

To a stranger the city is exceedingly interesting and I have spent the day in getting over the greater part of it. The most interesting thing I found were the cemeteries. These are different from any other in that the bodies are all deposited above ground in private vaults. Many of them are of costly design and must cost many thousand. Those of the poorer class are of brick—finished in cement. Everything is kept in the best order and plenty of white wash is used so that everything looks white. Such a wealth of flowers I have never seen; every tomb is liberally supplied with either natural or artificial flowers and every effort is made to present a pleasing effect.

The dead here fare better than the living."

El Paso, Texas Nov. 7th, 1901

"Arrived here at 8:40 this morning after a 24 hour ride from San Antonio. They make the slowest time here I ever saw, and all the old cars that went out of date 20 years ago in the east, are on this road. From San Austere to El Paso is 640 miles-24 hours. From Chicago to New Orleans is 962 miles in 24 hours.

Crossed the Pecos river bridge about sundown. It is the highest bridge in the U.S.-342 feet. The whole country is covered with cactus, thistles and mesquite. The cattle look bad to me, but cattlemen here say they are looking well. The smallest piece of the toughest meat on my whole trip I have had in Texas.

Hoping this will find you all in good health as it leaves me.
I am as ever the bum, Otto"

When Otto returned home from his wonderful trip, he found plenty of work to do. Windmills—the wonderful devices that bring water up from the ground, needed frequent repairs. The windmill on the Adobe Ranch, which was eight miles away, needed some work.

Otto wrote in his diary:

"Immediately after breakfast I started per bike for the adobe ranch to inspect the windmill, which is out of commission. I made a quick trip and directly came back home. I took down the windmill in the garden at home and put same in good condition—preparing to mount same in the adobe house. The next day I finished repairing the windmill. I hitched a wagon to my bike—loaded in the windmill, and went down to the ranch to put it up. I took the old mill down and while I was so engaged a furious North wind started—making

further work impossible. I left the windmill unfinished and came home on my bike—towing behind the wagon. The fierce wind made for a very difficult ride."

He concluded the year with a tragic entry: *"Frank Bishofberger was run over by his lumber wagon and died seven hours later. Father and I went to his funeral, which was very well attended. There were 68 carriages in the procession. And the year goes on—rain comes—and comes—water is everywhere."*

Otto had taken on a new responsibility:

"I'm involved with another of Brack's developments—the Telephone Co. I'm on the board and in charge of establishing the lines from Brack's Landing all the way into Lodi. We call them "Farmer's Lines," largely because farmers are the only people out there. The lines are actually owned by the farmers, with as many as ten to a line. They own them, but I'm in charge of maintaining them and collecting the money to pay for them. This is just what I needed, more work. I must say I do enjoy the work. I like the close contact this gives everyone who has one of the Talk a Phones."

TO MAKE IT EASIER FOR PEOPLE TO REMEMBER HIM, OTTO CHOSE A "PROPER" CALLING CARD.

THE OAK GROVE

OTTO HAD MANY RESPONSIBILITIES DURING THIS TIME, and the future looked bright. His favorite task was organizing events in the oak grove. Local organizations would contact Otto and arrange for the use of the grove for special events. Otto put up swings in the grove to add to the fun, and one such event even included a merry-go-round.

St. Peter's Lutheran Church of Lodi had its official formation in Joseph's grove. Services had been held at Henderson School one Sunday a month, and on the other three Sundays, worshippers had to travel to Stockton. One Sunday in September 1896, during a combined picnic and official meeting at the grove, they formed their own congregation of the German Lutheran Church. Jessie and Otto were both members of this congregation and were very happy about the decision.

May was one of the best times for picnics in the grove. Carpets of wildflowers nestled among the fresh green grasses, and a faint green glow haloed the lacy tips of the giant oaks. The glow became more pronounced and slowly turned to a dark, rich green as summer days drew near. The sheltering canopy that formed provided a shade-protected area for both the wild inhabitants of the grove and the people who sought its sanctuary.

Otto took pictures and wrote about picnics in the oak grove.

Otto is second from the left in the front row. In 1906 he wrote: *"Today was the W.A.C. picnic in the oak grove, a fine crowd and a good time. I was awarded the prize as the handsomest? man on the grounds! A good one on me."*[4]

[4] The W. A. C. was the Women's Auxiliary Corps—the Women's Auxiliary of the Grand Army of the Republic, a Civil War Union veterans' group.

"Our second picnic for the season was put on by classes from the Lodi Normal Institute on a cool and cloudy day in the morning—turning warm in the afternoon. They had the largest crowd yet. They came early and stayed all day. I had a good time, but didn't feel at home in the crowd.

The Women's Auxiliary will spend time in our grove. They anticipate about 1,000 people will attend. That would be our largest gathering ever. Hattie Woock is the lady dressed in white."

SECOND ANNUAL

GRANGE PICNIC

AT SPENKER'S GROVE

Near Woodbridge,

Saturday, May 14th, 1898.

PRESIDENT OF DAY, OTTO SPENKER.

xxx PROGRAMME xxx

(FORENOON, 10:30 A. M.)

Music ....Orchestra
Vocal Selection..
Recitation..Birdie Childs
Music ....Orchestra
Recitation..Hazel LeMoin
Vocal Selection..
Recitation...Lela Parsons
Recitation..Lulu Villinger
Oration...Rev. T. A. Boyer

(AFTERNOON.)

Boys' Race, 50 yds, 5 yrs, Box Candy, by Deaver's Kitchen
Boys' Sack Race, 50 yds, 12 yrs, Book, "Five Years ....Before the Mast," by Joe Friedberger
Fat Men's Race, 50 yds, Hay Rake........by Henderson Bros.
Boys' Race, 10 yrs, Pocket Knife..............by E. M. Percival
Free for All Bicycle Race, Luggage Carrier....by Lillie Bros.
Married Ladies' Race, 50 yds, Can Baking Powder ....by Thompson & Krause
Ladies' Race, over 20, Dress Pattern.............S. K. D. G. Co.
Girls' Race, 10 to 15, Child's Rocking Chair, by F. O. Hale
Boys' and Girls' Race, under 8, Box Candy,..H. Hollingsworth
Married Men's Race, free for all, Year's Subscription ....to Lodi Sentinel
Girls' Race, 16 to 18, Hand Painted Hk'f, by R. L. Graham
Girls' Race, 15 to 17, Pair Fine Shoes..............by G. Peirano
Married Men's Race, free for all, Hair Cut and Shave ....by Louis Rieffle
Young Ladies' Race, under 20, Box Writing Paper ....by Dr. L. H. Thompson
Married Ladies' Race, Fine Hat........by Miss E. L. Channell
Most Popular Young Lady, Shirt Waist Set...by Friedberger & Kaiser
Girls' Race, 15 to 20, Silver Jewel Case............by G. W. Hill
Single Men's Race, Hair Cut and Shave....by Scott Robbins

Refreshments Served on Grounds.

Dancing in Pavilion After 1 O'clock.

"The Grange held their second annual picnic at Spenker's Grove. It was a splendid occasion."

CHAPTER FOUR

The Valley and the Wider World

LIFE IN THE SAN JOAQUIN VALLEY was increasingly connected with life in the wider world beyond. In part, connection always had existed for immigrants who still had relatives in the old country, but modern modes of transportation made correspondence quicker and easier.

The Beckman family was connected to events in Germany for the next half-century and more by its correspondence with a man named John Westphalen. When John heard of Henry's marriage, he sent a letter to Jessie to explain how they had met.

"In 1894, I sailed on a sailing ship by name of Cutty Sark from Liverpool around the horn to San Francisco as boatswain. There I cleared out, there was little and very bad grub. In Frisco I met a German out of Berlin—a goldsmith who made double filigree work. He said to me, "Come along with me, for you speak English, which I do not understand. We sell them double gold rings." He had a little cart with two horses, so I rode one horse and went with him from village to village, selling, hunting a bit and so forth. At last we came to your place. There was a big haystack, we made a little fire to cook some dinner and the horses took the hay. Then came Mr. H. Beckman and said, "Don't make the fire so close to the haystack!" The goldsmith muttered and pulled the rifle on Mr. Beckman. I jumped up and took the rifle away from that crazy fellow—telling him to go his way alone! This he did. Mr. Beckman told me "If you like, come to my farm." So I did. I worked about a year on the farm and then I went back to Germany."

On November 22, 1899, Henry received another letter from John Westphalen.

"How is it about your family dear Henry? Is everything alright?—at least I hope it is. About the war I need not tell you any news, only that we all sympathize with the Boers, and I hope that England will get licked! How is it about your crop this year? If you had some of your hogs here you would make a pile of money on them. For good pork we have to pay about 25 cents the pound. I am working in a big machine factory as blacksmith and have a dollar a day by 10 hours work. That is very much for this place. I pay two dollars a month for my family for rooms and I manage well so I am satisfied. I hope dear Henry that you will write to me as soon as possible."

JOHN WESTPHALEN

JOHN WESTPHALEN, 1899 IN GERMANY

Jessie also received letters from Germany. She had a cousin, Hartwig, who was near her own age, and they had corresponded off and on through the years. He was a soldier in the German army, and his brother was in the marines. Hartwig felt he made more money and had more freedom than his brother. On October 24, 1897 he wrote a letter to Jessie from Berlin.

"At my request I got to go to Berlin on Oct. 1. So now I live in the Emperor (Kaiser) City of Berlin. You know, dear cousin, it is quite different from a little town. The hustle and bustle is very stressful. You have to watch out so you don't get run over. And all what there is to see!! Whenever I'm off, either during the day or even night, I slowly walk the streets and window shop, and watch all the people hurry about. Most everything happens in the Friedrichsstrasse and Unter den Linden. Friedrichsstrasse is the longest street, it takes a good hour to walk it. It doesn't matter if it's 8:00 p.m. or 10:00 p.m. or 3:00 a.m., it's always crowded with people. Whenever I leave at 5:00 a.m. to work, I see all the night owls, strolling along, as if the night would go on for who knows how long. If you go to a concert or to a pub, it is so beautifully appointed. I can't imagine it's like this anywhere else. It's part of the classy tone of the city. I will tell you more about Berlin in my next letter."

On January 27, 1898, Jessie received another letter from her cousin.

"New Years Eve everyone celebrated in a big way, with song and dance until the morning hours. The streets were full of people and the trolley ran all night. In some of the bigger streets the crowds were so large around midnight, you could not move at times. I can't even explain it, you have to experience it yourself to understand. Some coffeehouses and restaurants were closed by the police to avoid trouble. It is here customary to round up the troublemakers quickly. Sometimes it's fun to watch, however it can be painful for those involved. I have only seen a few, because on New Years night the police patrols every 20 minutes. If one is too loud and won't cooperate, he will be taken to the station. As I said, you have to see it for yourself. It is very cold here now and we are happy to be at home in a warm room. How nice it must be for you, since your summer will be arriving soon. I have thought about taking 8 weeks vacation in the year 1901 so I can visit you. That is, if I can save that much money until then, otherwise it's not possible of course. I would love to get to know your country. My father would surely agree to the trip and I assume you would not mind putting me up for a few weeks. But it's a long time away.

How is your brother Otto? You haven't written in a long time. Siegfried likes the marines, but he has to work very hard. But that's the same everywhere. We had a nice birthday celebration for the "Kaiser" (Wilhelm). I saw him in the afternoon "Unter den Linden" (a popular place in Berlin) with his wife. They were in a carriage pulled by 4 white horses. He took a little trip to the "beer-garden." Lots of dignitaries and royalty came to visit. In the evening all the store windows were lit. From 6 to 10 o'clock at night you could hardly move along the streets. It's much fun for the young people. They have to be there, come rain or shine. They shouted excitedly every time the Kaiser came to the window. I could tell you so much more, but I have to close. It's almost time to go to work. How does it look for the harvest? Will it be plentiful this year? They expect it to be meager here again. Too much flood water. But let's hope for the best."[1]

On April 16, 1900, Jessie received a letter from her cousin Fritz Spenker. Hartwig had passed away very unexpectedly from influenza on Good Friday. He was only twenty-four years old. Hartwig's parents were devastated, and Jessie shared their deep sorrow.

[1] These letters were written in German and translated by Gabriele Libhart and her mother, Charlotte Eisenmann. The majority of John Westphalen's letters were also written in German and translated by Gabriele and Charlotte.

MOTHERHOOD

FAMILY LIFE FORMED THE CENTER around which all these wider connections revolved, and the size of Jessie's family had increased. On January 27, 1900, after a previous still birth in 1898, Jessie gave birth to a healthy baby girl. Jessie and Henry named their new daughter Anita.

"What will her middle names be?" Anna asked Jessie. Anna and Joseph had named Jessie, Anna Jessie Marie Spenker, but Jessie always felt she had too many names. *"Her name will simply be Anita. When she gets married, she can use her maiden name for her middle name,"* Jessie replied.

HENRY HOLDING ANITA IN JANUARY OF 1900

JESSIE AND ANITA

Anita loved music and took piano lessons from a very early age. A gifted pianist, she performed at many church and school functions. She also enjoyed the ranch animals, but would rather care for them than ride one of them.

AFTER THE RECITAL

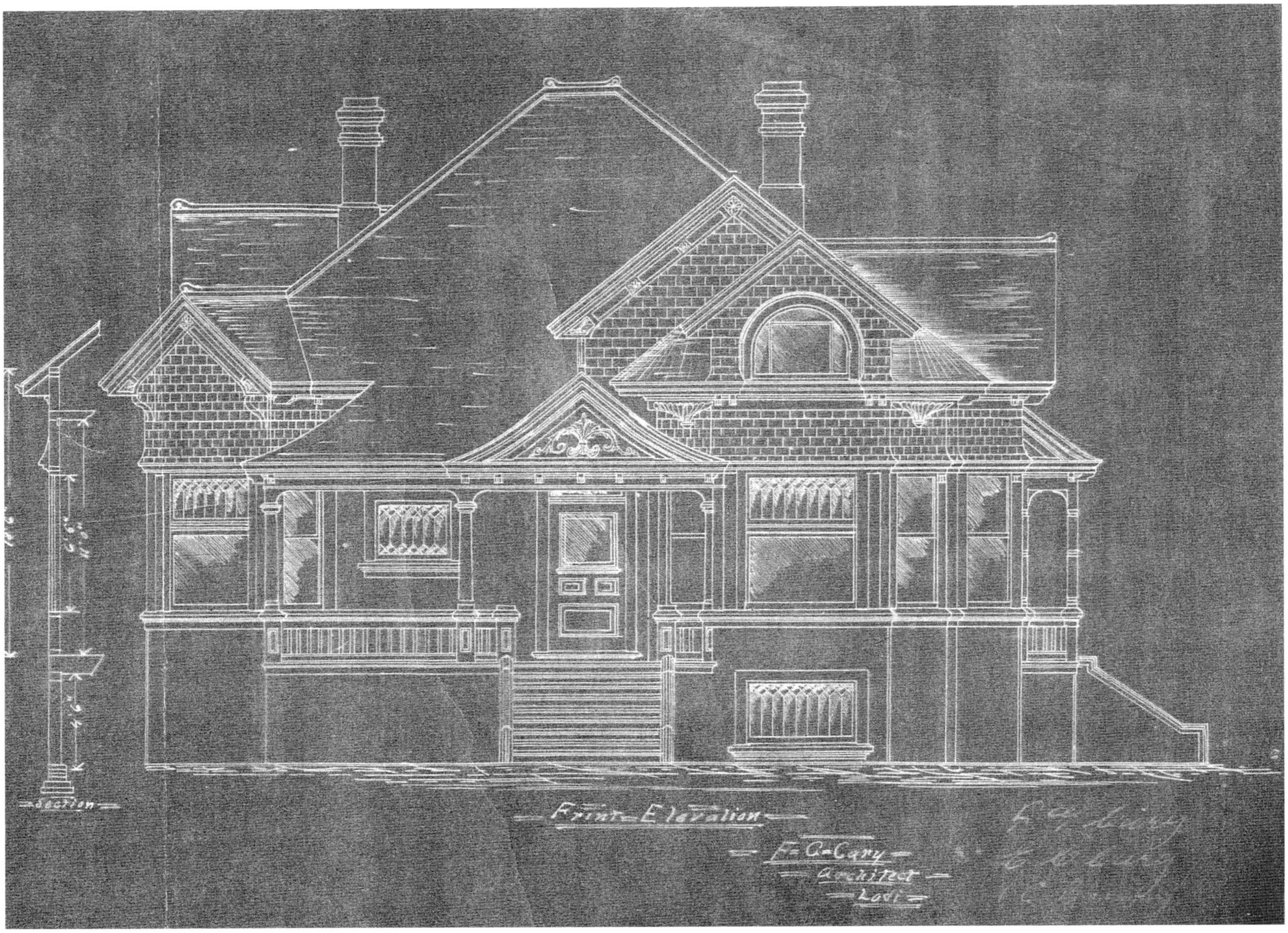

JESSIE SAVED THE BLUEPRINT FOR THEIR NEW HOME.

Henry was building a home for his new family. On April 9, 1901, he signed a contract with a firm in Lodi called Cary Brothers to build a 2,450-square-foot, two-story house for $2,950—paid in gold coins of the United States. The contract stated: *"To be paid in the manner following: $737.50 when the frame is up; $737.50 when the building is enclosed; $737.50 when the brown mortar is put on; $737.50 thirty five days after completion and acceptance of said building."* The Lodi paper reported the event on April 30, 1901: *"H. C. Beckman, the well known farmer—residing 2 miles South of Lodi, is constructing a beautiful eight room residence which will be one of the most attractive homes in the northern part of the county."* Jessie observed that the paper seemed to be happy to report anything they could about her family. They even reported how high the windmill was—sixty feet, and what it was made of—wood!

THE NEW BECKMAN RESIDENCE WITH THE (AS REPORTED) SIXTY FOOT TALL WINDMILL MADE OF WOOD

On Christmas Eve, 1901, twenty-three months after the birth of Anita, Jessie gave birth to a second baby girl—Vera. Vera, who had a deep love for animals, was ideally suited to life on a ranch. While Anita was taking music lessons, Vera would be out riding a horse or training a group of cats to all sit up at the same time. She had a German shepherd, Loiya, who was her constant companion. Vera had a very happy, ideal childhood, which gave her an enthusiasm for living all the 102 plus years of her life.

VERA LOVED HORSES ALL HER LONG LIFE.

LOIYA—VERA'S FAVORITE DOG

VERA'S TRAINED CATS

LENA KREBS

In 1902, Jessie was extremely busy trying to cope with all the duties of her new life. She had found it a challenge before the birth of Anita, but now with the new baby and her mother-in-law being confined to a wheelchair, Jessie was overwhelmed. Henry knew just who to call for help. Her name was Lena Krebs. Lena moved into the household and eased the burden for Jessie.

Otto had gone down to the Adobe Ranch, where he was trying to repair the first home of Anna and Joseph. This was the home where he had been born. He wrote to Jessie:

Adobe Ranch Dec. 2nd, 1902

Hello Sis:

As I have a few minutes to spare this morning, and it's not pleasant out, I thought it would be well to let you know how things are going at this delightful winter resort. I have the roof and windows pretty well nailed up now so that we can tell whether we are on the inside or outside of the house without looking to see. The first night here I couldn't tell the difference as the room was full of fog in the morning.

Cooking is fine work only I would be glad to let someone else enjoy the pleasure. I'm getting somewhat used to it now and as we are half done, I guess I can stick it out but I have come to the conclusion not to let it happen again.

Spent awhile over at Uncle Hansens last Sunday evening and had an enjoyable evening. Enjoyed a few selections—carefully selected—on the organ by Prof. Weiss and some artistic renditions on the accordion by Sig. Dohrman. Mrs. H. also raised her glad voice in song, and Mr. H. cracked his old chestnut about the cannibals which was highly enjoyed by at least two of the company. I don't know whether the rest saw the point or not.

Best regards to all from—Otto

THERE WAS A NEW TOY FOR THE CHILDREN THIS CHRISTMAS OF 1902 THAT JESSIE THOROUGHLY ENJOYED. THEY WERE LITTLE STUFFED BEARS CALLED "TEDDY BEARS", BEING NAMED AFTER PRESIDENT THEODORE ROOSEVELT. ANITA AND VERA EACH RECEIVED ONE. THEY CERTAINLY WERE ONE OF THE MOST POPULAR GIFTS FOR CHRISTMAS IN 1902, AND JESSIE COULD WELL IMAGINE THEY WOULD REMAIN POPULAR FOR MANY MORE YEARS TO COME.

POSTCARD—JESSIE'S COLLECTION

In the fall of 1903, Jessie was expecting another baby—perhaps this would be the son Henry longed for. Henry loved his two daughters, but he hoped for a son to carry on the family name. On October 23, 1903, Jessie indeed gave birth to a son, and Henry was happy beyond all his expectations. They named him Joseph Christopher Beckman.

Joe, as everyone called him, was born into a life that could not have had more love, adventure, opportunity, security, and challenge—the challenge to follow in the footsteps of such a man as his maternal grandfather and namesake, Joseph Spenker. Joe had a wonderful life laid out for him and two sisters who adored him.

JOSEPH CHRISTOPHER BECKMAN

MEDICINE—1905

IN 1905, WHEN JESSIE'S LIFE WAS COMPLICATED by three very young children to care for, plus a mother-in-law whose health was rapidly deteriorating, Henry became ill. The doctor told him the problem could be caused by his heart, but there was no medical treatment available at the time. Jessie tried to get him to take Beecham's Pills—they were supposed to solve so many complaints, but Henry wasn't interested.

The doctor suggested a visit to one of the local hot springs. He was to rest and bathe in the healing waters. Many people went to the springs for "the cure." Some even drank the water as a tonic. Jessie always thought it smelled like rotten eggs and never took a sip.

One of Henry's friends gave him an advertisement for Duffy's Malt Whiskey. He claimed a few good drinks of this in the evening makes all his aches and pains go away. *"The one whiskey that has been authorized by the Government as medicine."*

BEECHAM'S PILLS—THE PERFECT PILLS TO TAKE FOR ANY COMPLAINT

Duffy's Pure Malt Whiskey

is the only true medicinal whiskey that is commended by chemists for its absolute purity. Being entirely free from fusel oil, it is the one whiskey that has been recognized by the Government as a medicine. Uniformly prescribed by physicians of all schools as a tonic stimulant, Duffy's Pure Malt Whiskey is used exclusively in the foremost hospitals. Above all it has a record of cures unparalleled in the history of medicine for diseases of the throat and lungs, dyspepsia and all stomach troubles, nervousness, malaria and low fevers.

TAKE DUFFY'S. NO OTHER

IT CURES DISEASE

Beware of cheap imitations and so-called malt whiskey substitutes. They are harmful. Demand Duffy's. It is the one absolutely pure whiskey, containing medicinal, health giving qualities. Duffy's Pure Malt Whiskey is sold in sealed bottles only, never in bulk. The Duffy bottle is patented and has "The Duffy Malt Whiskey Company" blown in the glass. When purchasing, see that the newspaper, "Duffy's Annual," is wrapped around the package. Be certain that the seal over the cork is unbroken. Again, look for the trade mark, "The Old Chemist," on the label. These are the safeguards that stand for purity and health. Do not accept the medicine unless they are present.

At grocers and druggists, or direct, $1.00 a bottle. Medical Booklet free by addressing Duffy Malt Whiskey Co., Rochester, N. Y.

Get the Genuine

There were more and more products available for people who were ill. Jessie knew Henry wouldn't take either of these medicines, but she thought perhaps one of them would help his mother, Marie.

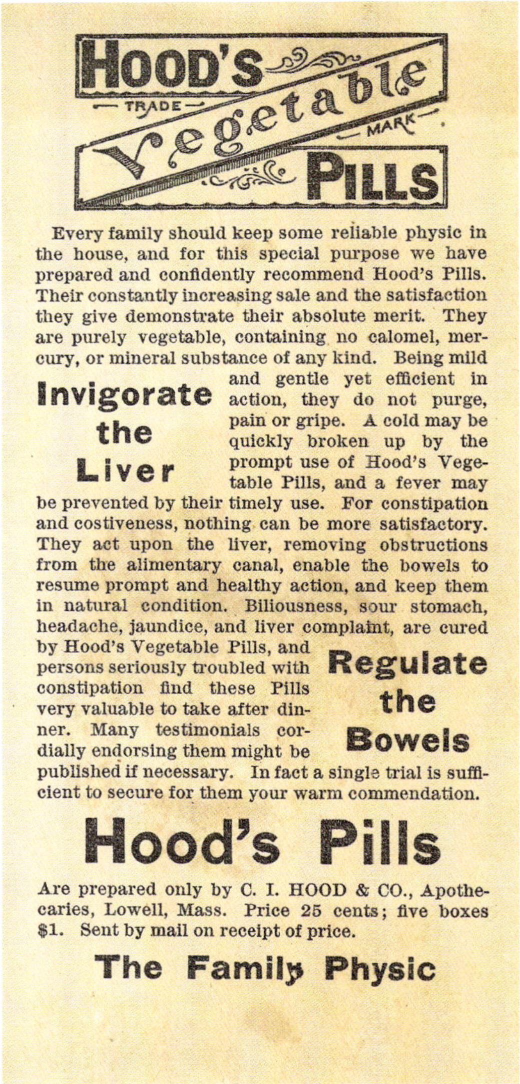

HOOD'S Vegetable PILLS

TRADE MARK

Every family should keep some reliable physic in the house, and for this special purpose we have prepared and confidently recommend Hood's Pills. Their constantly increasing sale and the satisfaction they give demonstrate their absolute merit. They are purely vegetable, containing no calomel, mercury, or mineral substance of any kind. Being mild and gentle yet efficient in action, they do not purge, pain or gripe. A cold may be quickly broken up by the prompt use of Hood's Vegetable Pills, and a fever may be prevented by their timely use. For constipation and costiveness, nothing can be more satisfactory. They act upon the liver, removing obstructions from the alimentary canal, enable the bowels to resume prompt and healthy action, and keep them in natural condition. Biliousness, sour stomach, headache, jaundice, and liver complaint, are cured by Hood's Vegetable Pills, and persons seriously troubled with constipation find these Pills very valuable to take after dinner. Many testimonials cordially endorsing them might be published if necessary. In fact a single trial is sufficient to secure for them your warm commendation.

Invigorate the Liver

Regulate the Bowels

Hood's Pills

Are prepared only by C. I. HOOD & CO., Apothecaries, Lowell, Mass. Price 25 cents; five boxes $1. Sent by mail on receipt of price.

The Family Physic

HOOD'S VEGETABLE PILLS AND AYER'S SARSAPARILLA PROMISED THEY COULD CURE ANYTHING, BUT HENRY REFUSED TO TRY THEM.

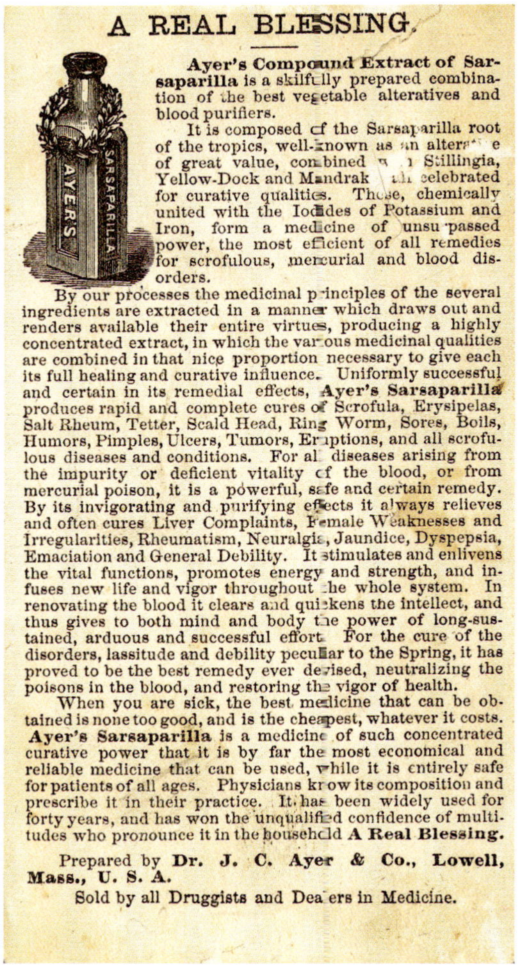

A REAL BLESSING.

Ayer's Compound Extract of Sarsaparilla is a skilfully prepared combination of the best vegetable alteratives and blood purifiers.

It is composed of the Sarsaparilla root of the tropics, well-known as an alterative of great value, combined [illegible] Stillingia, Yellow-Dock and Mandrake, all celebrated for curative qualities. These, chemically united with the Iodides of Potassium and Iron, form a medicine of unsurpassed power, the most efficient of all remedies for scrofulous, mercurial and blood disorders.

By our processes the medicinal principles of the several ingredients are extracted in a manner which draws out and renders available their entire virtues, producing a highly concentrated extract, in which the various medicinal qualities are combined in that nice proportion necessary to give each its full healing and curative influence. Uniformly successful and certain in its remedial effects, **Ayer's Sarsaparilla** produces rapid and complete cures of Scrofula, Erysipelas, Salt Rheum, Tetter, Scald Head, Ring Worm, Sores, Boils, Humors, Pimples, Ulcers, Tumors, Eruptions, and all scrofulous diseases and conditions. For all diseases arising from the impurity or deficient vitality of the blood, or from mercurial poison, it is a powerful, safe and certain remedy. By its invigorating and purifying effects it always relieves and often cures Liver Complaints, Female Weaknesses and Irregularities, Rheumatism, Neuralgia, Jaundice, Dyspepsia, Emaciation and General Debility. It stimulates and enlivens the vital functions, promotes energy and strength, and infuses new life and vigor throughout the whole system. In renovating the blood it clears and quickens the intellect, and thus gives to both mind and body the power of long-sustained, arduous and successful effort. For the cure of the disorders, lassitude and debility peculiar to the Spring, it has proved to be the best remedy ever devised, neutralizing the poisons in the blood, and restoring the vigor of health.

When you are sick, the best medicine that can be obtained is none too good, and is the cheapest, whatever it costs. **Ayer's Sarsaparilla** is a medicine of such concentrated curative power that it is by far the most economical and reliable medicine that can be used, while it is entirely safe for patients of all ages. Physicians know its composition and prescribe it in their practice. It has been widely used for forty years, and has won the unqualified confidence of multitudes who pronounce it in the household **A Real Blessing.**

Prepared by **Dr. J. C. Ayer & Co., Lowell, Mass., U. S. A.**

Sold by all Druggists and Dealers in Medicine.

BACK SIDE

SWAMP ROOT COULD BE THE ANSWER TO ALL YOUR PROBLEMS.

BUILDINGS DEVOTED EXCLUSIVELY TO THE SWAMP-ROOT BUSINESS

THE OLD HOME OF SWAMP-ROOT

OUR NEW HOME---ABSOLUTELY FIREPROOF

★Denotes where we commenced business.

Remember the name, **Swamp-Root,** Dr. Kilmer's Swamp-Root, and the address **Binghamton, N. Y.,** on every bottle.

When you ask for Dr. Kilmer's Swamp-Root, the great kidney, liver and bladder remedy, don't be persuaded to take something else.

Beware of the druggist or clerk who tries to sell you some other remedy to take the place of Dr. Kilmer's Swamp-Root.

They talk for a little more profit. They wish to sell you something on which they make more money.

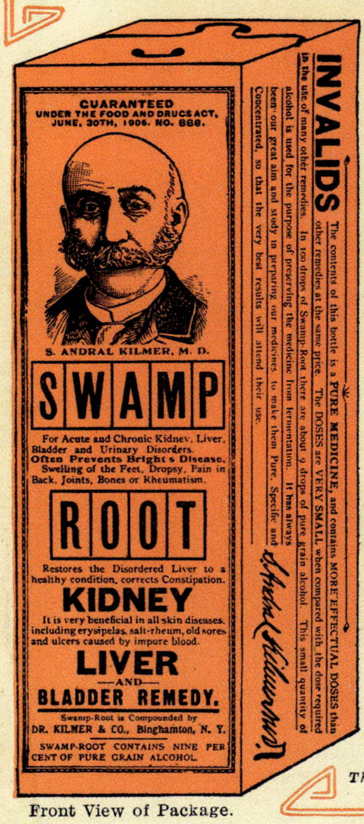

Front View of Package.

Patronize the store where they do not try to substitute something else for Dr. Kilmer's Swamp-Root.

Every bottle of Swamp-Root contains the same high standard of purity, strength and excellence.

SOLD BY DRUGGISTS AT 50 CTS. AND $1.00

A Sample Bottle Free.

You may have a sample bottle of Swamp-Root by mail free—if you have not already had one. Address

DR. KILMER & CO., Binghamton, N. Y.

French, German, Spanish, Polish and Swedish Directions with Each Bottle.

These cartoons are like the Swamp-Root Package in both Style and Color.

The 50-cent package is three times larger.

The $1 Package is more than six times larger.

Get the Genuine.

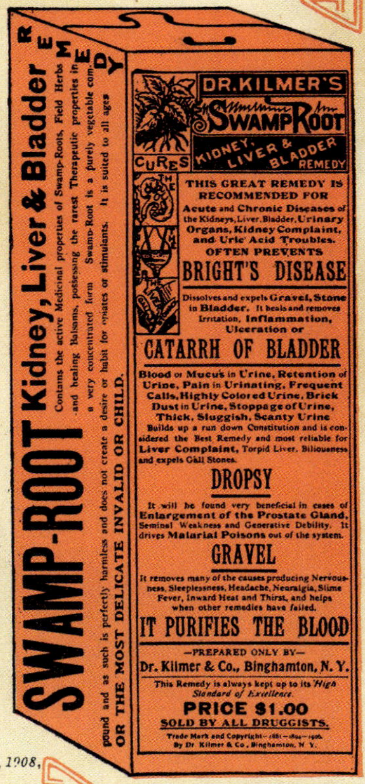

Back View of Package.

This book, cover and pictures, copyrighted, 1908, by Dr. K. & Co.

J. B. SAVAGE PRESS, CLEVELAND

Henry ignored all such suggestions and went to the springs in Cantara to take "the cure." Henry is on the lower left.

Henry wrote a letter to Jessie, dated August 3, 1905.

Dear Wife,

I am situated now in this "wondeful resort" hot springs. I slept good last night. It is nice and cold where my bed is. The tent is open so I get lots for fresh air. I have had 3 meals hear now and they were all good, but the accomodations is bad otherwise. When you want to—after breakfast, you haft to take a walk, and get in behind a log, tree or rock. Mr. Mey says this is not a natural hot springs because they haft to heat the watter, but the watter will draw out anything that is impure, or as one of the gests says that it will draw a nail out of a bord even if it is klinched on the other side. I am sitting down by the crick on a rock writing a few lines. I do love to see the watter run over the rocks. It is as clear as a cristol, and the lofty ferns all around me, this surely is a spot in the woods. Rattlesnakes, the woods are full of them, they killed 7 last week around the camp, one of them was killed in the kitchen. Ask Lena if she would not like to cook hear.

I'll close for this time. Donot worry about me for I ame all right.

H.C.B.

HENRY (LOWER LEFT) AT CANTARA

Jessie responded:

Dear Henry, don't you think you ought to write Otto a letter? He would be pleased to hear from you. You must address to Otto Spenker, Lodi, R.F.D. #3 and as Dear Bro. inside. But my dear, don't make any mistakes in your spelling. I know you make a few so I want to guard you, you see. You can see in my letters how to spell most any word. I am doing this because I think they would like to hear from you directly once.
Your loving wife
Jessie

Henry returned home from taking "The Cure". His health remained precarious and it was later diagnosed the problem was his heart.

OVER THE HILLS BY "MACHINE"

THE SPRINGS AT CANTARA, near Mount Shasta in Northern California, were right on the railroad running north along the Sacramento River. Access to other parts of California, the Sierra for example, most often required a long, difficult trip. That, however, was also changing . At the turn of the century, automobiles were being produced for the public to purchase. The rapid and enthusiastic acceptance of the automobile meant that what once had been many days' difficult journey was now closer at hand.

Jessie and her friends quickly adopted the nickname of "machine" in reference to these new and exciting wonders. The word "car" was not commonly used until years later. In 1900, roughly four thousand automobiles were produced in the United States. By 1904, the entire country seemed to be going into a frenzy about the machines. More and more of them were seen everywhere—not only on the streets, but on postcards which was the latest way to communicate since publishers, the post office, and artists got together. The machines were in the music people listened to and in their conversations. Otto's ideal way to travel short distances however, was still with his bicycle—especially since 1890, when rubber tires were added. That change greatly improved the comfort of the ride. But Otto admired all the inventions that were connected with the machines—those men were making history.

Jessie's husband could hardly wait to buy a machine. On May 24, 1904, the *Lodi Sentinel* reported: *"Henry Beckman has purchased a new Auto car through the agency of Lillie Bros. This powerful ten-horse, two-cylinder liner cost in the neighborhood of $1,800."*

"...NOTHING QUITE EQUALS THE THRILL THAT YOU FEEL AS YOU SPEED THROUGH THE LAND IN AN AUTOMOBILE." POSTCARD—JESSIE'S COLLECTION

POSTCARD—JESSIE'S COLLECTION

HENRY BECKMAN'S TEN-HORSE, TWO-CYLINDER "LINER"

Once Henry's purchase was reported in the *Lodi Sentinel*, he started receiving letters from dealers involved with this industry. Henry was pleased that such well-recognized companies could solve all his problems.

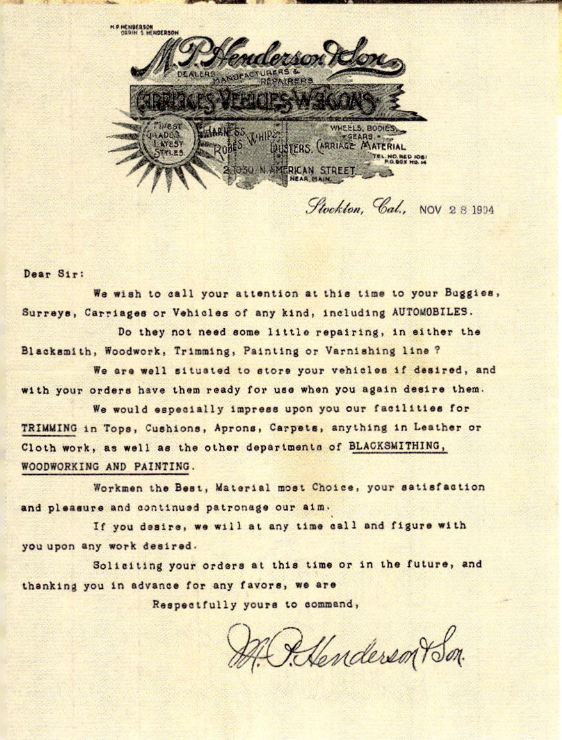

M P HENDERSON
ORRIN S HENDERSON

M. P. Henderson & Son
DEALERS MANUFACTURERS & REPAIRERS
CARRIAGES · VEHICLES · WAGONS
FINEST GRADES LATEST STYLES
HARNESS ROBES WHIPS DUSTERS.
WHEELS, BODIES, GEARS, CARRIAGE MATERIAL
TEL. NO. RED 1061
P.O. BOX NO. 14
2 1030 N. AMERICAN STREET NEAR MAIN.

Stockton, Cal., NOV 28 1904

Dear Sir:

We wish to call your attention at this time to your Buggies, Surreys, Carriages or Vehicles of any kind, including AUTOMOBILES.

Do they not need some little repairing, in either the Blacksmith, Woodwork, Trimming, Painting or Varnishing line ?

We are well situated to store your vehicles if desired, and with your orders have them ready for use when you again desire them.

We would especially impress upon you our facilities for TRIMMING in Tops, Cushions, Aprons, Carpets, anything in Leather or Cloth work, as well as the other departments of BLACKSMITHING, WOODWORKING AND PAINTING.

Workmen the Best, Material most Choice, your satisfaction and pleasure and continued patronage our aim.

If you desire, we will at any time call and figure with you upon any work desired.

Soliciting your orders at this time or in the future, and thanking you in advance for any favors, we are

Respectfully yours to command,

M. P. Henderson & Son.

M. P. HENDERSON SENT HENRY A PHOTOGRAPH OF HIS "MACHINE" AND A LETTER ABOUT HIS STORE IN STOCKTON.

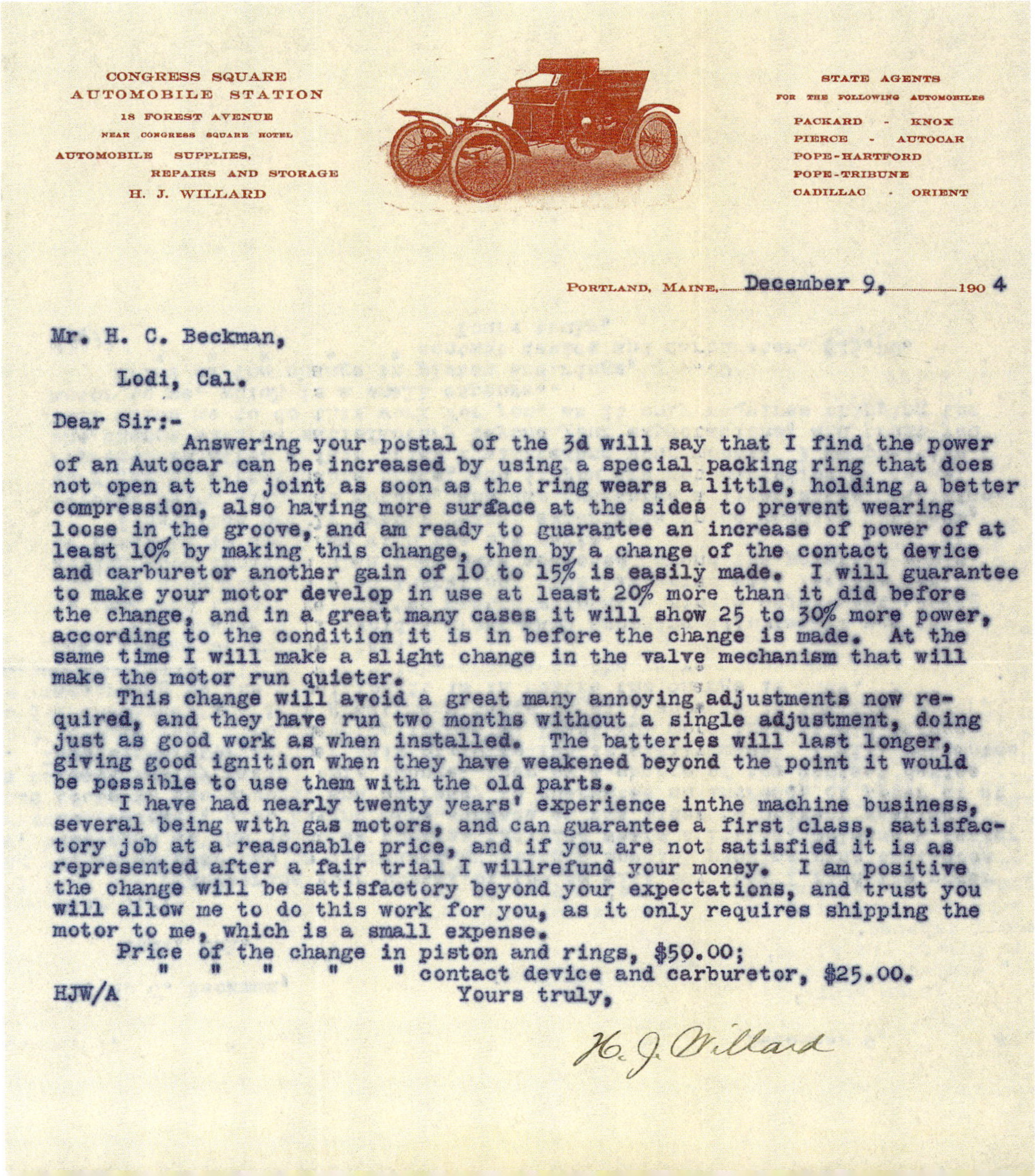

CONGRESS SQUARE
AUTOMOBILE STATION
18 FOREST AVENUE
NEAR CONGRESS SQUARE HOTEL
AUTOMOBILE SUPPLIES,
REPAIRS AND STORAGE
H. J. WILLARD

STATE AGENTS
FOR THE FOLLOWING AUTOMOBILES
PACKARD - KNOX
PIERCE - AUTOCAR
POPE-HARTFORD
POPE-TRIBUNE
CADILLAC - ORIENT

PORTLAND, MAINE, December 9, 1904

Mr. H. C. Beckman,

Lodi, Cal.

Dear Sir:-

Answering your postal of the 3d will say that I find the power of an Autocar can be increased by using a special packing ring that does not open at the joint as soon as the ring wears a little, holding a better compression, also having more surface at the sides to prevent wearing loose in the groove, and am ready to guarantee an increase of power of at least 10% by making this change, then by a change of the contact device and carburetor another gain of 10 to 15% is easily made. I will guarantee to make your motor develop in use at least 20% more than it did before the change, and in a great many cases it will show 25 to 30% more power, according to the condition it is in before the change is made. At the same time I will make a slight change in the valve mechanism that will make the motor run quieter.

This change will avoid a great many annoying adjustments now required, and they have run two months without a single adjustment, doing just as good work as when installed. The batteries will last longer, giving good ignition when they have weakened beyond the point it would be possible to use them with the old parts.

I have had nearly twenty years' experience inthe machine business, several being with gas motors, and can guarantee a first class, satisfactory job at a reasonable price, and if you are not satisfied it is as represented after a fair trial I willrefund your money. I am positive the change will be satisfactory beyond your expectations, and trust you will allow me to do this work for you, as it only requires shipping the motor to me, which is a small expense.

Price of the change in piston and rings, $59.00;

" " " " " contact device and carburetor, $25.00.

HJW/A

Yours truly,

H. J. Willard

HENRY FELT HIS AUTOCAR SHOULD HAVE MORE POWER, SO HE WROTE TO A COMPANY IN PORTLAND, MAINE FOR SOME SUGGESTIONS. THEY REPLIED WITH THIS LETTER (RIGHT).

THE WHOLE COUNTRY WAS FASCINATED WITH THE MACHINES, BUT JOSEPH SPENKER STILL PREFERRED HORSE POWER

TABLE OF STATE REGISTRATION AND SPEED LAWS.—Corrected to January 1, 1906.

STATE.	License Fee.	Non-Residents.	Apply for Blanks to	Tags Required.	Speed Limits in Miles per Hour. Cities (close)	Cities (open)	Country.
Alabama	$ .25	Not exempt	Probate Judge of County	None	8		8
Arkansas		(No State Law)					
California	2.00	Exempt‡	Sec'y of State, Sacramento	tag and seal	10	15	20
Colorado		(No State Law)					
Connecticut	1.00	Exempt‡	Sec'y of State, Hartford	2 tags	12		20
Delaware	2.00	Exempt*	Sec'y of State, Dover	1 tag	8½	10	20
District of Columbia		Not exempt	Board of Examiners of Steam Engineers	1 tag	12	(6, crossing car tracks)	15
Florida	2.00	Exempt°	Sec'y of State, Tallahassee	1 tag	Reasonable considering traffic		
Georgia		(No State Law)					
Idaho		(No State Law)					
Illinois		(Cities and villages permitted to pass local ordinances)			15	15	
Indiana	1.00	Exempt‡	Sec'y of State, Indianapolis	1 tag	8	15	20
Iowa	1.00	Exempt‡	Sec'y of State, Des Moines	tag and seal	10	15	20
Kansas		(Cities permitted to make local ordinances)			10		20
Kentucky		(No registration required)			(6 miles at crossings, etc.)		15
Louisiana		(No State Law)					
Maine	2.00	Exempt‡	Sec'y of State, Augusta	2 tags	8		15
Maryland	1.00	Not Exempt	Sec'y of State, Annapolis	1 tag	6		10
Massachusetts	2 00	Exempt†	State Highway Comm'r, Boston	2 tags	10		15
Michigan	2.00	Exempt‡	Sec'y of State, Lansing	tag and seal	8	15	25
Minnesota	2.00	Not Exempt	State Boiler Inspector	1 tag	8		25
Missouri	2.00	Not Exempt	License Comm'r or County Clerk	1 tag			9
Mississippi		(No State Law)					
Montana		(No registration required)			8		20
Nebraska	1.00	Exempt‡	Sec'y of State, Lincoln	tag and seal	10	15	20
Nevada		(No State Law)					
New Hampshire	3.00	Exempt‡	Sec'y of State, Concord	2 tags	8		20
New Jersey	1.00	Not Exempt	Sec'y of State, Trenton	2 tags	Reasonable considering traffic		20
New York	2.00	Exempt‡	Sec'y of State, Albany	tag and seal	10	15	20
North Carolina		(County comm's authorized to pass speed regulations)					
North Dakota		(No registration required)			8		15
Ohio		(No registration required)			8	15	20
Oregon	3.00	Exempt‡	Sec'y of State, Portland	1 tag	8		24
Pennsylvania	3.00	Not Exempt	State Highway Commissioner, Harrisburg	2 tags	10		20
Rhode Island	2.00	Exempt‡	Sec'y of State, Providence	1 tag	Not exceeding common pace		

JOSEPH DIDN'T HAVE TO WORRY ABOUT SPEED LIMITS.

HENRY BOUGHT AN E. M. STUDABAKER IN 1911. LEFT TO RIGHT—VERA, ANITA, HENRY AND JESSIE.

TWO MARVELS

THE MUSIC OF THE DAY REFLECTED THE LOVE AFFAIR WITH THE AUTOMOBILE.
THIS IS FROM ANITA BECKMAN'S COLLECTION, DATED 1908.

"HE'D HAVE TO GET UNDER
GET OUT AND GET UNDER
TO FIX HIS LITTLE MACHINE,
HE WAS JUST DYING TO CUDDLE HIS QUEEN
BUT EVERY MINUTE WHEN HE'D BEGIN IT,
HE'D HAVE TO GET UNDER
GET OUT AND GET UNDER,
THEN HE'D GET BACK AT THE WHEEL
A DOZEN TIMES THEY'D START TO HUG AND KISS—
AND THEN THE DARNED OLD ENGINE WOULD
START TO MISS
SO—HE'D HAVE TO GET UNDER
GET OUT AND GET UNDER
AND FIX UP HIS AUTOMOBILE.

"Splendid" improvements had been made in the few short years that automobiles had been available to the public, and excitement reigned everywhere. One man was determined to build an automobile that could be afforded by the average American. That man was Henry Ford. He built his first automobile in 1896—the Quadricycle, and proceeded from there to experiment with other designs and a different kind of steel used in Europe. This steel, with a vanadium alloy, was lighter and stronger than the steel being used by contemporary American auto makers. The use of vanadium alloy steel in his cars is considered one of the reasons so many Model T Fords have survived today. He built a mill to produce this steel, refined techniques on the assembly line, and started the dramatic story of the American automobile. On October 1, 1908, the first Model T Ford was built at his plant in Detroit. This basic model was a 20-horsepower, four-cylinder car that featured a semi-automatic transmission. A speedometer, windshield wipers, and side doors were optional features. The car was an immediate sensation, and in 1909, Ford sold more than ten thousand at $950 each. To keep up with the demand, he further refined the assembly-line system, and production rose from 78,440 cars in 1912 to 300,000 cars in 1914. By 1917, he was selling the Model T for $345—later he lowered the price to $290. From 1909 to 1927, the Ford Motor Company built more than fifteen million Model T cars. Henry Ford changed the social and economic lives of all American citizens in the twentieth century.

It definitely took some time for the public to get used to these machines, however. A police report from Chicago for 1916 gave some interesting statistics: "Horse drawn vehicles caused 79 deaths with 46,662 vehicles being involved. Motor vehicles caused 235 deaths in the same year, with 65,651 vehicles being involved." As the 1916 *Superintendent of Police's Annual Report* illustrates, "It was rarely the horse's fault":

"Throughout the first thirty years of the century when the automobile death rate was highest, conditions were quite different than today. Pedestrians and drivers alike had a poor understanding of automobiles or their dangers. Drivers didn't always have to be licensed or tested. Automobiles were designed as if drawn by horses. Traffic laws were sketchy and based on an incomplete understanding of automobiles. Enforcement was often a problem. Courts required a formal physical arrest of traffic offenders. This was impossible for foot patrolmen trying to stop speeders. What few traffic lights there were did not function alike or even use the same colors to mean the same thing. Local funeral parlors ran the ambulance services and lacked incentive to train drivers so that their charges would arrive alive.

It should also be noted that horses were not only safer, but they were better at finding their way home. In 1916, of the 1,215 horses that strayed or were stolen, all except 26 were recovered. However of the 3,295 automobiles which were lost or stolen, only 2,366 were recovered, leaving 959 missing."[2]

Otto was looking for a machine. "I've been looking for a Rambler for my private use. The salesman gave me a fine ride in one. It was the best machine of all, but too expensive. The Woock boys drove their machine to the last picnic in the grove, but they had to spend 2 hours repairing one of the tires. All these new machines need improvements."

[2] The Chicago Public Library, compiled by Ellen O'Brien and Lyle Benedict, reference librarians in the Municipal Reference Collection.

Jessie felt that driving was dangerous. She had one bad experience, and that was the end of her career as a driver. In 1913, she and Henry were driving home from Lodi in their E.M.F. Studebaker when Henry stopped the car and said to her, *"Jessie I think it would be a good idea if you learned how to drive."* She agreed, and after a short time under his careful instructions, she did very well. She drove the rest of the way to the south entrance of their home. Henry said, *"Jessie you're doing so good, drive on in and park the car in the garage."* She proceeded down the lane, made the big curve, went into the garage and out the back through closed hanging doors. Jessie flew out of the car and landed on top of a rose bush, not breaking it or any part of herself, but severely denting both the bush and her pride. She never drove again.

ANITA AND JESSIE IN THE SAFER WAY TO TRAVEL

A FRIEND OF HENRY SENT HIM INFORMATION ABOUT A NEW, VERY MODERN PRODUCT TO HELP HIM KEEP HIS MACHINE LOOKING NEW.

1915 FORD TOURING CAR
(NOTE THE SMOOTH ROUNDED REAR PANELS)

JESSIE ADDS ANOTHER CARD TO HER COLLECTION

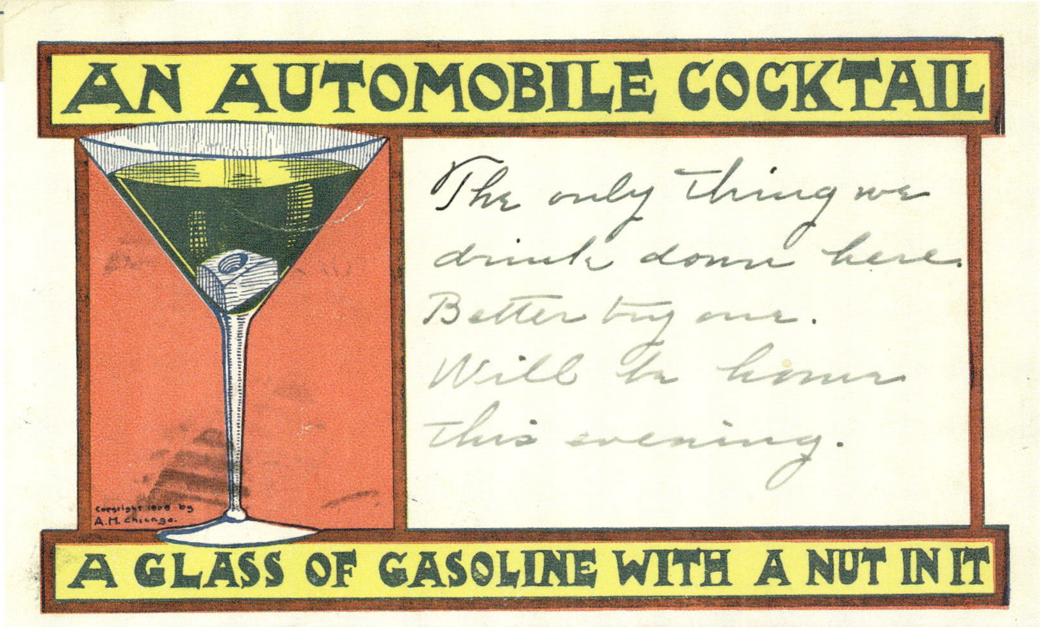

In 1917, Jessie decided to buy Henry an automobile for his 50th birthday. They wanted a machine so the whole family could take a trip together. She and Henry decided on a seven-passenger touring car, a Packard Twin Six. The price was a staggering $3,225.

THE NEW BECKMAN CAR—
A 1917 PACKARD TWIN SIX

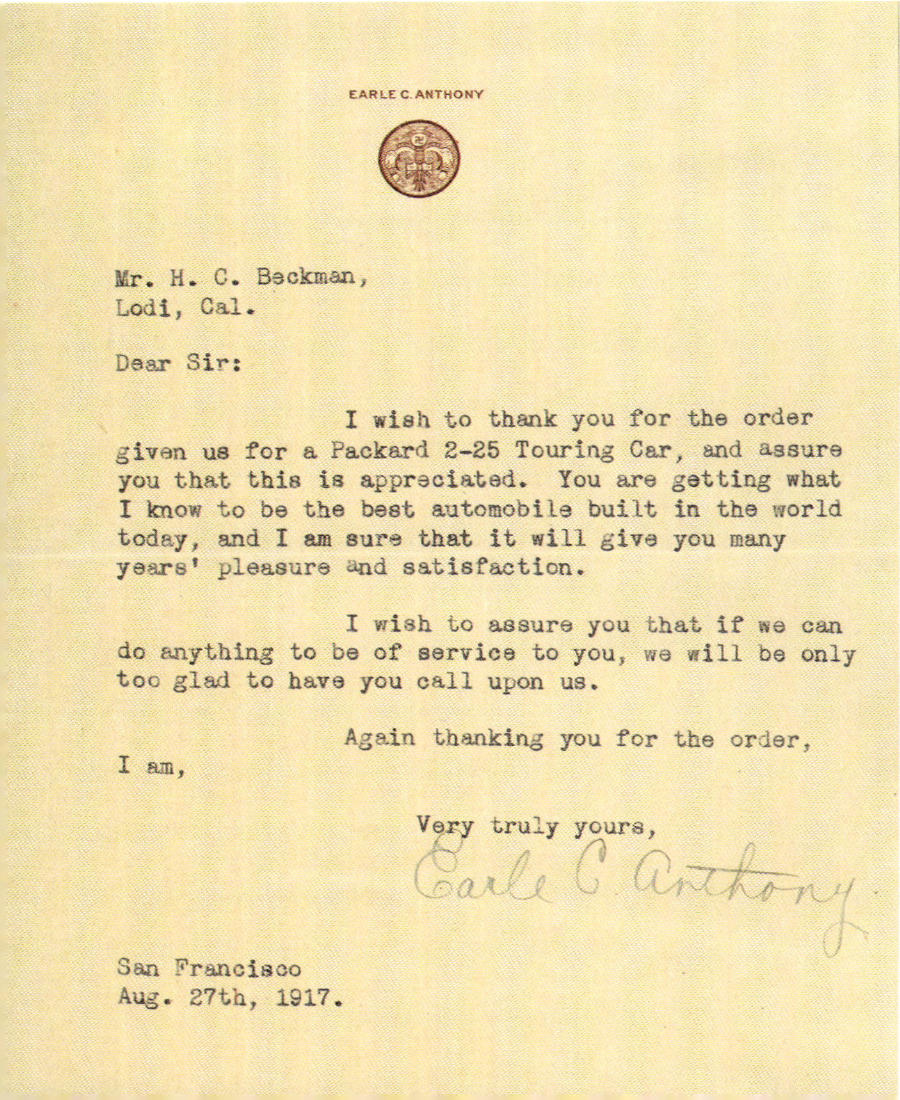

EARLE C. ANTHONY

Mr. H. C. Beckman,
Lodi, Cal.

Dear Sir:

I wish to thank you for the order given us for a Packard 2-25 Touring Car, and assure you that this is appreciated. You are getting what I know to be the best automobile built in the world today, and I am sure that it will give you many years' pleasure and satisfaction.

I wish to assure you that if we can do anything to be of service to you, we will be only too glad to have you call upon us.

Again thanking you for the order, I am,

Very truly yours,
Earle C. Anthony

San Francisco
Aug. 27th, 1917.

THEY RECEIVED A LETTER FROM THE COMPANY DATED AUGUST 27, 1917.

THE PACKARD IN FRONT OF THE GARAGE

Jessie made some entries in the Packard's log book to record a few short trips the family had taken. On August 26, 1917, they took a trip to San Francisco to see Henry's grandmother Hacke. The log recorded that it took them seven hours to make the trip, and *"they saw many tourists on the road."*

On September 16, 1917, they went from Lodi to San Joaquin City, approximately 44 miles, in two and one-third hours, and *"coming home they counted 110 machines from Tuxedo to home."*

On September 23, 1917, *"we were right in back of a machine that bumped into a street car. The machine was crippled."*

INTRODUCTORY TO THE LOG BOOK OF A MOTOR CAR.

In presenting this " Log Book of a Motor Car " to automobilists the object of the Ætna Life Insurance Company has been to give them something that not only will be helpful and convenient while being used, but also will be instructive, and the means of calling up many pleasant memories in the future. An old diary is always refreshing reading, and this book will be equally so in years to come.

Without notes it is almost impossible for a tourist to remember as much about the details and incidents of a trip as he would wish to. It is hoped that this book will make the recording of the details of a tour so easy and convenient that every motorist, whether he makes long or short trips, will use it and get full enjoyment therefrom in later years.

As this is an individual " log book " its pages are left blank, to be filled up in one's own way; but in presenting it indulgence is asked for the making of a few simple suggestions in the form of " don'ts ":

DON'T start on a tour without preparation for any and all emergencies. Carry extra tires and parts. Provide against the weather. Carry plenty of tools. Be sure your car is in good shape, and then keep it so.

DON'T carry too many passengers. You will be more comfortable with fewer people and carrying your baggage with you than with so many people that you have to ship it.

DON'T map out your tour like a railroad time-table and try to keep to the schedule. Select your objective and lay out the route with reference to roads, hotels, etc. Map out roughly about where you expect to stop, and then make up your mind to go where you please and stop when you feel like it.

DON'T try to make fast time. Take it easy and enjoy the country.

DON'T drive fast over rough roads. It injures your engine, car, and tires, and wears you and your passengers out.

DON'T go too far without stopping. A short stop will rest not only you and the passengers but the engine and tires as well, and the balance of the trip will be all the more enjoyable.

DON'T fail to stop if everything about the car is not going just right. "A stitch in time saves nine,' and five minutes by the roadside may save fifty dollars in the shop.

DON'T forget your gasoline. It is better to stop and fill up while you know you have plenty than to run out five miles from any supply.

DON'T be dissatisfied with the car, or the roads, or the weather, or the hotels. Take things as they come and get the most out of everything.

DON'T hurry. Take plenty of time for meals. Start at a comfortable time in the morning and stop for the night before you are tired out.

DON'T forget to take out liability insurance before you start. You are not likely to run over or collide with any one, but a horse may take fright at the car and through no fault of your own you may become involved in an expensive lawsuit. If you *should* cause an accident

DON'T tell the injured party that you are insured or refer them to the Company.

DON'T give information about an accident to anyone except the police and the Company's representative.

DON'T let witnesses get away without taking their names and addresses.

DON'T treat a claimant or his representative discourteously or decline to consider their claim. Hear them, express sympathy if you feel it, promise consideration of the case, — but don't commit yourself further.

DON'T forget to immediately report in writing to the Company every accident, no matter how slight the injury, and if it is a fatal case telegraph or telephone.

DON'T be inconsiderate of others using the highways. Their appreciation of any little courtesies you may show them, and the satisfaction of knowing that you have made friends rather than enemies for your favorite sport will be among the pleasantest remembrances of your trip.

DON'T openly disregard speed laws and ordinances. Flagrant violation of them may mean arrest, expense, and delay, and is sure to cause prejudice against the automobile. There is a tendency on the part of the public toward a liberal interpretation of speed laws and limits which should be fostered by decency rather than discouraged by abuse.

DON'T forget your registration and licenses when starting on a tour. Your own state license may protect you in other states, and it may not. The following table will tell you:

4

THE PACKARD CAME WITH A LOG BOOK FOR THE MOTOR CAR. IT HAD SEVERAL PAGES OF VERY GOOD ADVICE.

ANITA TRIED OUT A 1918 OVERLAND ROADSTER WHEN SHE TURNED EIGHTEEN. SHE THOUGHT IT WOULD MAKE A MARVELOUS BIRTHDAY PRESENT.

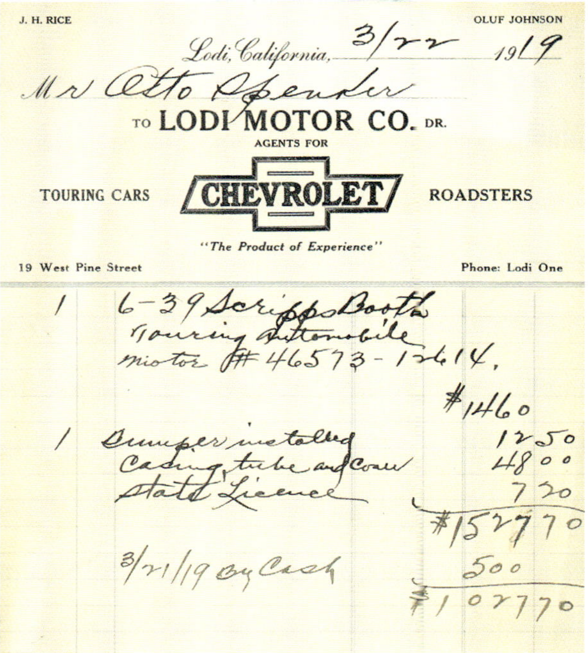

J. H. RICE — OLUF JOHNSON

Lodi, California, 3/22 1919

Mr Otto Spenker

TO LODI MOTOR CO. DR.

AGENTS FOR

TOURING CARS — CHEVROLET — ROADSTERS

"The Product of Experience"

19 West Pine Street — Phone: Lodi One

1	6-39 Scripps Booth Touring Automobile motor #46573-12614.	
		$1460
1	Bumper installed	12 50
	Casing, tube and cover	48 00
	State Licence	7 20
		$1527 70
	3/21/19 By Cash	500
		$1027 70

OTTO'S CAR COST $1,027.70!

OTTO BOUGHT A "SPLENDID" MACHINE IN 1919—A SCRIPPS BOOTH TOURING CAR.

MACHINES CAN GO ANYWHERE!

WHAT A THRILL—ON TOP OF AN AUTOMOBILE!

OTTO FOUND THE "MACHINES" TO BE A FASCINATING SUBJECT FOR HIS CAMERA.

OOPS!

YOU CAN CLIMB TO THE MOST BEAUTIFUL VIEWS IN AN AUTOMOBILE.

POSTCARD FROM JESSIE'S COLLECTION

HOW MANY PEOPLE CAN ONE MACHINE HOLD?

ANITA LOOKS AT A HUDSON.

WHEN NECESSARY WE CAN ALWAYS GO IN THE TRUCK.

BE SURE TO LEARN WHERE THEY SELL THE GASOLINE.

I THOUGHT YOU WERE GOING TO BRING THE GAS!

POST CARD—JESSIE'S COLLECTION

WHO WANTS TO GET OUT OF THE MACHINE AND SIT IN THOSE BLEACHERS?

MACHINES START APPEARING IN STOCKTON.

EVERYONE DRIVES MACHINES THESE DAYS.

AT TIMES YOU STILL NEED MANPOWER.

BEST TO STAY ON THE ROAD!

—A GOOD ROAD, THAT IS—

I THOUGHT THIS WAS SUPPOSED TO BE A GOOD ROAD!

AT TIMES YOU STILL NEED HORSE POWER.

STUDENTS WERE DRIVING TO LODI HIGH SCHOOL IN THEIR AUTOMOBILES.

YOSEMITE

TRAVEL BY "MACHINE" always could be exciting, and you never knew what could happen. It also enabled people to go places they had never gone to before, and to experience some of the natural wonders of the nation that had been out of reach in the past because of distance.

In 1919, Jessie planned a family camping trip to Yosemite. The family's 1917 Packard twin Six seemed dependable and large enough for both the family and camping supplies. Otto was also included in the plans, along with Herb Woock. Jessie wanted to get to know Herb Woock better, because he and Anita seemed to be developing a close relationship.

On July 21, 1919, at 4:40 in the morning, the group started out. Otto drove his new machine and Herb rode with him. Jessie carefully recorded in the log book each town they went through. They had hoped to get to Yosemite in the early afternoon to set up camp.

They did, the only problem was it took to the afternoon of the next day! Everything had been going fine on the trip, until they got to Knight's Ferry. From that point on to Hazel Creek, Otto's machine had three blowouts! Everyone was surprised because Otto had the newest machine. They camped overnight at Hazel Creek and took off early the next morning for Yosemite. Along the way Otto's fourth tire blew out! Luckily Otto had carried along two spares, Henry loaned him one of his, and Otto was able to purchase two more tires along the way. They finally arrived in Yosemite at 2:40 PM and set up their camp.

The camping trip of 1919 was beautifully recorded by Otto's photography.

INSPIRATION POINT

INSPIRATICN POINT

HERBERT WOOCK

JESSIE AND JOE IN CAMP BECKMAN

YOSEMITE FALLS

MIRROR LAKE—BACK ROW: JESSIE, HENRY, JOE; FRONT ROW: HERBERT WOOCK, VERA, ANITA, OTTO

KINGSBURY GRADE THE HARD WAY

HERBERT WOOCK HAD BOUGHT A NEW AUTOMOBILE IN 1922, a Hudson—a fine-looking machine. He invited Henry and Otto to go on what was supposed to be a short trip over the Sierras to Minden, Nevada.

Herb wanted to give his new machine a good test, because the company had used some of his ideas in the designing and building of the automobile. The three men took off in grand style, planning on camping just one night in Minden and returning home the next day.

They left at daylight and had an excellent run up the grade to Lake Tahoe. The weather was beautiful, all was going well, and Herbert was very proud of his machine. They crossed into Nevada and made the short climb to the top of Kingsbury Grade. Herbert stopped to check that everything was ready for the steep descent. He verified the machine was in fine shape, and they started down the grade. They went a short distance, seeming to go faster and faster. Herb exclaimed in a worried voice, *"I'm losing the brakes!"* Fortunately, they had rounded a curve and came to an up rise in the grade. This incline enabled Herb to bring the machine to a complete stop. Everyone got out, extremely relieved, but concerned. How were they going to descend the rest of the grade?

Herbert said, *"I have a little braking power, but not nearly enough for this steep grade. We need to drag something behind the car to help slow it down."* They searched the area and finally found a stump that was large and yet light enough to move. All three of them dragged it over behind the machine. Herb got a rope, and soon they had it securely attached—tied behind the automobile. Herb said, *"I don't think it's big enough, but with my added weight maybe it will succeed in slowing the machine down to a safe speed. If one of you will drive the car, I'll ride on this thing and that added weight could be enough to give us a safe descent."*

Henry volunteered to drive, and he and Otto got into the machine, giving Herb one last concerned look as he straddled the log. *"Try to keep the speed down!"* Herb said as they closed the doors.

"TRY TO KEEP THE SPEED DOWN!"—HERB WOOCK, THE HUMAN BRAKE

Off they went—as slowly as possible, and in this fashion they finally made it to the bottom of the giant grade. So there they were, in the little town of Minden, Nevada, with a complicated machine that needed a major overhaul before they could attempt the return home over those same high mountains.

They set up camp and proceeded to take the machine apart. Fortunately, Herb and Otto were not without mechanical skills. The next day they felt they had found the source of the problem, but now they needed parts. Otto volunteered to stay at the camp with the machine while Henry and Herb made the trip to Reno, where they hoped the parts would be available. They heard a man was driving to Reno the next day, and they arranged a ride. Days went by. Otto wrote to Jessie about their predicament, and she replied:

Dear Bro: We rec'd a pack of mail today and note that you (with the little love you express for Nevada) have still taken up your abode in the little village of Minden. It is a nice little place, I know it may have an attractive climate also. Now you are getting a good look at Nevada anyway, but I must say it didn't take me so many days to see enough of it.

Christine Raab and family of Carson were here. They had trouble with their Fliver[3] *on the way, and Christine and the youngsters had the pleasure of taking the Meyers Grade at their own speed—on foot! So there are others besides you folks that choose walking. Well to say the least you all know that I understand your situation and no one feels more sorry for you all then I do—but one has to just keep cool and await better conditions.*

Don't worry! Tell Herbert I feel sorry for him especially, for I think the owner of the car feels it most keenly. My best to you all, Sis

Herbert and Henry finally arrived with the needed parts. After the necessary corrections were made to the machine, they took off for home. All went well on their return trip, and they arrived in Lodi without further incident.

AUTHOR'S NOTE: This story was the favorite of my father, Herbert Woock. I heard it again and again and never believed it, until I found these pictures in Vera's closet 40 years later.

[3] Fliver was the popular name for the new machines, and was used before the word "car" became more common.

A FINE MACHINE, IT JUST NEEDED A FEW ADJUSTMENTS.

CHAPTER FIVE

Changes in the Valley

WHEAT FARMING WAS SO EASY—scratch in the seed and watch it grow. Now and then, however, the boom in wheat reminded Joseph of the gold fields. He had been taken in once by a "sure thing," and was determined this would not happen to him again.

Wheat certainly was king, but for how long? Joseph heard that vast fields were being planted farther east, in the country he had crossed by wagon twenty years earlier. Wheat flourished everywhere, and sure enough, the price started dropping. The price dropped, and the tonnage per acre dropped as well. At the Grange meeting, they said wheat tonnage was dropping because planting the same crop year after year depletes the soil. Many farmers had hopes the prices would go back up and kept on with wheat, but Joseph and Otto were looking for a better crop to grow on their land.

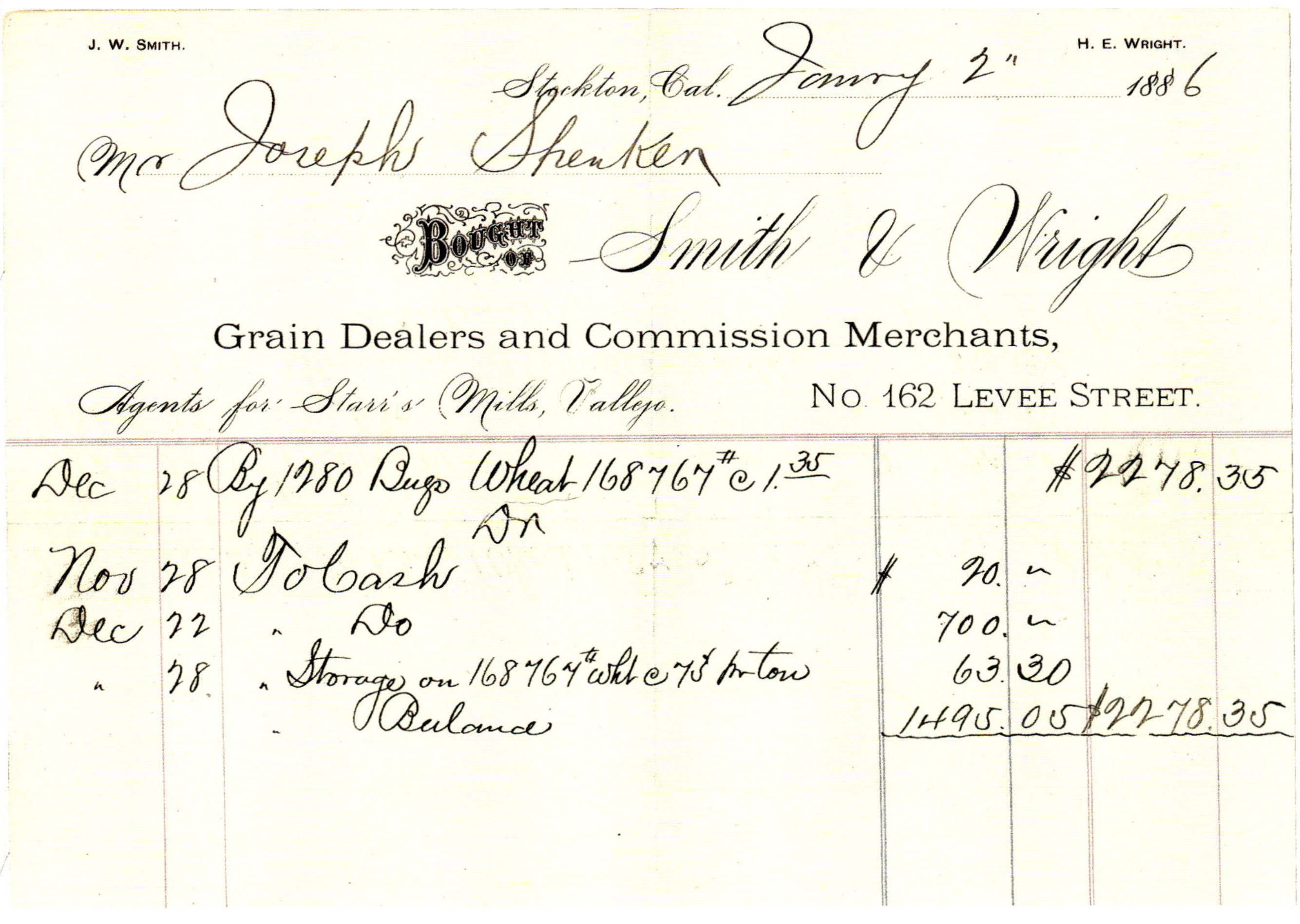

J. W. SMITH. H. E. WRIGHT.

Stockton, Cal. Janry 2" 1886

Mr Joseph Shenken

Bought of Smith & Wright

Grain Dealers and Commission Merchants,

Agents for Starr's Mills, Vallejo. No. 162 Levee Street.

Dec	28	By 1480 Bags Wheat 168767# @ 1.35		$2278.35
		Dr		
Nov	28	To Cash	$ 90.	
Dec	22	" Do	700.	
"	28	" Storage on 168764# wht @ 75 per ton	63.30	
		" Balance	1495.05	$2278.35

WHEAT RECEIPT FOR JANUARY, 1886

THE POPULAR POSTCARDS WERE HELPING TO PROMOTE CALIFORNIA AGRICULTURE. AT TIMES THEY TENDED TO EXAGGERATE A LITTLE!

In 1887, one farmer planted forty acres of watermelons. Everyone watched him with great interest. At first, when the melons didn't seem to grow, people started laughing at him, but then they took off. He had an amazing crop, which was surpassed only by the amount of money he took to the bank after harvest. He cleared $20,000 from his forty acres the first year[1] and he did well the next year. The "Lodi melon" became famous.

[1] *Stockton Daily Independent*, 1887.

EVERYONE WAS EATING WATERMELONS: ANITA, LENA, JOE, JESSIE, VERA AND HENRY

Soon everyone started planting melons throughout the valley. Other areas grew them and called them "Lodi melons," but they were not the same quality—not even close. People quickly became wary of all melons, and that, along with over planting, caused the price to plunge.

Joseph had planted a few acres of the popular melon, but without enthusiasm, even though some of the melons in Lodi grew to twenty-five pounds each. Joseph wanted to plant something that would be profitable, but a crop that would stay in the ground year after year. Joseph was thinking about planting grapes.

JOSEPH WOULD PLANT GRAPES ON HIS RANCH

FROM WHEAT TO GRAPES

JOSEPH MET WILLIAM WEST, who owned a nursery in Stockton where he grew trees from all over the world. Trees were one thing Joseph didn't need, however Joseph admired the pine grove in front of West's nursery. Joseph and West shared a love for trees. Joseph told him about his oak grove, and West made plans to visit his ranch.

William West and his brother George started their first nursery in the San Joaquin Valley in 1853, when most people were still focused on the gold fields. The nursery struggled for the first few years, but in 1866, it began to be profitable—shipping its stock as far away as San Diego and Texas. The West brothers carried different varieties of trees, especially pears and apples, and they also carried grapevines. In 1885, William West started one of the first commercial wineries in California, two miles north of Stockton. He named it El Pinal after the grove that he planted in front of his nursery.

West talked to Joseph about the winery and showed him all the different grape cuttings he had available. Joseph was interested. West told him the popular grapes now were Madeline, Black Hamburg, Sweetwater, Black Ferra, and Emperor.[2] Another variety he had available was Cinsault, also called Black Malvoisier. Joseph had heard about this grape and purchased enough vines for 20 acres. He established his first vineyard north of the oak grove, which placed it in the middle, or heart, of his ranch. Joseph remarked in later years he felt that was a good place to start a new venture.

In 1889, Joseph planted five acres of Zinfandel cuttings he bought from West. For this vineyard, he chose the ground on the south side of his oak grove.[3] Joseph was in the grape business and excited about the different varieties he could grow. He liked the way the vines looked on his ranch and the fact they were to stay in the ground for many, many years to come. He knew his soil was good, some of the best around, and with the Lodi climate, he was convinced that raising grapes was the direction he wanted to pursue in farming. The next year he would plant additional acres of grapes.

In 1890, Joseph increased his vineyard by planting just over seven acres of Black Prince and twenty-two acres of a new variety called Flame Tokay.[4]

Many acres of land on the ranch had to be reserved for growing alfalfa. The dairy consumed an amazing amount of this nutritious grass, as did the cattle, not to mention the sixty to eighty horses needed to run the harvesters. Alfalfa was a basic necessity and required level ground because the nourishing crop had to be flood irrigated. When it was mature, it was cut, raked, dried in the field, and then stacked in a mound or barn in a high mountain of hay. In 1909, a horse-powered hay bailer was

HAULING IN THE HAY WITH THE SAMSON TRUCK

---

[2] *An Illustrated History of San Joaquin County, California* (Chicago: Lewis Publishing Co., 1890), p. 120.
[3] This vineyard, still productive after well over 100 years, produces the grapes used to make Jessie's Grove Winery's "Royal-tee" Zinfandel.
[4] Recorded in the California Department of Agriculture in Sacramento by Marian Dameran.

A FRESNO SCRAPER USED TO LEVEL THE LAND SO IT COULD BE FLOOD IRRIGATED FOR ALFALFA.

MOWING THE ALFALFA.

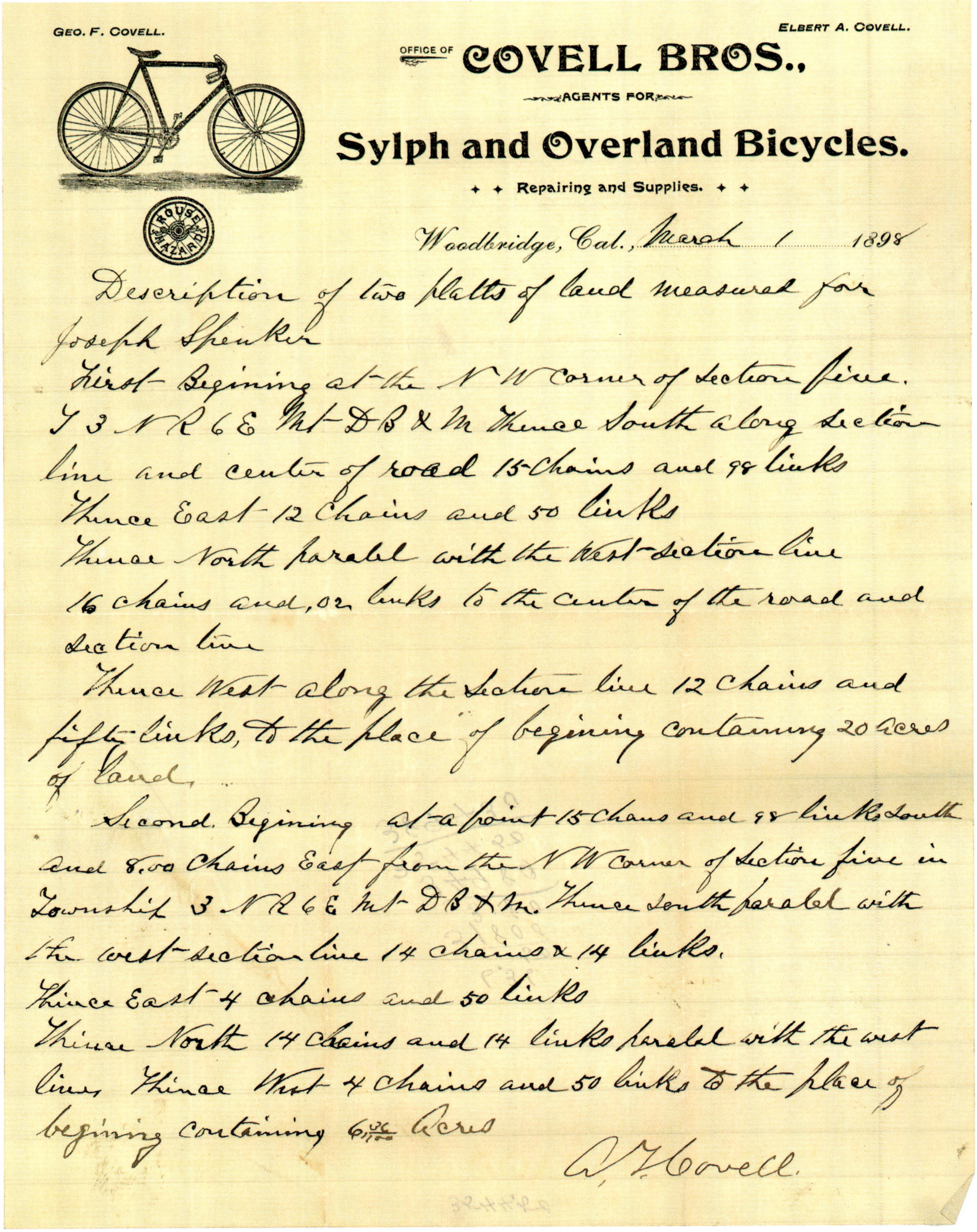

GEO. F. COVELL. ELBERT A. COVELL.

OFFICE OF **COVELL BROS.,**

AGENTS FOR

Sylph and Overland Bicycles.

Repairing and Supplies.

Woodbridge, Cal., March 1 1898

Description of two platts of land measured for Joseph Spenker

First Begining at the N W corner of section five. T 3 N R 6 E Mt D B & M Thence South along section line and center of road 15 Chains and 98 links

Thence East 12 Chains and 50 links

Thence North paralel with the West section line 16 chains and ,02 links to the center of the road and section line

Thence West along the section line 12 Chains and fifty links, to the place of begining containing 20 acres of land.

Second. Begining at a point 15 Chains and 98 links South and 8.00 Chains East from the N W corner of section five in Township 3 N R 6 E Mt D B & M. Thence South paralel with the west section line 14 chains & 14 links.

Thence East 4 chains and 50 links

Thence North 14 chains and 14 links paralel with the west line, Thence West 4 chains and 50 links to the place of begining containing 6 36/100 Acres

A. F. Covell.

JOSEPH WAS INTERESTED IN BUYING SOME MORE LAND TO PLANT ADDITIONAL ALFALFA. IN 1898 HE HAD A PIECE OF GROUND SURVEYED.

developed and was used on many ranches, but Joseph continued with the old way of bringing in the hay.

The grapes did well. Joseph and Otto visited West's nursery many times trying to make the critical decision as to which grapes to put in next. In 1900, they decided to plant sixteen more acres of Zinfandel, five acres of Carignane, and eight acres of Mission grapes.[5] They believed these grapes could be used for wine or could be packed and shipped from Lodi by railroad. Joseph laughed and told Otto that in 1879, the first grapes shipped from Lodi by the railroad—a load of Black Prince, took sixteen days to get to New York. The development of refrigeration for freight cars would be a boon to the grape industry. Farmers would be able to ship grapes to the East Coast and have them arrive in excellent condition. They were both glad that the method of transporting grapes was showing signs of improvement. The future of the grape industry looked promising.

By 1900, the grape industry was booming, and soon there would be another winery to which they could ship their crop. Jacob Brack, Joseph's and Otto's friend, was developing a winery in Lodi. He had talked to Joseph and other farmers about his idea, and everyone was excited and hopeful for his success. He told them he was tired of the stranglehold that West and Sons had on the grape industry. Farmers hauled their grapes to the El Pinal Winery and West paid them $4.00 a ton. With no one else buying grapes locally, West could say "Take the price or go elsewhere," but there was no "elsewhere."

Jacob Brack was trying to change all that. He told the grape growers that when he and his partners opened their winery in Lodi, they would give them a decent price for their grapes—as much as $20.00 a ton. Even though Joseph had known West for many years, he was happy to hear the news. This price increase was just what the grape industry needed. Brack hoped to process the first grapes by the 1900 harvest, and Joseph wished him all success. If any man could complete this complex undertaking and make it work, Jacob Brack would be that man. Brack told them he would name his winery The Urgon.

In 1903, however, Brack's dream collapsed, along with the hopes of all the farmers with whom he dealt. Jacob Brack lost his winery after being in business only three years. There were many stories circulating around as to why this happened.

The easiest explanation was that no one could pay that much money for grapes and still make enough money to keep the winery profitable. He had paid growers from $20.00 to $22.00 a ton for the last three years. West had been paying $4.00 a ton. Now that West had bought Brack's winery he announced he would pay $3.50 a ton! It seemed to many farmers, including Joseph, that West intended to get even with the farmers now that he again had total control of the grape market.

In response, a group of growers formed the Woodbridge Vineyard Association near the close of 1904 and opened the first cooperative winery. Farmers in the association could ship their grapes to the winery and pay for the grapes to be processed and stored. When the wine was eventually sold, the farmers would share in the profit in direct relation to the amount of grapes they had delivered. This was an excellent idea, one that many believed was long overdue. Joseph thought the close of Brack's Urgon Winery pushed them into action.

The Woodbridge Vineyard Association crushed their first grapes in 1905. They started off by paying growers $5.00 a ton. The association records note that Otto Spenker delivered twenty-six tons of grapes. A total of 3,138 tons were crushed in 1905 for the Woodbridge Vineyard Association.[6]

[5] Also recorded by Marian Dameran in the Calif. Dept. of Ag. in Sac., California.
[6] Woodbridge Vineyard Association records for 1905.

Once farmers began planting grapes and other crops instead of wheat, water became a major issue. Wheat had thrived with no additional water, but many grapes needed irrigation, as did alfalfa and fruit trees. The need to provide the water brought about the formation of the Woodbridge Canal and Irrigation Company on April 27, 1889. Stock in this company was issued at $1.00 per share. They built their first dam in 1891 and established 24 miles of canals. This was the year the canal was put in along the north side of the oak grove on the Spenker Ranch. In 1895, however, because of their inability to pump adequate water into the canals with their steam-driven pumps, the company failed. All their property and water rights were sold to the Stockton Mokelumne Canal Company on March 4, 1899. In 1910, this company replaced the wood dam built in 1901 with a concrete dam.[7]

Otto wrote: *"After church I drove by way of Woodbridge and stopped for several hours watching the construction of the new concrete dam. The work is going slow—a major project but one so desperately needed. They appear to be about one third finished. The rainy season will be starting soon, so good luck to the crews to get it finished in time."*

WOODBRIDGE DAM

Joseph was interested in planting more Tokays, while other farmers tried other varieties or different crops. Farmers are probably the most independent thinking people in business. Deciding what to grow is always their biggest problem. They can work years developing a crop and then realize it is no good, no one wants it, and the market has disappeared. This was the most discussed subject at the Grange meetings.

There was no easy solution. When Brack's winery operation ran into trouble, some farmers were having money problems, and Joseph loaned them money because the banks turned them down. So many were borrowing money, it became a major accounting job for Otto. By 1906, eleven farmers had borrowed a total of $80,000 from Joseph. He charged them 7 percent interest, with a mortgage on the specific pieces of property. The document was written by the county recorder and all signatures were notarized. Otto had become vice president of the new First National Bank on Pine Street in Lodi, which had opened on September 12, 1905. This position and his father's financial dealings, gave Otto excellent banking experience.

Leasing land for other people's animals also brought in money to the Spenker Ranch, and if the ground was available, why not? Otto thought it was more trouble than it was worth, so Joseph showed him his records:

Pasture of 9 cattle—Feb 8th to May 10th	$27.00
Pasture of 1 black horse—3 months	4.75
Pasture of 1 roan horse—2 months	2.80
Pasture due from Hansen on 1 cow	3.50

For some reason, though, Joseph couldn't get Otto interested—even when he told him for a horse, he charged $1.50 a month. Joseph had many horses out to pasture. He felt that any horse that had worked hard for him all his life, should enjoy his last days sleeping and eating the grass. Jessie was proud of the fact that Joseph never put a horse down because of age.

[7] Hunter and Morton Report, Completed August 16, 1914, Woodbridge Irrigation District Office, Woodbridge, California; *San Joaquin County Records*, vol. 20 (1914), p. 341.

Grapes had become the crop of choice, without a doubt, and farmers planted hundreds of acres. However, grapes had their problems, and they were far more complicated to grow than wheat. Grapes needed extensive care: cultivating, watering, pruning, and dusting with sulfur to prevent mildew, and then sometimes a vineyard would die anyway because of their vulnerability to pests and diseases. Phylloxera, the "root louse," a destructive pest found in the ground that specifically infests grapevines, often caused this destruction. This increasing problem concerned Joseph, and so he investigated a resistant root stock being grown in France. He wrote to the company and received a reply.

December 25th 1906

Telephone No. 2

Telegraphic:

Salmon-Thornery

Gentlemen,

It has occurred to us that you are about to establish vineries and to do this in a proper manner a certain length of time is necessary to get up the land. The earliest date at which you could have the ground ready to put in your plants is next fall.

But another difficulty, and a very serious one too, presents itself and that is, the rapidity with which phyloxera attacks the California vines.

There is only one way of providing against this enemy and it is, to plant only those vines which have been grafted, united and rooted on to resistant stocks.

If planted in a section where phyloxera is known to exist, salmon's plants will never be attacked, and their immunity from the ravages of this terrible pest will ensure the vine grower a full and plenteous vintage, whilst his neighbors; who had not taken the precaution to plant salmon's unattackable vines, waste their time and money in endeavoring to check the evil and save their crops when it is too late; a striking example of the truth of the old adage:

"prevention is better than cure"

We deliver them to any depot in the State of California free of all costs for freight, duties and at an average cost of $35.00 per 1000.

NOTE THE ADDRESS ON THE ENVELOPE AND THE TELEPHONE NUMBER ON THE LETTER.

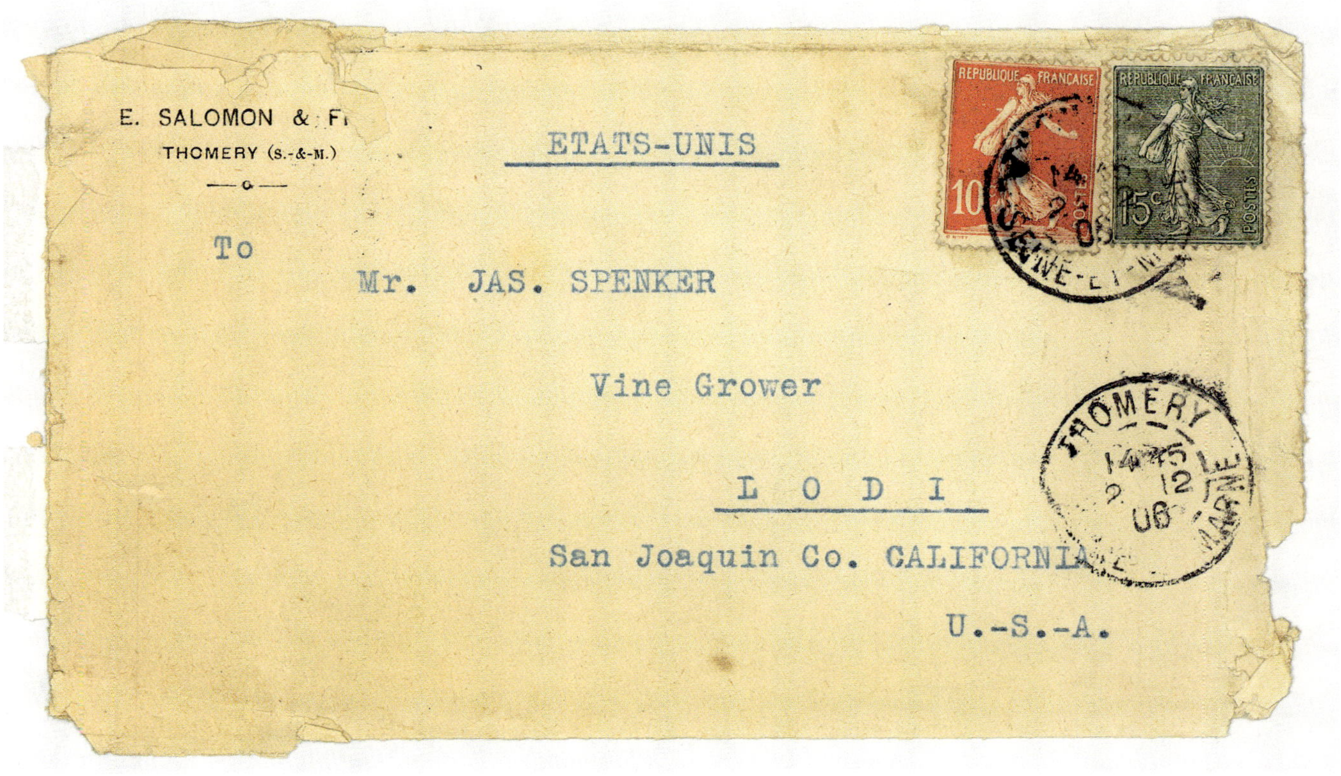

Joseph was sure he would plant more grapes—especially when there was a root stock that could resist such a destructive disease as phyloxera. That fact strengthened his determination to stay in the grape business. He also decided he would plant more Tokays, which did so well in Lodi.

Leon D. Adams wrote: *"Tokays were planted at the turn of the century. Then eastern fruit auctions, supplied by trains of new refrigerated cars, made cross-country shipping of fresh grapes possible. In two decades Lodi, with its brilliant red Tokays, became the most prosperous grape district in the United States."*[8]

Leon D. Adams continued with the following quote in *The Wines of America*:

"The Lodi district is viticulturally unique. Vines grow to enormous size in its deep, sandy loam soil, washed down from the mountains for centuries. Many vines around Lodi area are eight feet tall and have trunks as large as trees. Summer days in the San Joaquin County are less torrid than in the main Central Valley. At Lodi, however, the vines are further cooled at night by moist, westerly winds from the nearby Delta, with its thousand miles of tidewater rivers, bays and sloughs. This combination produces fruit unique to the area. It was because of these conditions Lodi produced such an outstanding watermelon that could not be copied anywhere else. Another product was soon to make Lodi famous because of these natural conditions—the Flame Tokay grape. In Lodi it turned a beautiful dark ruby red color, a few miles to the south, north, east or west, it stayed a yellowish-green color."[9]

8 Leon D. Adams, *The Wines of America*, 2nd Edition, 1978, p. 409.
9 Ibid, p. 410.

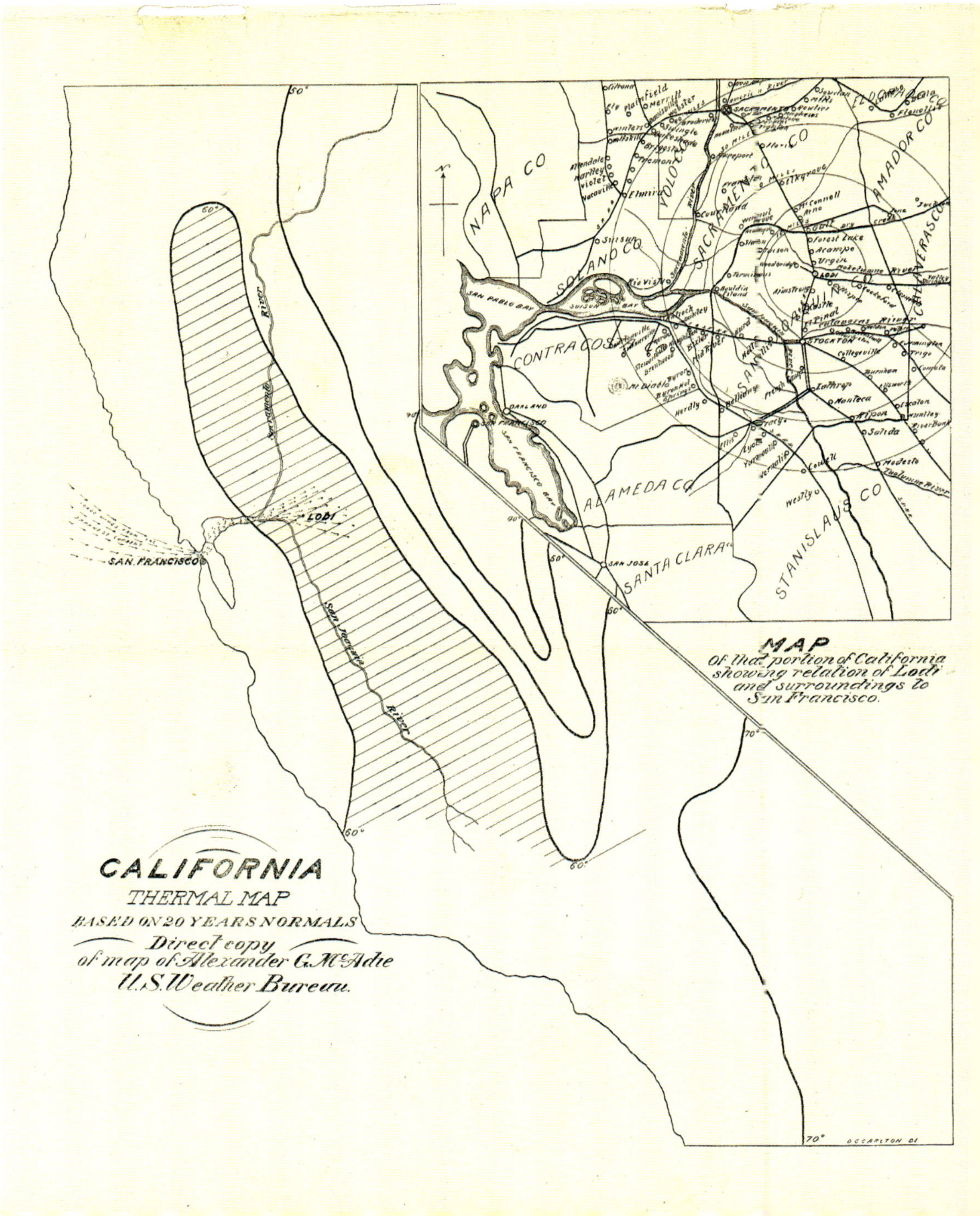

THE DELTA LANDS OF
CALIFORNIA 1904

JOSEPH WOULD PLANT MORE GRAPES. THE FACT THERE WAS A ROOT STOCK AVAILABLE THAT WOULD RESIST THE DEVASTATING DISEASE PHYLOXERA, STRENGTHENED HIS DETERMINATION TO INCREASE HIS ACREAGE.
—POSTCARD FROM JESSIE'S COLLECTION

The Tokay grape did wonderful things for the grape industry and Lodi became known as the Tokay Capital of the World. This beautiful grape was a delight to eat fresh and also made outstanding wine and brandy. In 1907, Lodi staged a festival to celebrate this noble grape. Otto planned on taking in some of the activities at the Tokay Carnival and appreciated receiving the program from Hale's—"Stockton's Greatest Store"

"Queen Zinfandel"

Miss Bertha de Almado

QUEEN OF THE
TOKAY CARNIVAL

September 19, 20 and 21, 1907
Lodi, California

THIS WAS THE PROGRAM FOR THE FIRST GRAPE FESTIVAL HELD IN LODI. NOW CALLED THE LODI GRAPE FESTIVAL, IT REMAINS A POPULAR YEARLY EVENT.

The grape industry was growing and gaining respect throughout the state. On July 22, 1908, the Grape Growers of California was established in San Francisco and they sent Joseph a copy of their Bulletin No. I. The following are excerpts from that bulletin.

Remember: God Helps Those Who Help Themselves.

The Grape Growers of California

Bulletin No. 1. *December 15, 1908.*

Organization

Since the original mass meeting held in San Francisco last July, when the Grape Growers of California came into existence, eighteen coöperative associations have been formed, the grape growers voluntarily assessing themselves 25 cents an acre to help the central organization carry on its excellent work. There are effective organizations in the counties of Sonoma, Napa, Santa Clara, Alameda, Contra Costa, Lake, Santa Cruz, Yolo, Sacramento, San Joaquin, Stanislaus, and also in Southern California.

What Has Been Done

Over eight thousand copies of "The Fight for True Temperance," written by President Andrea Sbarboro, have been distributed to all the leading newspapers of the United States, to every member of the co-operating organizations established throughout the State, and to hundreds of individuals who have sent in requests for the book from Maine to Florida, and British Columbia to Mexico. The book has also been sent to many prominent people abroad and has created a great amount of discussion. A copy will be sent to any address upon application.

Despite the fact that prohibition has made rapid strides in the Southern States, several of them have passed measures discriminating in favor of the manufacture and sale of wines. The Byrd License Law which passed a few months ago in Virginia, while prohibiting spirits, allows the manufacture and sale of wines, and makes a distinction in the licenses for the sale of wines. The prohibition law which goes into effect in North Carolina on January 1, 1909, makes an exception in favor of the manufacture and sale of wines. The Shattuck bill, which passed the Louisiana Legislature last June, makes the licenses for wine only one-half of the amount charged for liquors.

Now that the organization of the grape growers of California is practically complete, the real educational work will begin. Everything that human agency can do to return to the grape growers the prosperity they deserve will be done by the central organization. They intend to bring California wines prominently before the people of the United States; they will preach loyalty to American wines; they will teach the American people how to drink wine intelligently. They intend to ask for legislation that will bring the product of our vineyards to the attention of the world and awaken a new interest in the growing of grapes. But in order to accomplish all this, the grape growers throughout the State must continue to give this worthy association their financial and moral support. They must rise in their might and ask for what is due them. They are entitled to recognition. They can have it, if they will only pull together. In union there is strength.

What Must Be Done

One of the chief reasons why the viticultural industry has been ignored by the State authorities has been the absolute indifference of the vineyardist himself. Here are some figures showing the appropriations awarded various commissions during the last two sessions of the legislature that ought to make the grape grower wake up to the necessity of asking for his just deserts. In 1905 the fish commission was allowed $71,400; horticultural commission, $33,000; State agricultural society, $36,000; State mining, $46,000; viticulture, $10,000. In 1907 horticulture was allowed $35,000; fish, $81,000; State dairy, $10,000; forestry, $22,100; mining, $51,000; viticulture, nothing. The grape growers of California intend to have representatives appear before our next legislature and demand recognition for our industry; to ascertain why the fish commission, for example, should receive an appropriation of $81,000 to further its interests, while the viticultural industry, representing an invested capital of $100,000,000, should be cut off without a cent.

We have urged upon the California Congressional delegation at Washington, D. C., the necessity of at once taking steps to secure the passage of a law next March that will permit patent medicine manufacturers to use American sweet wines as medicinal components. It is of vital importance to the grape growers of the sweet wine districts of this State that this ambiguous law be properly interpreted. It means, if the ruling is not permanently suspended, that the California grape growers will lose millions of dollars each year.

President Andrea Sbarboro, who has been abroad since the beginning of October, has returned to Italy from Switzerland. He succeeded in securing valuable letters from our consuls at Milan, Naples, and Genoa, showing that the people of Italy are temperate and drunkenness is almost unknown. Mr. Sbarboro has been asked to make several addresses in England, which he will visit before he returns to California about the first of February.

The Grape Growers of California are cosily located in room 216, 460 Montgomery Street, San Francisco. This office is open to every grape grower who visits San Francisco. He will find it a convenient place to meet his friends, use the telephone, or write a letter. Do not hesitate to visit us. You will always be welcome.

For further information address,

SECRETARY
GRAPE GROWERS OF CALIFORNIA
460 MONTGOMERY STREET, ROOM 216
SAN FRANCISCO, CAL.

GROWERS IN THE SAN JOAQUIN VALLEY WERE PLEASED THERE WAS A STATE ORGANIZATION THAT COULD LOOK OUT FOR THEIR INTERESTS IN THE GRAPE INDUSTRY.

Joseph had been communicating with some of his cousins who had come to America in the 1880s. One, his cousin John, settled in Modesto and raised hogs. In November 1896, John wrote a letter addressed to Joseph and his "sister-in-law" describing a day at the market. He wrote he took thirty-one swine to be sold. Thirteen became sick and couldn't be sold, so he kept them. One died, and the others sold for three cents a pound. Joseph stated he'd rather raise grapes any day. He had a few hogs, but since he knew Otto hated the critters, he kept them to a minimum.

Another cousin, Fritz Spenker, bought a piece of property from Joseph on October 20th, 1902.[10] The property was about a mile from Joseph's ranch. Fritz was going to plant grapes.

Wilhelm Spenker, also decided to follow Joseph's lead and settled in Lodi. Joseph enjoyed having relatives move close to him, and so he sold him a piece of ground across the road from Fritz Spenker's vineyard. They finalized the deal with a written agreement dated October 5, 1903.

The grape industry in the Lodi area continued to grow. In 1910, Joseph and Otto attended a Grape Grower's Association meeting in Woodbridge, and Otto noted that the hall was filled with many new members. The major topic of discussion was the shipping of grapes by rail. Now that the trains had refrigerated cars, shipping grapes east was a profitable way to go. The grapes arrived at their destination in fine shape. This was starting to bring the farmers a better price than the wineries wanted to pay. The one grape that continued to develop a name for itself was the versatile Tokay. Joseph and Otto were happy they had planted more Tokays in 1890. As part of the meeting, Otto was elected to the board of directors of the Table Grape Association.

The grape business sounded wonderful, and then the season started. Otto wrote entries in his diary about the season—these are a few:

"August 15—We are near mid August and the grapes will be starting. Kobayashi and partner called and contracted to pick grapes. He'll charge $1.75 per ton for the old vines and $1.80 for the young vines. We'll start in the Black Prince and move onto the Tokays. I went to town for a load of boxes, one of many needed trips. I hauled two loads of Tokays to the packing shed and had to wait two hours to get them packed out. Then I went by the winery as our driver had reported our grapes were too green. So I laid all the pickers off. The grape business is the worst its been in years! Everything is gone to __________!

September 12—All was going as well as can be expected with poor prices and low tonnage. Some grapes are barely making one ton per acre. We were all working along and then Fritz had a Mishap with the grape wagon. He was struck by a run away team and broke the tongue off the wagon. Fortunately, that was all that got damaged, but it took us about three hours to replace it with a new tongue.

September 28—We picked more the next day, but the winery was so full we had to leave the wagon at the winery unloaded. Then we had to quit taking grapes to the packing shed as they were too soft and prices are so bum anyway it's not worthwhile. And so goes the grape business!"

Otto's comments at times in his journals suggested that labor issues were a problem in California, and the grape business was no exception. From 1850 to the early 1880s, the labor force in California was largely composed of Chinese immigrants. They were industrious, would work for low wages, and would do menial jobs. They were used extensively in the building of the transcontinental

[10] Fritz Spenker managed his ranch well and it has stayed in the family for two more generations. At this time, his grandson, Chuck Spenker, has developed a winery on the ranch that has won many awards. He and his wife Betty Ann manage the ranch and the Spenker Winery.

railroad, and many people feel that if it hadn't been for the Chinese, the success of the railroad would have been in jeopardy. When this vast project was completed in 1869, however, more than ten thousand Chinese workers were instantly thrown into the general labor market primarily on the West Coast, competing with other workers and driving down their wages. The resulting social unrest led to the Chinese Exclusion Act of 1882, which with periodic reinstatements stayed in force until 1943. The original passage of this act stimulated the flow of Japanese immigrants to the United States, so by the time that the grape business began to dominate San Joaquin Valley agriculture, the Japanese workers made up much of the labor force. Other immigrants were encouraged to come to California in those early years by the formation in 1881 of an Immigration Association in San Francisco. Joseph had received a document from them which gave "encouraging" advice to immigrants. On the subject of wages, they stated: *"ordinary day laborers range from $1.00 to $2.00 per day, or $12.00 per week. Regular farm hands with board, per month $20 to $30."*[11] Joseph had received $20 a month with room and board in 1859. In 1910, the average wage for farm workers was 12 cents an hour, and remained low until 1920 when the average per hour raised to 31 cents. In the years of the Great Depression, wages dropped down to 14 cents per hour.

Weather was another concern for the grape farmer. In 1910, initially, the crops looked fine, and there were high hopes for a good season. Otto wrote:

"August 17—The grape season is starting. Ashley and Goddard called to inspect our grape crop. They pronounced them good. We agreed on 45 cents per crate. The grapes were good, everything was going well—harvest time is such a wonderful time of the year—and then it started to rain. Unseasonable rain and crops will be damaged. I spent all day turning the alfalfa hay. It had gotten wet all the way through and is turning rotten—it smells bad. We'll haul the hay out in a few days to the cows and scatter it in the fields.

September 17—Rain is damaging the grapes. I went to the winery this morning to see how the grapes were doing. There were ten teams in line and everyone loaded with rotten grapes. The grape situation looks bad. I hauled a 2 horse load in myself in the afternoon to help clear up what was picked."

Keeping the vines healthy was a main concern for the farmers, and sulfur dust was proven to be valuable. Very early it was discovered sulfur can prevent the mildew that causes the grapes to rot. Sulfur is effective, but difficult to apply. One common method, perhaps the only early method, was to have a man walk through the vineyard with a pack on his back to apply the sulfur. This pack contained the sulfur in a tin box with a bellows underneath. The sulfur would flow down into the bellows and come out through the attached hose. The man pumped air into the bellows with one hand and directed the hose with his other. He was to give a good blast one-fourth of the way down the vine and another up near the top. It was very exhausting labor to walk the vineyards on the soft, cultivated ground with a heavy pack on your back. Otto's inventive mind was working on an idea to improve this process. He was building a sulfur machine that would be built upon a cart and directed by a man sitting on the cart, all pulled by one horse through the vineyards. He described in his diary the process of developing this idea. On February 13, 1911, Otto wrote:

"I've gotten an idea as to the building of a sulfur machine—one that will be far superior to existing models. I've worked a whole day on it and got very little accomplished except for the blower. Now I have made the valve and connections for the blower. I'll try it out tomorrow.

[11] State of California Immigration Association. Office No. 10 California St. San Francisco, 1881.

The sulfur machine was a total failure. I think it will work, however, if I use larger pipes for the sulfur and for the wind. I'll build it again.

A kid from the dairy came over for a job. I got him to hoe grapes at 6 cents a row.

Working again on the sulfur machine. I've rebuilt it from one end to the other and I think I have met with good success. I hitched a team to it and it worked in splendid fashion. I think it will give satisfaction.

Tried the sulfur machine again, and except for a few slight changes I find it entirely satisfactory. The principal is right. Now it needs: more wind, wider wheels and a drive from both wheels. I also need something to spread the sulfur wider. I tried it again—ran into some trouble and spend the rest of the day making the necessary changes.

After spending more time on my sulfur machine, it is working nicely. I sulfured about 12 acres of grapes in 4 hours this morning. I proceeded to another field and broke the machine by driving over a stump."

In 1912, Otto continued working on his sulfur machine. He wrote: *"I've been thinking about it off and on since last season and feel I can make some adjustments and changes to improve its performance. I tried the sulfur machine this A.M and am well pleased with it. Great improvement over last year."*

"Sulfuring time is here and the machine is working in excellent fashion. I started at 4:30 and sulfured till noon doing more than 25 acres. Then I cleaned it up and painted it red. I have been asked to put it in the 4th of July parade.

It was an ideal 4th of July. I awoke at 4 and got the sulfur machine ready for the parade and started off about 8:00. There was a fine large crowd for the parade. I got started O.K., but went only a short distance when the fan broke and put the machine out of business for the rest of the parade."

SULFUR MACHINE

SULFUR MACHINE IN ACTION

THE NEW SPENKER HOUSE

ANNA AND JOSEPH DREAMED ABOUT A NEW HOME ever since their marriage in 1870. This home would have all the rooms Joseph originally described to Anna when they first moved onto the ranch in 1872.

Joseph and Otto carefully watched the construction on Jessie and Henry's new home in 1901, and felt confident they could build one of their own. Henry warned them about the expense of building and showed Otto a receipt from some lumber he had purchased in 1896.

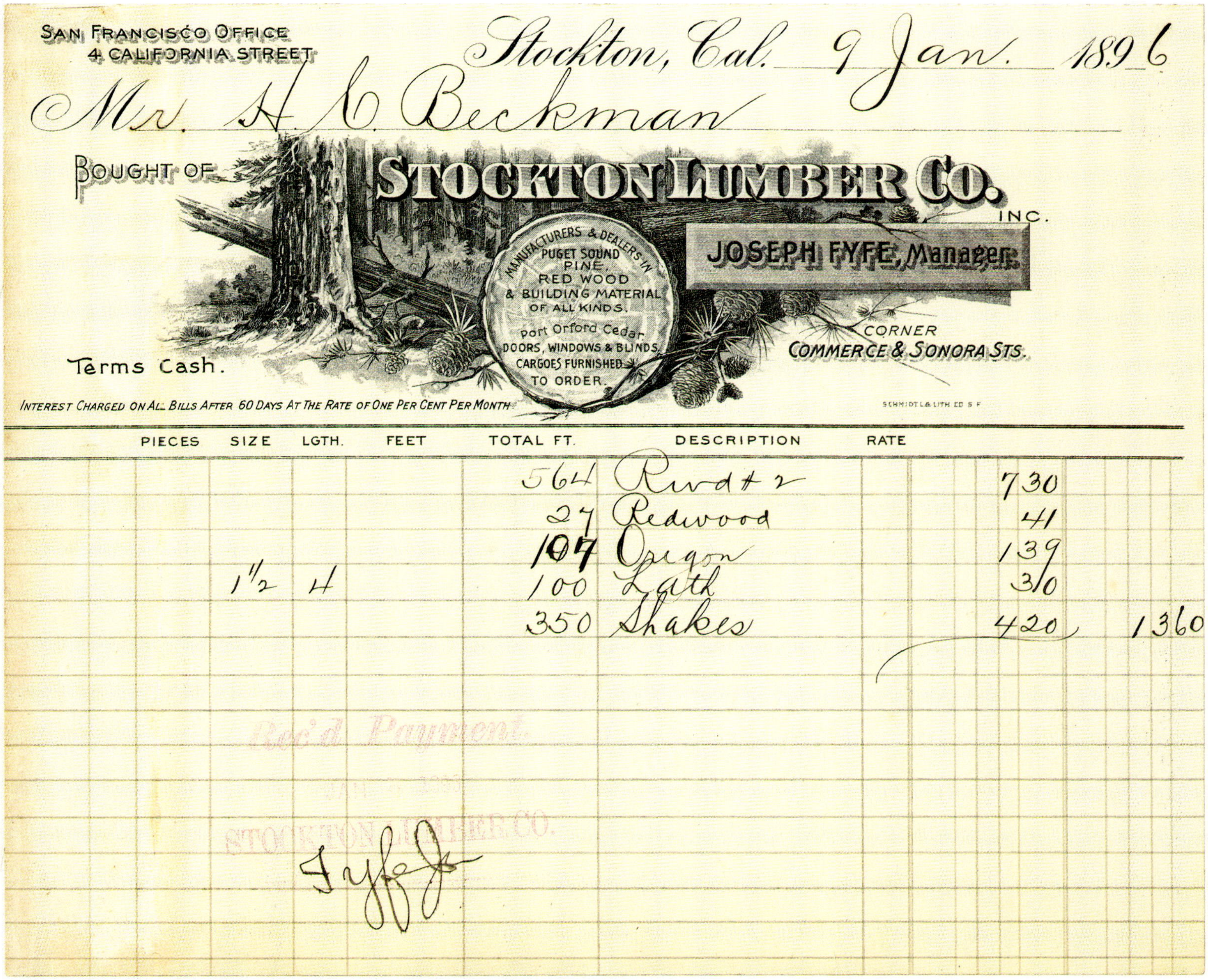

SAN FRANCISCO OFFICE
4 CALIFORNIA STREET

Stockton, Cal. 9 Jan. 1896

Mr. H. C. Beckman

BOUGHT OF STOCKTON LUMBER CO. INC.

JOSEPH FYFE, Manager.

MANUFACTURERS & DEALERS IN PUGET SOUND PINE, RED WOOD & BUILDING MATERIAL OF ALL KINDS. Port Orford Cedar. DOORS, WINDOWS & BLINDS. CARGOES FURNISHED TO ORDER.

CORNER COMMERCE & SONORA STS.

Terms Cash.

INTEREST CHARGED ON ALL BILLS AFTER 60 DAYS AT THE RATE OF ONE PER CENT PER MONTH.

SCHMIDT L. & LITH. CO. S. F.

PIECES	SIZE	LGTH.	FEET	TOTAL FT.	DESCRIPTION	RATE		
				564	Rwd # 2		730	
				27	Redwood		41	
				107	Oregon		139	
	1½	4		100	Lath		310	
				350	Shakes		420	1360

Rec'd Payment
Jan 1896
STOCKTON LUMBER CO.
Fyfe Jr

THE PRICE OF LUMBER IN 1896

Joseph and Otto started construction in 1905. Otto was mainly in charge, and this is what he wrote about the project in 1906.

"The major project on the ranch now is the house—it is well underway. I would say I make at least one trip to town everyday for home purchases. It is fascinating to watch the progress—you can actually go up the stairs now. It will be wonderful for mother to finally have a proper kitchen, parlor, and bedroom—enough for company. She is very excited. She'll even have a basement to keep things cool.

Work on the house is progressing at a good pace. I went to Lodi today for a wagon load of finish lumber. The plasterers are moving right along with their very messy job, and soon we'll be ready for painting. I hope I'll be able to find all the leaks in the roof before they start to paint. Unfortunately, there are numerous leaks and they are extremely difficult to locate. In the last heavy rain I could see that all my fixing attempts have met with little to no success.

Now the main focus is on the Water Works. Cromwell called to submit a bid on the tank house—$3400, we accepted and he's hard at work. He had five men working to bore the well, and now they'll start to raise the tower. Father had ordered a 3,000 gallon tank for the project.

Work is proceeding on the pump-house. We finally got the tower finished and then it was time to put the windmill in place. Everything was in great shape—but the tower was too short! The windmill didn't clear the roof of the tank house! Cromwell had to take it down and add more height to the tower. I'm amazed he couldn't figure this out before all the efforts getting the windmill in place.

The next day we had plenty of men working on the ranch; six workers planting Tokays, 4 painters, 2 carpenters, 2 brick layers and 3 farm hands.

"THE WATER WORKS"

The house—the house—a grand day it was for the house. I assisted the men in placing the gas fixtures into place. We turned everything on for the first time. There was an abundance of light—it made a grand showing, a fine birthday present for Father who turned 72 today, 3/29/06.

The house is finished!—all except moving the water closet over to the back yard. I have tried to talk Father into developing a complete bathroom inside, but he is reluctant to trying this new invention. I thought when he saw the bathroom Henry Beckman put in he would reconsider, but evidently it didn't impress him enough to want to try the idea. Jessie's water closet seems to work well enough. After using the apparatus you just pull the chain and the water rushes down from the tank over head and all goes outside through the pipes. Father thinks it's better to put things of that nature directly in a hole into the ground where they belong and be done with it! You can always cover the hole and move the water closet to a new location. At least we have a room available if he changes his mind.

Our furniture for the new house arrived today. Mother had a grand time placing the various pieces. We also had the men move some of the furniture from the old house that we had decided to use.

I took Mother and Father to the Lodi Opera House the next evening to celebrate his birthday."

PROGRAM FROM THE LODI OPERA HOUSE, 1906

THE LODI OPERA HOUSE

FRED H. LEE, Lessee and Manager

Friday and Saturday, March 30-31

MINSTREL MAIDS

In a Double Bill of Minstrelsy, Farce Comedy and Vaudeville

Synopsis of Act I—The scene is laid in the grounds of a young ladies' seminary. No men are allowed to enter the grounds. Arathusa, one of the young ladies, is out shooting and encounters Mr. Smith, who by accident has been strolling through the grounds. He speaks to her, she flies, he gives chase, is finally captured by the girls and some lively sport follows. They arrange to play a trick on him. One of their number appears to him as a spirit. Her unconventional remarks are due to the fact that she is impersonating Luna, the maid from the moon, and knows nothing of the ways of our world.

PROGRAMME

Act I, Scene I—Arathusa Pursued. Specialties introduced:
"In Vacation Time," "The Rose of Riviera," "I Love You All the Time," "I Kinder Likes to Have You Fussing' 'Round," "There's Nobody Just Like You," "A Picnic for Two."

Scene II—In which the Intruder is captured and made a prisoner, and a plot is laid for his discomfort.

——SPECIALTIES——

"I'm Mighty Glad I'm Living and That's All," "Why Don't You Try?" "Peggy Brady," "Lindy," "Peter Piper."

Scene III—Introducing "Smith, the Society God," and Luna, "the Girl From the Moon."

ACT II—OLIO OF MINSTRELSY

Interlocutor—Maria Anderson

FUNMAKERS

BONES .... Para Dice, Lillian Rustle, Funny Davenport
TAMBOS .... Adalina Paddy, Sorry Bernhardt, Inky White

"Get Happy"........... Introducing the jig-footed Jesters, Minstrel Maids
"The Goo-Goo Man" .... A Team of Goo-Goos
"Just a Little Rocking Chair and You" .... Pinky Panky Poo
"Won't You Come Down From the Big Fig Tree"......The Chocolate Twins
Mondolin Specialties .... Ragtime Sisters
"Buzzing 'Round" .... Isa Good Thing
"It Takes Me Back to Home Sweet Home". Madamoiselle De Kankee De Koko
"Georgie, I Love You" .... The Pretty Jilted Octaroon
"Fly Ye Blackbirds" .... Clementina Bigfoot
"Keep Away From the Hoodoo Tree" .... The Little Hoodoos

CLOSING WITH AN OLD TIME HOE DOWN

Press of The Lodi Sentinel

On May 15, 1906, Otto wrote: *"Completed moving into the new house. Had supper there for the first time. Herbert and Willie Hansen came over to drive some calves to the Adobe. They helped us move the safe. Spent most of the day getting things in place. Takes longer to move than I expected."*

JOSEPH AND ANNA SPENKER'S NEW HOME, 1906

POSTCARDS FROM A CHANGING WORLD

AROUND THE TURN OF THE CENTURY and rapidly accelerating between 1905 and 1910, postcards were considered the way to communicate. They were also used for advertisements. It had taken the post office, artists, and photographers a while to put this all together, but when they succeeded, a craze swept the country. The vast collection, which Jessie compiled throughout her life, chronicled contemporary social attitudes and changing values.

Jessie noted that often a postcard artist would get their ideas from the newspapers. On December 10, 1901, the *Lodi Sentinel* ran this article on the front page with the headline "THE COUNTRY INFESTED WITH CITY TRAMPS." The article went on to state:

"The festive bum who proves such an annoyance to the good-hearted housekeeper, has been few and far between for many moons past; but now the officers state that they find lots of them traveling through the country, and that in nearly all cases they hail from the city.

About every six months the city officers become extra vigilant and then the chair warmers and hand-out rustlers must look elsewhere to ply their daily graft.

As a rule they wander out into the country for a few weeks, and then gradually drift back to the cities.

There is plenty of work to be had, and in fact men are scarce, but the honest farmer man is not favorable to giving employment to the confirmed hobo -and the latter is not hurting himself in the effort to get busy at manual labor."

Jessie collected a card that she believed was a direct result of such articles.

THE ANNOYANCE OF THE "GOOD-HEARTED HOUSEKEEPER" AT THE "FESTIVE BUMS" FROM THE CITY.

Postcards reflected contemporary concerns and enthusiasms precisely because they served as a popular way to send a greeting to a friend, or to provoke a laugh.

Children were often depicted in advertisements. They seem so cute and innocent, no one seemed to object if once in a while their little bare bottoms were showing. This tactic certainly attracted attention.

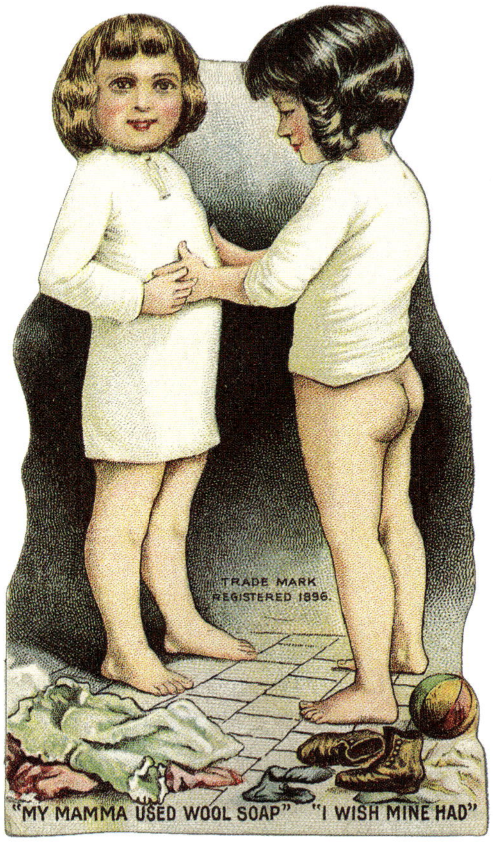

IT'S IMPORTANT TO USE THE CORRECT SOAP FOR WOOLEN UNDIES.

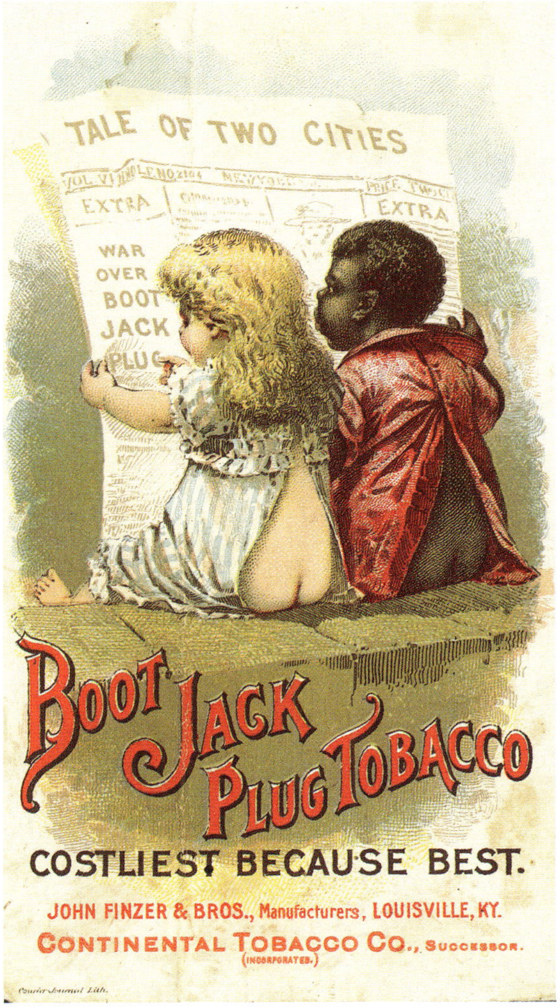

THE BOOT JACK PLUG TOBACCO AD WAS HENRY'S FAVORITE, EVEN THOUGH HE DIDN'T USE THE PRODUCT.

ONE OF THE OLDEST CARDS IN JESSIE'S COLLECTION, DATED 1882

THE CLARK AD REMAINED ONE OF JESSIE'S FAVORITES

Young children were used more and more during the early part of 1900s. They often were shown in adult situations. The basic cuteness of the child was being used to convey messages or sell products.

CHILDREN EVEN HELPED PROMOTE THE DRINKING OF WINE.

Later cards from 1911 on showed a trend toward using people of an appropriate age for the situations illustrated. Jessie was pleased about the change.

100 PERCENT PURE—
YOU CAN BELIEVE IT!

THE FIGURES IN SOME ADS BECAME FAMOUS. THE "GOLD DUST TWINS" COULD HELP WITH ANY CLEANING THE HOUSEWIFE HAD TO DO—BECAUSE, AS THE POSTCARD STATES, "WHEN YOU'RE MARRIED YOUR TROUBLE BEGINS." THESE TWINS COULD HELP SOLVE ANY PROBLEM. THE CARD WAS COPYRIGHTED IN 1907.

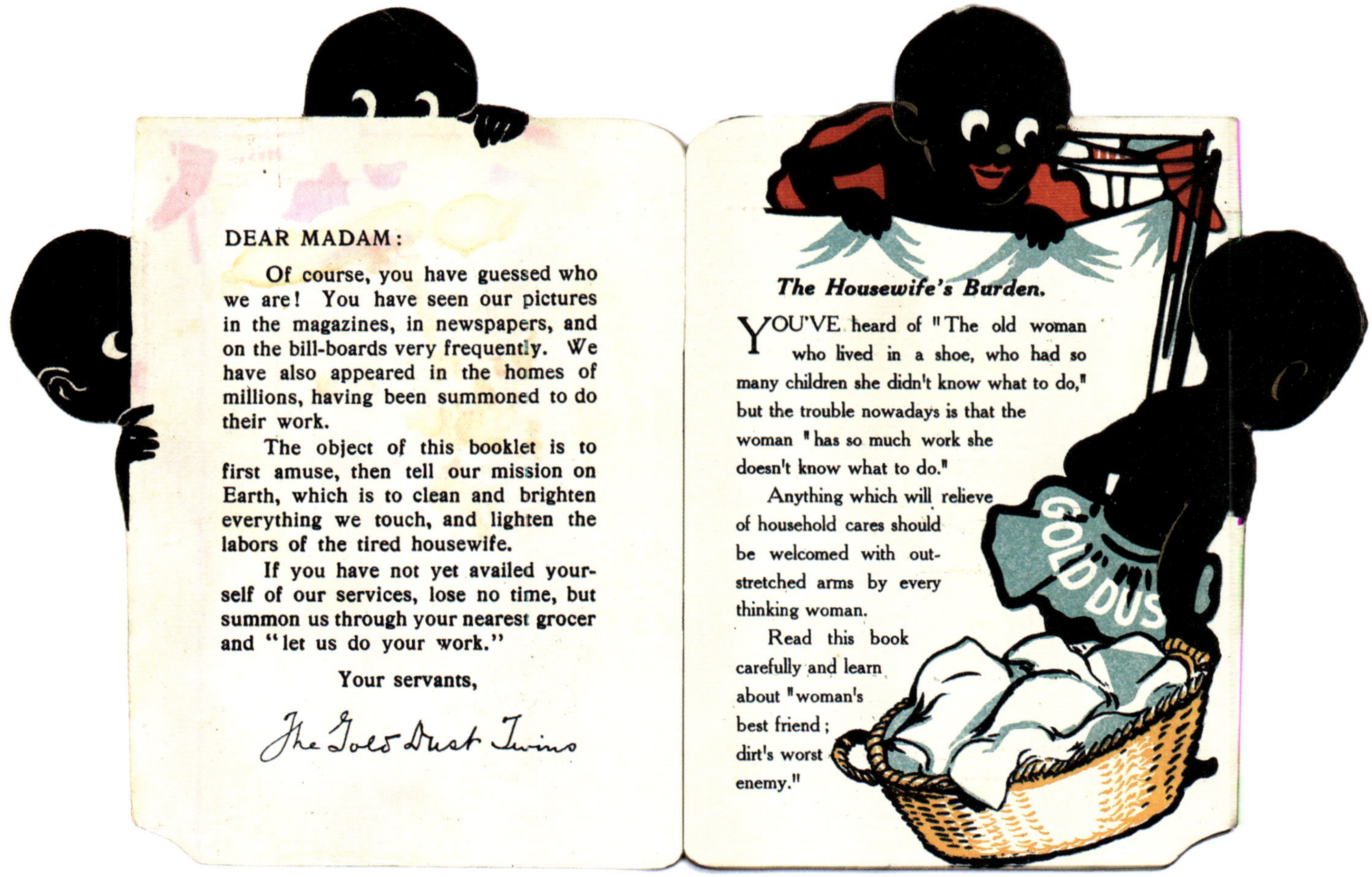

THIS HIRES ROOT BEER AD WAS ANOTHER OF JESSIE'S FAVORITES. IT WAS PRINTED IN 1883.

ON THE BACK OF THE CARD, HIRES ROOT BEER GAVE SOME "WONDERFUL" PROMISES. THEY CLAIMED THEY WERE THE "BEST BLOOD PURIFIER IN THE WORLD". IT WAS INEXPENSIVE AS WELL. FOR TWENTY-FIVE CENTS YOU COULD RECEIVE A SMALL BOX THAT WOULD MAKE FIVE GALLONS. "AN ENTHUSIASTIC LADY" WAS QUOTED AS SAYING IF SHE HADN'T GIVEN HIRES ROOT BEER TO HER CHILDREN THEY COULD HAVE DIED! IT SEEMED TO JESSIE THEY COULD SAY ALMOST ANYTHING IN THE ADS.

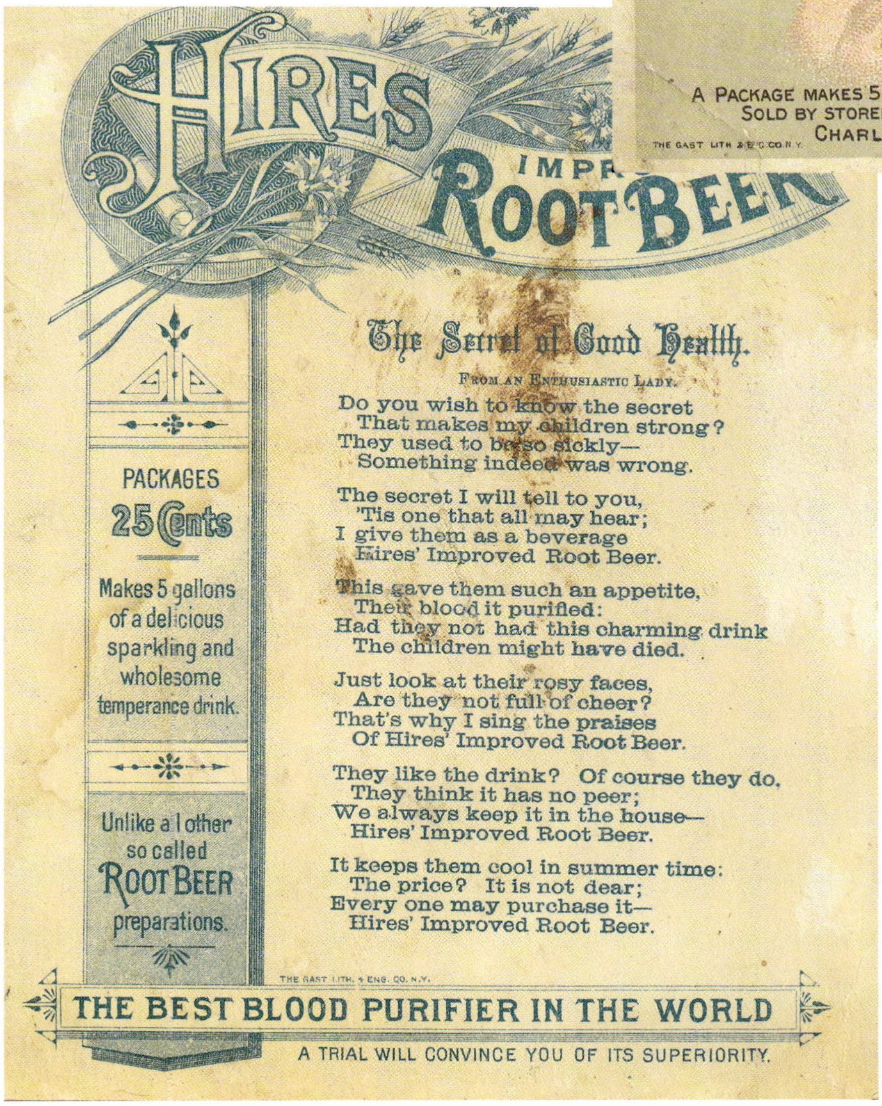

In 1914, when the United States government created the Federal Trade Commission, it became illegal to claim biased results merely to sell a product. The commission was to help export trade and prevent unfair methods of competition. Finally there would be truth to the advertisements.

Postcards also began to repeat messages to younger people that traditionally had been conveyed by parents, churches, and teachers, perhaps reflecting that in this changing world of the early part of the twentieth century, when life was moving at a dramatically faster pace, more caution was necessary.

ANITA AND VERA RECEIVED SOME WORDS OF WISDOM.

A FRIEND SENT A POSTCARD TO ANITA WITH SOME VALUABLE ADVICE.

MORE ADVICE FOR THE GIRLS

PROFESSIONAL PHOTOGRAPHY

JESSIE HAD A FAMILY PORTRAIT TAKEN AND PRINTED ON POST-CARDS TO SEND TO FRIENDS, A POPULAR WAY TO COMMUNICATE. VERA, HENRY, ANITA, JOE, JESSIE

OTTO PHOTOGRAPHY

VERA, ANITA AND JOE

CHAPTER SIX

Years of Upheaval

IT WASN'T JUST POPULAR ATTITUDES that were in flux. The Earth itself would not stay still, and rivers abandoned the confines of their banks. At home, social and technical progress created new opportunities and fulfilled dreams, but in Europe, political upheavals were again causing turmoil, and war appeared to be inevitable.

THE 1906 EARTHQUAKE

On April 18, 1906, at 5:15 in the morning, a devastating earthquake shook the ground. Jessie said she was in her bed, afraid to move. Would it happen again? Would it get worse? She and Henry slowly got up and looked for damage. All seemed well, but there was an eerie calm—all was so quiet. The birds were silent, the chickens were quiet, and it seemed like the world was holding its breath. Jessie said she spent a very uneasy day, and later that evening Henry came rushing into the house. *"Jessie, look to the west! San Francisco is burning!"*

Jessie went out to the back porch, which was about fifteen feet off the ground. A glowing orange radiance had crept into the evening sky. Jessie's heart was gripped with fear, Henry's grandmother Hacke lived in San Francisco. The next day all Jessie could do was think about the fire and the Hacke family as she watched a smoky blanket hover over the western horizon. That night the fire appeared larger and was plainly visible.

Days passed before they heard any news. Finally they heard that the Hackes had survived, but Grandmother Hacke's house had burned down in the aftermath of the earthquake. This was the home where Christopher and Marie, Henry's parents, were married in 1864. Harold Hacke had built a new home on Carl Street, and when the earthquake hit, his two-story chimney collapsed. Harold, sleeping in an upstairs bedroom adjacent to the chimney, could not get out because bricks blocked the door. He had to climb down the outside of the building. After the earthquake, hundreds of people moved to Golden Gate Park, including the Hacke family, who lived in the park for over a week. Jessie was very grateful to know they were safe.

Jessie's minister gave her a copy of a letter he had received from the Evangelical Lutheran pastor G. A. Bernthal. He was the minister of a large church on Eddy Street in San Francisco. The letter is dated May 8, 1906.

"I am writing this letter to you by candlelight, at this time there is no gas or electricity in San Francisco, and oil lamps are not allowed.

Tomorrow it will be 3 weeks since that terrible day—it was on the Wednesday after Easter, April 18th, that early in the morning we were shaken out of our sleep. Our house cracked and rattled, spit and jumped, and everything fell into a heap. Breaking glass clattered, vases and the like crashed down and there was such a noise that we thought Judgement Day was here. The 48 seconds seemed to be hours. I called to my wife and children to be sure to stay in their rooms, as I immediately thought about the chimney. And that was fortunate, since many people who ran out into the street were killed by falling stones. We dressed quickly and then went out into the street. Oh what an awful sight! The street swarmed with people in their nightclothes, and on all sides we heard their cries. In many places fires started to break out. Under the circumstances, our neighborhood got by better since we lived on a hill. In the lower parts of town innumerable houses collapsed in a heap. I headed immediately for the city hospital which in our big city was only 6 blocks away from us, but lo and behold, the entire building was in a heap of ruins. In a hurry a large hall near the hospital was opened and I was the first pastor that arrived there to speak words of comfort to the poor people. Whole wagon-loads of injured and dying were constantly coming in, such as could be pulled out of the ruins. I stood for hours at the operating tables and was splattered with blood—again and again legs, arms were amputated. The screams and groans were dreadful. How could I stand it, I myself do not know, but finally my senses became completely numb. Again and again there were new earthquakes and the whole building made a cracking noise and the people screamed in terror. Adding to their fears was the news the fires were coming closer. These had been pretty much under control, but a stupid woman tried to light a fire in her stove even though the chimney had fallen in. In an instant, the house was in flames and a strong wind shipped the fire onward. Unfortunately, most of the water mains had been broken by the earthquake and we had no water to put out the fire which rushed on unhindered and now was already very close to the wooden buildings in which we found ourselves with the hundreds of the injured, dead and dying. Only one side was the way still clear. In all haste, the injured were loaded on all kinds of wagons and were evacuated. It was like a wild retreat after a lost battle. The dead bodies remained behind. Hardly had we gotten away when the whole building stood in flames and in 10 minutes was completely leveled. I now went back home. The fire continued to be driven from the south side toward our church property—and no water. Buildings by the dozen were blown into the air by tons of dynamite before the fire reached them, in order to form a firebreak. But all was in vain. They also wanted to dynamite our church. Then there appeared a wonderful act of God. The water lines to our church had water. So from here all the might of two machines pumped water and the fire was halted 1½ blocks from us and then went in an easterly direction. For the time being we were saved.

By morning, hundreds of the finest buildings in the city stood in flames. It was like a hell. The strongest buildings collapsed together like cardboard boxes. Then the fire turned again from the eastside towards us. I will never forget the moment when with tearful eyes I looked back at our beautiful church which stood there high and isolated by a sea of fire. Yet, in a wonderful way, our water line was still holding out. The fire was again arrested, and hardly had that happened when we had not a drop of water anymore. That was obviously wrought by the hand of God, and the people were utterly amazed by this sign of divine protection.

We opened the doors of our church for use as a temporary hospital, and have as of now taken in and cared for over 3,000 people.

What are we to do now? How we will get through it for the time, only the Lord knows.

We all send our sincere greetings and ask you to include us in your prayers.

Your brother, Georg"[1]

[1] Pastor Bernthal was the great-uncle of Pastor Robert Fickenscher. At the time of the quake, this letter was mailed to family members and shared with ministers of other churches.

On April 20, Joseph went to Stockton to pay their taxes, but found all the banks were closed. Business was suspended because of the fire in San Francisco. No money was available anywhere.

On June 10, Otto wrote: *"Took the 6:50 train with Jessie for San Francisco to view the ruins of the greatest fire ever seen. The destruction is beyond comprehension. I cannot describe it in words, the pictures I take will have to speak for themselves. Here we are with a new home—almost ready to move in, and a few miles to the West is total destruction."*

SAN FRANCISCO
CITY HALL

JESSIE LOOKS OUT OVER THE RUINS OF THE ONCE BEAUTIFUL CITY.

TO LEASE

THE RUINS OF THE SPRECKELS BUILDING

"DEVASTATION WAS EVERYWHERE"

AFTER THE FIRE

ST. PAULUS GERMAN LUTHERAN CHURCH FROM JEFFERSON SQUARE

Jessie heard about the rebuilding of San Francisco from some of her friends. On August 29, 1906, Jessie received a letter: *"San Francisco has been a very busy place these last few months. You should see all the fine new stores (temporary ones, of course) on Van Ness Avenue and all about the City. In fact it does one's heart good to look at the window displays of beautiful things, and there are scores of purchasers and money seems to be brisk."*

On November. 23, 1906, another friend living in the city wrote:

"Our car system is still in a most deplorable condition, and oh what a lot of patience the delays require. One simply cannot keep an appointment on time. We simply do the best we can. The City is building up wonderfully. Out in the Mission and up at North Beach one would hardly know there had ever been a fire. Of course, there are very few large buildings as yet, but it is only a question of time when they will go up."

It was later reported that 674 people were killed instantly when the quake hit. If the Richter Scale had been in existence, it is estimated the quake would have measured approximately 8.25, which is classified by them as a "Great earthquake." The tremor was said to have lasted forty-eight seconds, and many said the ground moved in a swirling motion. The worst damage to San Francisco was caused by the horrific fire that couldn't be put out because of all the ruptured water lines. The combined tragedies caused the destruction of over 28,000 buildings and the deaths of over 3,000 people. This quake still stands as a monumental catastrophy today throughout the world.

FLOOD

THE GREAT 1906 SAN FRANCISCO EARTHQUAKE wasn't the end of the upheavals that nature had in store. On March 21, 1907, The *Lodi Sentinel's* headline read "Flood Water From Mountains Causes Damage in the Valley. Woodbridge Submerged at a Depth of From One to Five Feet."

The article continued:

"One of the greatest storms since 1869 that has swept over this section of the State raged Sunday, Monday and a portion of Tuesday. The over-flow from the Mokelumne River commenced early Tuesday morning to creep into Woodbridge and by noon the town was almost submerged. By noon, the higher points of Woodbridge formed an island and those who either left or came into the little town did so by boat. . . . Near the east turn at Smith's Lake[2] there is a drop in the middle of the road of nearly three feet, by afternoon it was fully six feet deep. In one hour's time at that point in the road Tuesday the water rose to a depth sufficient to swim a horse."

Jessie and Henry read the paper with grave concern. There were many stories to read in the paper over the next two days.

"Al McComb, the baggage master at the Southern Pacific depot, responded to the plea for succor, arriving on the scene with a duck boat. On the George Cox farm between Clements and Lockeford, two men, Bert Gaskill and Mr. Megerle were perched in the top of an oak tree. They had been down to the lowlands of the farm to round up a band of horses with a boat. Megerle was leading one of the animals by a halter from the boat. The horse came swimming along for awhile when it was suddenly overcome with a desire to climb into the boat. Of course there wasn't room for three and the expected happened. The two men went up a tree, the horse swam to higher ground and the boat was carried into the current and lost. Mr. McComb rowed to the tree and experienced little or no difficulty in rescuing the two men.

Yesterday afternoon John Peirano, brother of G. Peirano the grocery man, came into town in an excited frame of mind. He said that his house, foundation and all had sunk to a depth of seven feet. Peirano was almost frantic about the mishap and was asking nearly everyone he met to go out and assist him. A number of the houses out toward the flood waters in the western side of town have settled on account of the infirm land, and considerable damage has resulted."

It was the worst flood Stockton ever experienced, and with the exception of the blocks bounded by California, Clay, and Sacramento Streets and the Mormon canal, every portion of the city and the suburbs was inundated. The flood was from sixteen inches to four feet deep all over the city. Main, Market, and Weber Avenues were swift rivers two feet deep and yellow and thick with mud. Those streets were no exception to the rule. All streets were streams, and all sidewalks knee deep. Every basement was flooded. Probably not a single store in the city escaped the inundation of its ground floor.[3]

Jessie was horrified reading the stories. Thankfully, the Beckman Ranch was saved from any damage due to flooding. She was concerned about the Spenker Ranch, but Joseph had always said the ground was high enough to bypass any floodwaters. On March 25, however, Jessie received a letter from Otto.

---

[2] Now Lodi Lake.

[3] The conditions that led to the flood were partially corrected, at least for Stockton, with the construction of the Diverting Canal in 1910 and the construction of Hogan Dam in 1930.

Afloat Sunday PM

Dear Sis:

Have just taken a bike ride to Woodbridge to look at the break in the levee. They are closing it as fast as they can but that's slow enough. Under favorable circumstances they may succeed in a few days. If the water rises it's all off. The water in my yard is higher today than last Wed., but we built a dam this morning which may check it.

Have just ordered a separator to come up by express tomorrow. I have been skimming the top of the cans since the flood and making butter.

The roads are so soft it is dangerous to travel. Will try to find the break in our phone line today if the water isn't up to my mouth.

If anyone comes over in a day or so—bring the camera over as there are some interesting views!

Yours for dry weather—Otto

THE FLOOD WATERS ENCROACHING ON THE SPENKER RANCH

THIS PICTURE WAS TAKEN FROM UPSTAIRS IN THE NEW SPENKER HOUSE LOOKING TO THE NORTH.

OTTO AND LENA

JESSIE OFTEN EXPRESSED HER CONCERN about Otto still being single. In 1907, he remained unmarried at the age of thirty-six. She had hoped he would get married long ago, but a serious relationship had never developed. He had many friends, but a special lady friend was not in the picture. When she spoke to him about it, he replied: *"I can't even begin to think of anyone I want to marry. I'm so busy and I find life plenty exciting without the added complications of a wife."*

LENA

Jessie thought Lena would make an ideal wife for Otto. She was a beautiful young woman, a proven good worker in Jessie's household, wonderful with the children, and kind in her care of Henry's aging mother. Jessie talked to Otto again and again on the subject. After all, as she mentioned many times, he would be the one to carry on the family name.

These concerns of Jessie's were recorded in Otto's journals over the course of several years. The pressure placed upon him was evident in the dramatic change in his entries from happy descriptions through December 31, 1906, to fragmented, brief, almost illegible entries for January 1907. These continued, skipping many days and then there were only a few disjointed words, and finally nothing.

In 1909, Otto and Lena got married. They had the ceremony in Stockton at the courthouse, just as Joseph and Anna had done, and took up residence in the new Spenker house. Jessie was hoping they would take at least some type of honeymoon, but Otto said he didn't have time for that sort of thing.

After Otto and Lena were married, Jessie had never seen her brother so upset—he hardly spoke to her now. He should be happy! Jessie thought maybe it would just take time. Lena didn't seem happy either. She came over whenever possible and often stayed overnight. Henry was always so glad to see her, and he made her feel very welcome. He knew he should encourage Lena to stay home, but quite the opposite seemed to happen.

Otto finally started writing again in 1910.

"Ah yes—I was going to write in my journal each and everyday, but 1907 turned dark for me. I refuse to remember—let alone write down the incidents that pushed me into that dark world. I could blame this person, that person or myself, but what good would that do. Things have happened—my life has seemed to be in a jumble—people pushing me one way and then the other way, and why I couldn't stop it, I don't know. I am determined to get a grip on this—get back to the high spirits I usually associate with myself. Of course things are different now—I'm married!

January 19, 1910

Just happened to think—I have been married for three months today. After delaying the event for as long as I could I finally gave into sister and married Lena. She is a lovely girl—she deserves a better mate than I will ever be. I want to do what's right—I think that is one of my main problems. I listen to what others say and want for me and don't listen to myself. Mother seems happy to have Lena in the house—I'll try not to let her see how distressed I am.

Of course Lena is gone a lot and that does ease the tension. Just the other day she went to Beckmans and stayed several days. I'm sure she's pleased to stay away. So mother and I did the washing as my wife has not returned from H.C.B. The next day H.C.B. brought Lena home for a short stay."

Otto's and Lena's married life seemed tragic from the very beginning. On March 6, six months after they were married, Otto wrote:

"A very pleasant March day. I washed the buggy—first time in a year or so, and went to church alone. Lena has been staying at Beckmans again. She made a "short call" in the afternoon with H.C.B., Joe and Vera, but declined to stay. So off she went in the fancy car with "cavelarous" Henry.

The next afternoon I took a ride into Stockton to see Col. Johnson's flying exhibit in a Curtis biplane. It was at the old racetrack and he had an immense crowd. It was a very satisfactory performance. He has a wonderful machine—light and yet simple. I saw him make eight or ten very successful flights. I heard he flew again the next day but broke the machine by landing too hard.

LENA IS BACK AT THE BECKMANS.

After the flying exhibit—with happy heart I drove by Beckmans to hopefully pick up my wife. Lena declined to come with me and said she plans on staying with Beckmans indefinitely!

I was sick the rest of the day as I have never been before—One of the pleasures of being a husband and caring nothing for a wife."

The only entry that was at all cheerful was on July 27, 1910, when Otto took Lena into Stockton to select a new buggy. This appeared to be something Otto had wanted for a long time, and he let Lena make the selection. *"Think she made a good choice,"* He wrote. Lena learned to drive the buggy by herself, and this seemed to lead to more time spent at the Beckmans.

This pattern continued, and on March 3, 1911, Lena packed up her clothes and moved out for good.

On May 7, Lena wrote to Otto:

Dear Otto, Received both of your letters and was glad to hear from you, but could have appreciated the last one much more if you had only written something about how the Beckman's were—especially Mr. Beckman. I was afraid his heart would trouble him. Perhaps you think not mentioning him or his family will make me forget them, but I never could. As long as they treat me alright I shall always be the same to them. Their place seems just like home to me and they seem just like my own people, and I don't care what the people all say about me. I will talk to Mr. Beckman and be to him just the same as always, and don't care who sees me. Let them all blame me just as they do in your and my affair. They can't make me worse than they have already.

Otto continued to work on the ranch—trying to get his life back in order. Later in the year, Otto wrote:

The dairy—the dairy, always problems at the dairy. First one of our good cows had twins—they both died, and now it looks like the cow will die! Then the cream separator broke down, so I had to take it apart and order extra parts. We made arrangements with Harshners to skim our cream at his establishment in the meantime.

Yes we always have problems at the dairy, but they are fixable. My problem with Lena is without solution. We took a drive around Acampo and back—talking all the time. She had decided on a divorce and nothing else can be done. I practically agreed to let her get a divorce—I'm unable to do anything else with her. Now I'm feeling bum and don't care what happens. I'll write up an agreement and send it to her. I can see there has to be an end to this for both our sakes. I will keep a copy of this agreement in my private papers. I believe this should end the matter of a very sad experience for both of us.

In consideration of the sum of $3,000.00 to me paid and other valuable considerations, I solemnly promise and agree that within one week after I secure a decree of divorce from Otto Spenker, I will leave the city of Lodi and the immediate vicinity to take up residence elsewhere, never to return during the lifetime of the said Otto Spenker.

Signed this day of April 1912

_______________(sign here)

Lena responded with this letter, which Otto kept with his records.

April 27, 1912

Dear Otto,

As you can see I have not signed your paper and I don't intend to, and I'm sure I don't remember promising to do so.

I will not promise to leave within a week after I get my decree, but as soon as it is convenient for me. Saying "I will never return to live here"—I think that is going a little too far for a person can never tell what may happen in the future. When I told you the other night that I would leave, I didn't mean for all time.

Considering all things, how my life has been ruined, how I will be excluded from church, leave Lodi and everything, and how rich you will be someday, it is a very small sum you gave me. If I felt I had enough to live off and would not have to work always, it would seem different.

Nevertheless I thank you for what you have given me, but I don't like to sign a pledge that I am afraid I would regret too much in the future. Lena

A few months later, Otto wrote in his journal: *"On a warm sunny August Sunday, I took mother to H.C.B. and went to church. I had lunch with Rev. Jacobs and at 2 our quarterly meeting started. The main business was a call for a new teacher and my domestic troubles—they were brought before the congregation for action."*

This was the procedure in the Lutheran Church at this time when a couple wanted to get a divorce. The all-male voting body of the church would listen to the problems, and at times the woman was questioned by this group. I do not believe Lena had to go through that ordeal. I do know that Lena and Otto did get a divorce, and she moved out of town. Otto wrote:

"Lena has finally moved away so that terrible incident is at least not on the top of everyone's conversation. I'm afraid this bothered Father more than he would say. Sis is still in close contact with Lena, but I have no control over that. I know this has weakened a very strong bond that Sis and I used to have for each other. Things have never been the same since Lena came into our lives. We used to be so close—almost think as one, and now there is a cold distance."

The day after Christmas in that terrible year for Otto, the temperature dropped to twenty degrees. Otto took a picture of the Spenker Ranch with an unusual frosty covering, remarking that the ice was perfect for the mood he was in.

As the spring of the new year approached, however, work on the ranch intensified, and Otto struggled to put his life back together.

I wish I could supply more information about Lena—her background, why she was available to help Jessie. The truth, however, is that Lena was a subject you didn't discuss in my family. I have many ideas as to what happened between Lena and Otto, but since there is no clear evidence, I will refrain from speculating. After all, only Lena and Otto really know the answers.

THE ICY COLD WINTER OF OTTO'S DESPAIR

EQUAL RIGHTS

By Clyde Ludwick

EQUAL rights—if such a thing could be—mother would stay out at the club nights playing cards with the girls and come home seeing double and society wouldn't say a word. And just think! Daddie would be allowed to stay in and care for the baby and rule the home and call his time his own, although he would probably not devote much time to the war news or the sport page of the daily paper.

NEWSPAPER CLIPPING—JESSIE'S COLLECTION

EQUAL RIGHTS

BROAD SOCIAL AND POLITICAL UPHEAVALS were occurring, both in the United States and abroad. One important change in progress was the women's suffrage movement, to gain women the right to vote. Jessie was proud of the women in her country. As early as 1848, groups had organized to try to gain equal rights, and an equal say in the running of the government. Jessie felt this was so right she couldn't begin to understand all the opposition.

COPYRIGHT 1909

After the Civil War, many women felt they would be given the right to vote, but when Congress passed the Fourteenth Amendment, it stated that only males could vote. This was the first time a sexual qualification was placed in the United States Constitution. After the passage of the Fifteenth Amendment, newly freed black males could vote, but not women. The territory of Wyoming, gave women the right to vote in 1869. Jessie felt this was a trend that was bound to sweep across the country. Women should be treated as full and equal citizens everywhere in the United States and in the world.

Laura De Force Gordon was a woman Jessie knew and greatly admired. She had been working on the women's suffrage movement for years, in addition to carrying on a very successful law practice in Sacramento. Jessie was highly interested in the fact she also ran her family's ranch in Lodi. Why not? This idea had always appealed to Jessie, and she carefully observed and made notes about the progress and activities on all the ranches in her family. There could come a time when she would be placed in charge, and she would be ready.

Some senators in California were trying to get a constitutional amendment passed that would allow women to vote. This was encouraging, but it also brought out the opposition. On March 5, 1907, the *Lodi Sentinel* published an article that had Jessie outraged. The heading in bold type stated: "**Women Too Dainty To Vote**." As if that wasn't bad enough, a subhead continued: "A Creature, Says Senate, Man Cannot Live With Nor Live Without."

The article was mainly quoting Senator Willis of San Bernardino County. He actually had the nerve to give his version of how God created women. He said:

"The mighty creator gathered the strong materials of the earth and out of this solid substance he made a being of wondrous strength and beauty—man! When, however, He cast about for something out of which to make the companion of the wondrous being he could find nothing substantial, as all solid matter had been used up in the construction of man. Therefore He contented himself with things airy, ethereal and intangible.

He took the roundness of the moon, the splendid suppleness of the serpent, the warmth of the fire, the coldness of the iceberg, the firmness of the oak, the clinging of the vine, and to this was added the velvet of the rose, the sweetness of honey, the cruelty of the tigress, the tender cooing of the turtle dove, the stubbornness of the mule, and the chattering of the magpie! These he wove together with the tears of the mist and the result—Woman!

A companion to man, one who loves and torments, one who caresses and harasses, one who encourages and discourages, one who causes his greatest pleasure, his most poignant pain, a creature he cannot live with, a creature he cannot live without."

He continued, *"Now gentlemen, What do you think of this ethereal being mixing with us, the individuals in whom all the stuff that is solid is concentrated, at the polls? Would it not lower her status? Would we take off our hats to her? Would we step into the gutter and allow her the sidewalk? Could we venerate her as we do now?*

Women do not need to go to the polls to have a say in the government of the state or nation. They control the ballot as it is. Her influence is felt so much in the home that the man carries her impression with him when he goes to cast his vote. Politics is not for fair women. What would be the result if the Legislature grants her the right of suffrage? The majority will stay at home. Could the few that would vote have any greater influence than they do now? A clubwoman is not the woman we want to see at our fireside."

Jessie felt the statements were so outrageous the paper should not have put them in the newspaper. To change the words of the Bible for a political maneuver was unconscionable.

Another article to the side of this one stated: *"Ungallant Senators—But Few of Them Who Think That Women Should Vote."* Few? The paper listed the ayes, and there were eighteen that voted to grant women the right to vote in the state of California. The noes were also listed and added up to eleven. The bill needed a two-thirds vote to change the amendment, but the majority had voted to do so. The paper seemed reluctant to report progress. Jessie could see it was only a matter of time before women would be raised to the status of full and equal citizens.

Jessie enjoyed all the postcards that were coming out about women's suffrage. She collected them, but had the strong impression they were supporting the male view against suffrage. They were cute, however, and got people actively talking and considering this obvious needed change in our government.

Finally, in 1911, California passed an amendment granting women the right to vote in local and state elections. Actually, women in San Joaquin County were the first women to exercise this privilege in a local election. On December 14, 1911, Jessie cast her first official vote for the $150,000 bond to construct the badly needed Lodi High School building. She was very proud the bond passed.

By 1914, the contrast between the East and the West had become striking. All the states west of the Rockies had women's suffrage, while no state east of the Rockies did except for Kansas. Westerners proved far more willing than other Americans to welcome women as full and equal citizens. Jessie felt her girls were growing up in a time of opportunity unsurpassed in earlier years. Women were allowed to vote only in California elections, but Jessie felt that would soon be corrected. It took until 1920 before the Nineteenth Amendment was passed giving women the right to vote in national elections.

POSTCARDS FROM JESSIE'S COLLECTION

THE WORLD AT WAR, FROM THE COLLECTION OF DON PEIRANO.

WAR

In 1914, war broke out in Europe. The news was grim. Germany declared war on Russia on August 1, 1914 and declared war on France on August 3. Then Great Britain stepped in and declared war on Germany August 4th.

The war in Europe made Jessie heartsick—she couldn't begin to understand the reasons for it. She received some letters from her mother's sister, Lina Schirerak, who lived on a farm in Strolen, Germany. In May 1915 she wrote: *"It is still very cold here, it has been raining all day, but we need it. The hard time will be at harvest time, without the men. Almost every-one has a harvest machine, we don't have enough horses. Some use the cows on the plows. Pigs are expensive. We don't have anymore, they all died last fall. We'll try to get some again."*

In May 1915, a German U-boat [submarine] sank the passenger ship *Lusitania*, killing 1,201 civilians, including 128 Americans. Some Americans were clamoring for an immediate declaration of war, but President Wilson urged the country to stay at peace. Jessie was relieved when he won the election of 1916 with the slogan "He kept us out of war." The thought of her country fighting the birthplace of Anna and Joseph was more than she could bear.

Jessie followed all the war news with dread and horror. Where would this lead? What would America's role be? Everyone kept saying that it's so far away it won't affect us, but how would America react? What would happen to the people she knew and loved in Germany? Her dreams were filled with nightmares.

MODERN WARFARE, FROM THE COLLECTION OF DON PEIRANO

On Nov. 7, 1915, Jessie received another letter from her aunt.

My Dear Jessie,

I sit here with a sad heart ready to write another letter. I'm sorry you had to wait so long for my letter, but the letter I wrote to you in Sept. came back to me in October. I'm sending it again and hope the bad Englishman will let it pass this time. They are bad warring people. I'm sending today's newspaper along so you can read about everything yourself because your newspaper is probably lying to you. It is so sad in the German warfront. We can't even imagine. You wanted to know where my sons are. Heimrich is in Russia (officer), Wilhelm and Herman are in France. Herman apparently has been wounded. I don't know if he is still alive. I'm hurting so much, I can't even tell you. He took several bullets into the body. He is probably dead. I have not been able to find out. He wrote to my daughter in law on Oct. 5th, that was the last we heard. He wrote he can't sleep because of hunger. You can imagine my grief! Is he in enemy hands or already buried? So much hunger, no money. All the men are gone; so many fears for everyone. I can't write what I feel, my heart hurts too much.

Jessie was deeply troubled by this letter. She continued to send numerous letters to her aunt throughout the course of the war, but she never heard from her again.

Although war went on in Europe, people in the United States had the general feeling :"Surely we won't be involved. After all, the war is way across the ocean." In Lodi, life went on and people were building hotels.

Lodi was also adding a new bank to the community—The Farmer's and Merchants Bank opened their doors in 1916. Joseph and Otto were relieved that finally a bank that could look out for the interest of the farmers was available. They both felt this was a worthwhile addition to the community.

LODI WAS EXPANDING, AND OTTO RECIEVED AN INVITATION FOR THE GRAND OPENING OF "LODI'S MAGNIFICENT NEW HOTEL!"

Henry was worried about Jessie and her reaction to the terrible news coming from Europe, so he rented a flat in Santa Cruz. There, the family could escape the hot August days, and he hoped they could take Jessie's mind off the war for a few weeks. While they were there, Otto wrote them a letter that typifies how, despite the conflict raging in Europe, life went on in the San Joaquin Valley.

Dear Folks in Santa Cruz, Cal.
August 8, 1916

We have been very much delighted to receive your postals with the information that you arrived safe and sound after a most delightful trip, and that you are all enjoying good health and fish.

I suppose that Joe and H. C. catch all the fish, but am a little inclined to believe that they use a silver bait.

You ought to be thankful that you are down there as it was a hot one here last week, but now it is much cooler—almost cold this evening, and I think the hot spell is over for awhile.

We finished hauling hay this forenoon and start shipping barley tomorrow morning. I sent over and got your wagon today.

There was no meeting at church Sunday as there were not enough present for a quorum, probably because it was so hot.

After visiting awhile with Mr. Spoerke, I spent awhile at Smith's Lake (now called Lodi Lake) and tried to make believe it was Santa Cruz. It's about as near the real article as I can get this summer, and by allowing your imagination to supply a few deficiencies it will do very well for a substitute. The bathers and water are there anyway, and some fish too.

I guess it's no use to tell you any news as you certainly get the Sentinel or some other reliable ? Paper and it would only be a waste of time to tell you that Joe Maley has a new auto (Overland), and that the Harshner girls are getting married, and that Mr. Hartje went to sleep Sun. evening while going home and demolished his buggy by driving into Daniels mailbox post (never hurt the post), and that I have purchased 17 head of young cattle from the celebrated J. H. Pope herd of dairy stock. (took pity on the poor fellow and gave him a chance to pay off his mortgage). Etc. adlib Infanitum.

We are all enjoying good health, considering the fact that we are at home, and hope to continue so indefinitely. Father's leg is healed up nicely now and some days I am able to get around very nicely myself. Mother, of course, is always well.

I suppose by this time you are able to go down on the beach without feeling embarrassed at the sight of the swell suits—or maybe you have gotten up nerve enough to don one yourself.

Bet not one of you can swim yet or dive either.

I am enclosing a 2 cent stamp, so if you can borrow a piece of paper you could write a letter—if not too busy.

With regards from us all, and best wishes for your good health and enjoyment, I remain your Brother—
Otto

VERA SENT A CARD TO ANNA

Otto was correct in thinking none of the family could swim, let alone dive. Anita was the first to want to venture into the water. She and some of her friends rented swimsuits and had a grand time.

SEASIDE CO. RENTED SWIMMING SUITS.
ANITA IS ON THE RIGHT.

JESSIE DECLINED TO EVEN THINK ABOUT DONNING SUCH APPAREL. SHE AND VERA RECLINED ON THE BEACH PROPERLY DRESSED, AS ALWAYS.

THE END OF AN ERA

AS UPHEAVALS OF MANY KINDS troubled the tranquility of the San Joaquin Valley, the pioneers who had done so much to bring peace and prosperity to the area by their hard work and dedication to their families began to pass away.

The *Lodi Sentinel* reported: *"Marie Langhorst Beckman, born in Westphalia, Prussia, died in her home on April 25, 1911. She was the wife of the well known deceased pioneer Christopher Beckman. Arriving in this country at the age of twenty five, she had lived in Lodi since her marriage in 1864 on the Beckman estate. She was seventy two years old."*

Jessie was saddened by the loss of her mother-in-law. They had grown very close in the fifteen years during which they had shared the Beckman home. Jessie's mother Anna was going to miss her as well, and deeply mourned her passing. They had so much in common, and sincerely enjoyed each other's company.

MARIE BECKMAN

JOSEPH SPENKER

In Fall of the year 1916, Joseph Spenker died. He had developed another case of pneumonia, and in this year it led to his death. Joseph—the innovative, courageous pioneer man, shrewd in business and a Christian man in every step of his life, died on October 22, 1916. He was eighty years old.

Anna was overwhelmed with grief by the loss of her husband. They had been married for 46 years. Anna often stated to younger generations that those years had fulfilled her highest expectations of happiness. Her life would continue on, but in a sadly different way. Otto stepped in to try to help his mother as much as possible.

His son Otto wrote:

"Father has passed away! He contracted pneumonia again and in a few short weeks he was gone. He is gone and I will miss him everyday for the rest of my life. He is a giant of a man to follow: business ability, intelligence, generosity, a truly God fearing man. What he accomplished in his life—in the few short years that were allocated to him, very few men could come close to matching. He was an inspiration that God has greatly blessed me with. I also know in my heart, I can never live up to his image. I will carry on the business as best I can, cherish mother to her dying day, and always do the best I can for the ranch he's given me and for those around me."

Jessie was devastated by the loss of the father she so deeply loved. He was a man greatly respected and admired by countless people in the community. She felt humbled to have been so richly blessed with such a father. Jessie admired all the many things he had done, and resolved to continue in his stead wherever she possibly could. She had been blessed with so much, and some people had so little. Jessie made a vow to follow Joseph's lead and help as many people as she could. She also cherished her father's love of beauty—the way he nurtured and protected the oak grove. Jessie would continue that protection.

On October 23, 1916, the Lodi News wrote an article about Joseph that Jessie kept.

"Joseph Spenker was one of San Joaquin's most successful farmers, and during his many years residence in this locality had built up a wide circle of friends who will greatly regret his demise. He was noted for his generosity, and has probably held out a helping hand to more people in hard circumstances than any other one man in this end of the county."

The paper also covered the funeral:

"The funeral of Joseph Spenker, which was held from the family residence west of Woodbridge yesterday afternoon at 2 o'clock, was one of the largest funerals held in this section for a number of years. Friends who have known the pioneer for years came from far and near to attend the services. There was an abundance of beautiful floral offerings, and sacred selections were rendered by a choir. Rev. H. Wiemken officiated at the house and Rev. Jacobson at the grave."

Jessie received a letter from her cousin Emilie on October 28, 1916.

"I know what a good father he was to you, and how good and kind to everyone. I said to Rob that I am certain Uncle Joe never had made an enemy, he was good to everyone, and I am sure he is where there will be no more sorrow.

We all spoke of how glad we were that we saw him when he was at Mama's last, he was so full of life then. The last thing I spoke of to him was about riding home in the auto, he said we should wrap up warm. He said "Those things may be all right for you (meaning autos) but I think if I rode in one of them at night, it would kill me, the sharp air would go clear through me," and he put his hands on his chest, just where his weak place really was.

I know you know you have my most heart-felt sympathy, and that nothing I can say or do will help, only time can soften your grief."

JOSEPH AT REST IN THE OAK GROVE HE SO DEEPLY LOVED

JOSEPH'S GROVE

PHOTOGRAPH BY LEWIS KEMPER

THE RANCH AFTER JOSEPH

THE WAR CONTINUED ON IN EUROPE. The news was grim, but why should America join the conflict? Otto could not begin to see a reason for his country to get involved. Actually, he spent very little time thinking about it, because after Joseph's death, it was up to him to take charge of the business.

The ranch was in good shape—the fields were producing fine barley, hay, and grapes. The dairy was not expanding as earlier plans had anticipated, perhaps because of Otto's dislike for the operation. There was a fine herd of cattle, hogs, and *"ample horses to run all the equipment."* The financial future for the ranch looked secure, except for the prospects of some of the stocks in which Otto had invested. The companies did not look promising at this time, however, he maintained hope for their success.

The war in Europe concerned Otto, but not to the extent Jessie was experiencing. She appeared to be in a never-ending cloud of worry. She explained to Otto that it was not just concern about the people she knew in Europe that disturbed her, but mainly the fact that Germany had caused this terrible war. She could not relate the love she had for the Germany she knew to this war or begin to understand the reasons for the conflict. Otto didn't even try to figure out the reasons. Like so many people, he declared that the war was far away, so why worry about it? The Spenker Ranch now occupied all his attention.

Otto was working on his "secretarial duties," and he wrote to the Aggler and Musser Seed Company to find out the correct kinds of seeds to plant in his particular soil. He described his soil to them: *"deep sandy loam which made the Lodi watermelons famous twenty years ago, and is unexcelled for all crops such as melons, pumpkins, sweet potatoes, alfalfa and grapes. The only place we can find hard pan is in the dictionary."*

He also had to address a problem at the dairy with a hand separator. He ordered new parts and waited so long for them to arrive that he ended up fixing the separator himself. He wrote to the company:

"Necessity is the mother of invention, and as it has been up to me to keep the separator running without your rings for about a month I have found a substitute which gives better satisfaction at about one-tenth of the price. Therefore I have no further use for your rings. If it were not for the fact that the Sharples is such an excellent machine, and will take care of itself for months at a time without attention, your "service," if nothing else would soon put them on the junkpile. I have no intention to discourage the purchase of rings by others and will keep my discovery to myself."

In all fairness to the company, however, Otto did admit the order could have gotten lost because of the problems they were having with the mail carrier: *"our mail carrier has been sick and a green substitute took his place—got stuck with the Ford and served this part of the route by moonlight."*

The latest problem Otto was having at the dairy was the inspector. After he was at the dairy on an unprecedented visit, Otto wrote this letter to the central office in San Francisco.

Gentlemen: The state dairy inspector, Mr. Starkweather has been here and condemned my dairy from top to bottom, inside and out. As a certain change which he ordered on a previous visit was not carried out to his satisfaction I think he has it in for me on general principles.

My method of handling cream, which has given you "A" grade is roundly condemned and I will be arrested unless a cooler meeting with his approval is immediately installed.

We may not be antiseptic in our dairy management, but we do observe practical cleanliness, our friendly inspector not withstanding, and I would like to have an expression of opinion from you regarding the quality of the cream I have been sending you in the past.

What is the best make of cooler to purchase, all things considered, and which will stand the inspector?

I am anxious to improve the quality of my product and will do anything within reason to do so, but I will not be a football for any dairy inspector. Would sooner go out of the business.

Thanking you in advance I remain Very truly yours,

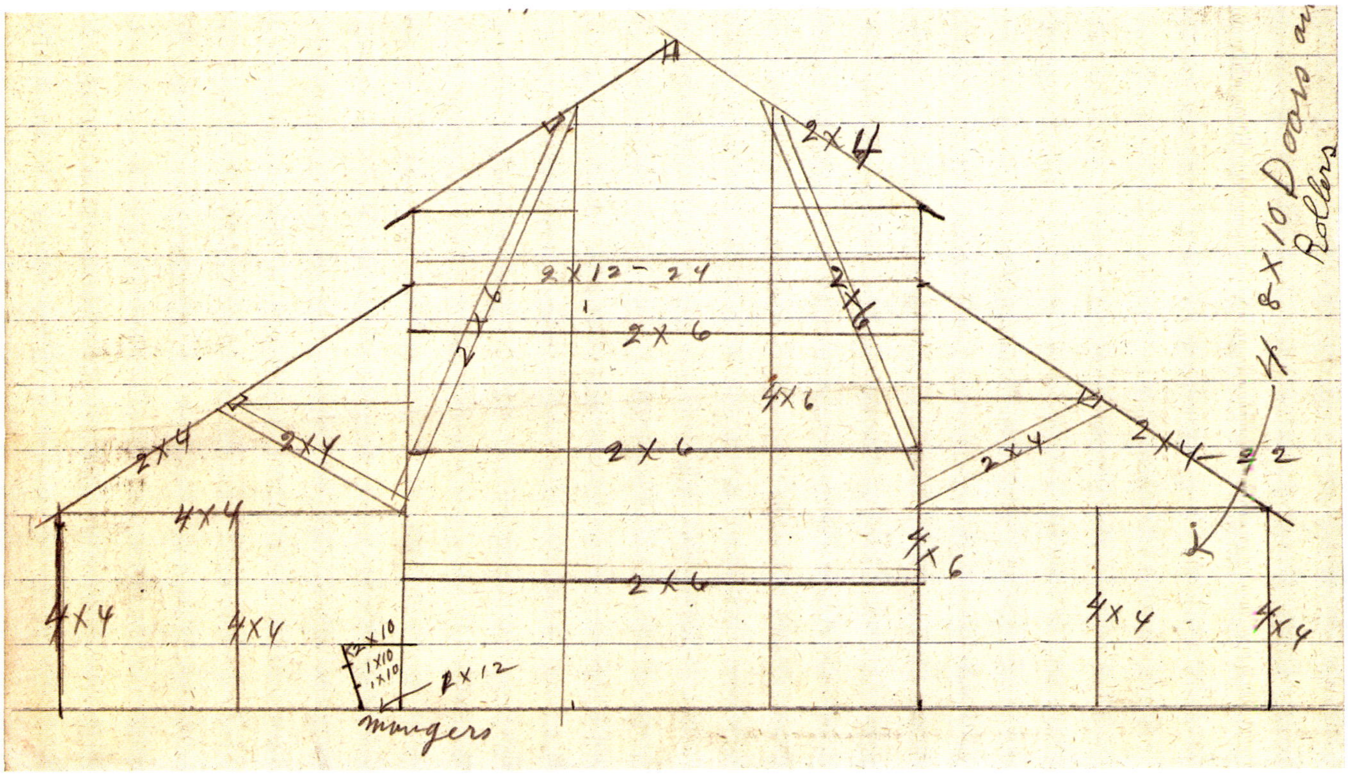

OTTO DECIDED TO BUILD THE BARN THAT JOSEPH HAD TALKED ABOUT FOR MANY YEARS.

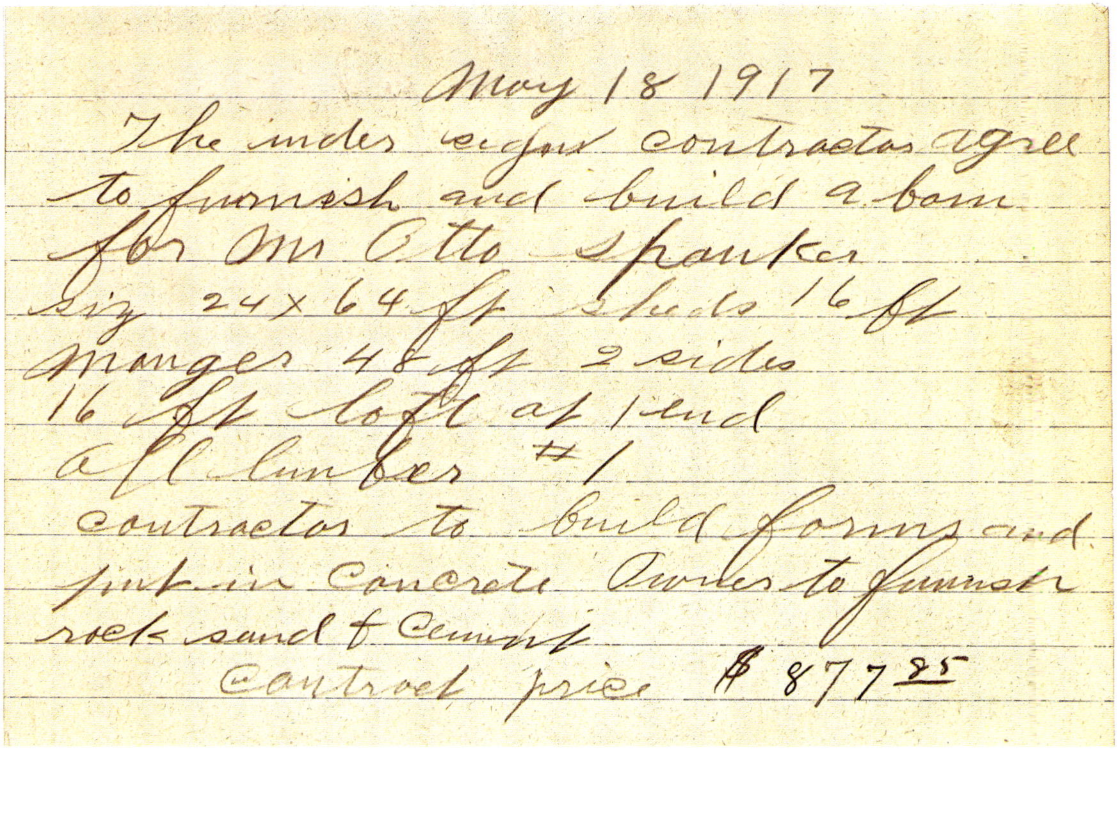

May 18 1917
The undersigned contractors agree
to furnish and build a barn
for Mr Otto Spanker
Siz 24 x 64 ft Sheds 16 ft
manger 48 ft 2 sides
16 ft loft at 1 end
all lumber #1
contractors to build forms and
put in Concrete Owner to furnish
rock sand & Cement
Contract price $ 877.25

THE GREAT WAR

THE ISOLATION OF THE UNITED STATES from the European war could not last, and as Otto labored to take his father's place managing the family ranch, Jessie's worst fears came true. By the spring of 1917, Germany's resumption of unrestricted submarine warfare, meaning any ship found in the war zone surrounding Britain would be sunk, regardless of nationality, caused President Wilson to ask Congress for a declaration of war. On April 6, 1917, the United States finally declared war on Germany. President Wilson promised the country that this would be "the war to end all wars." Within months, the United States had fighting forces in Europe, and American participation in The Great War had begun.

Jessie thought of her dear cousin Hartwig, he would have been in the middle of this conflict, fighting against her country. Perhaps his early death had been a blessing after all. Herbert Woock, Anita's admirer, was enlisting and would soon be on his way to Europe. Joe, Jessie's son, was thankfully too young to be involved. Otto was exempt because of the large ranch for which he was responsible.

Americans fought in Europe for nineteen terrible months. Finally, on November 11, 1918 an armistice was signed. The whole world breathed a sigh of relief. The troops commanded by John J. Pershing had been the deciding factor, giving victory to the Allies. Over one hundred thousand Americans had died to achieve this peace—sacrificing their lives would make the world safe for democracy. President Wilson had called this "the war to end all wars." History would call this war "The Great War" for twenty years—until the outbreak of World War II.

World War I greatly influenced the music of the day—people were singing the songs everywhere. All of the piano sheet music selections in this book are from the collection of Jessie's daughter, Anita Beckman.

DESPITE THE WAR, WORK CONTINUED ON THE SPENKER RANCH

TOMMY ATKINS

COURTESY OF
LESLIE'S WEEKLY
COPYRIGHTED

THE SONG THEY SING AS THEY MARCH ALONG

IT'S A LONG, LONG WAY TO TIPPERARY

WRITTEN AND COMPOSED BY
JACK JUDGE
AND
HARRY WILLIAMS

Price 60 Cents

For the United States of America
CHAPPELL & CO., LTD.
41 EAST 34TH ST., NEW YORK

For all other countries
B. FELDMAN & CO.
2 & 3 ARTHUR ST., W.C. LONDON, ENG.

SO LONG, MOTHER
AL. JOLSON'S
MOTHER SONG
U.S.
LYRIC BY
RAYMOND EGAN
AND
GUS KAHN
MUSIC BY
EGBERT
VAN ALSTYNE
5
JEROME H. REMICK & CO.
DETROIT NEW YORK

THE SENSATIONAL STAMMERING SONG SUCCESS
SUNG BY THE SOLDIERS AND SAILORS
K-K-K-Katy
By
Geoffrey O'Hara
Army Song Leader
— WAR EDITION —
To Co-operate with the Government and to conserve paper during the War, this song is issued in a smaller size than usual. Save! Save! Save is the watchword to-day. This is the spirit in which we are working and your co-operation will be very much appreciated.
LEO. FEIST, Inc.
POPULAR LEO. FEIST INC. EDITION NEW YORK
F. STANLEY SIEGFRIED
STATIONERY . ART
PIANOS, MUSIC
PICTURES and FRAMING
PHONE 380-J
Hotel Lodi Bldg.
LODI, CAL

IRVING BERLIN'S BUGLE SONG
OH! HOW I HATE TO GET UP
IN THE MORNING
US US
BY
IRVING
BERLIN
WATERSON-
BERLIN
&
SNYDER CO.
Music Publishers
Strand Theatre Bldg
Broadway at 47th St.
NEW YORK

THE OAK GROVE

THROUGHOUT THE YEARS OF CHANGE and the upheavals of the first decades of the twentieth century, the oak grove that Joseph Spenker had cherished and preserved continued to serve the whole Lodi community as an island of tranquility. It was a place to gather, celebrate, make plans, have fun and forget about the war.

Summer was a beautiful time of the year in the grove. The trees were in full leaf and provided dense shade for the visiting folk from town. Water was cascading over the dam, and the swimming hole was full, providing a tempting invitation for people to dive in.

WATER FUN AT SPENKER'S GROVE

THE SWIMMING HOLE

BACK FROM SWIMMING

THE BATHING BEAUTIES. JESSIE'S DAUGHTER ANITA IS THE SEVENTH FROM THE LEFT.

"As World War I was ending, it was apparent that the United States would never again be the same. By 1920, most Americans wanted to put the war and foreign affairs behind them and concentrate on domestic issues. The country would now return to an era of isolationism lasting nearly two decades. Nevertheless, the war had changed America socially, politically, and economically forever."[4] This was especially true for the soldiers coming home from Europe.

4 Steve Von Berg

PEACE WAS DECLARED AND PEOPLE WERE RETURNING TO THEIR OLD LIFESTYLES, BUT FOR SOME THAT WOULD BE DIFFICULT.

CHAPTER SEVEN

Years of Challenge

THE DECADES AFTER THE GREAT WAR posed a series of challenges for people like Jessie and Otto, both across the country and around the world. How they responded speaks volumes about their character. The Golden Twenties encouraged optimism, but also dangerous risk taking, and both rewards and disappointments followed in unexpected ways. The collapse of the economy that followed in the 1930s tested the character of everyone, worldwide, leading to the rise of totalitarianism in Europe and eventually to another world war. It was a difficult era, although the farmers in the San Joaquin Valley did their best to survive and to prevail.

PROHIBITION

In 1919, while the grape business continued to struggle, Congress passed the Eighteenth Amendment, prohibiting *"the manufacture, sale, or transportation of intoxicating liquors within, the importation thereof into, or the exportation thereof from the United States and all territory subject to the jurisdiction thereof for beverage purposes."* Grape growers were devastated.

Since the death of Joseph, Otto was managing the ranch on his own. He could well imagine what Joseph would have thought about this amendment to try to save the public from the evils of alcohol. As soon as the news arrived, some farmers pulled out their grapevines—all of them. Otto couldn't imagine what they thought they could grow in the place of the grapes—nothing was any good. He decided to continue farming his grapes as usual and see what happened. This was an easy decision when there wasn't anything better to plant. There was some talk about making a grape concentrate instead of wine. The government would allow them to do that and to ship it east. The wineries would be allowed to produce wine for medicinal or sacramental purposes, but that was all. They were also told that each head of the household could make up to 200 gallons of non-intoxicating fruit juice for use in the home. *"That's a huge amount of grape juice sitting around in people's houses—how much do they think one family could drink in a year anyway?"* Otto wrote in his journal.

THE EIGHTEENTH AMENDMENT. POSTCARD FROM JESSIE'S COLLECTION.

THESE POSTERS WERE SEEN EVERYWHERE. LEONARD THOMPSON COLLECTION.

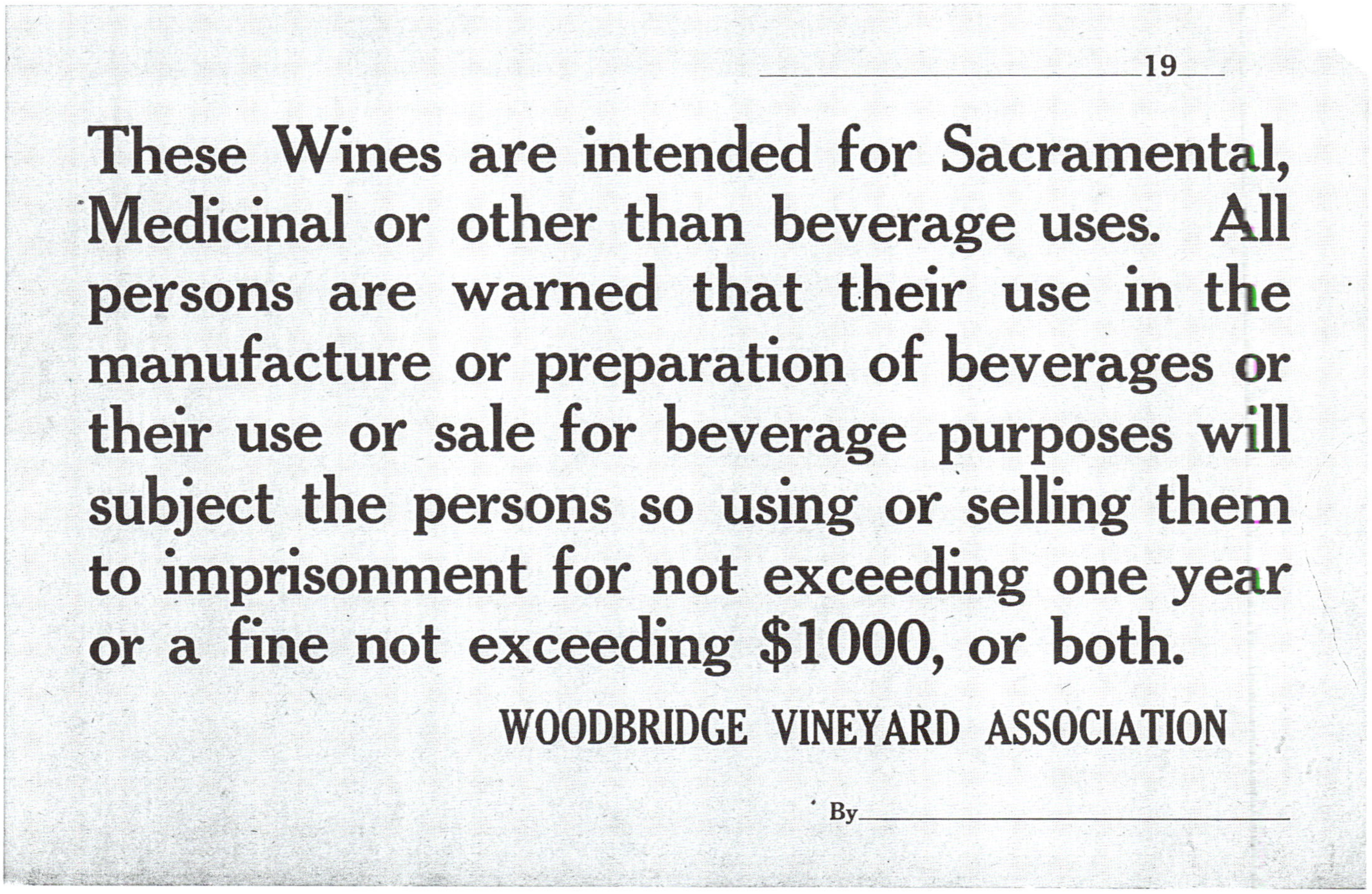

_______________19___

These Wines are intended for Sacramental, Medicinal or other than beverage uses. All persons are warned that their use in the manufacture or preparation of beverages or their use or sale for beverage purposes will subject the persons so using or selling them to imprisonment for not exceeding one year or a fine not exceeding $1000, or both.

WOODBRIDGE VINEYARD ASSOCIATION

By_______________

At least the cost of labor went down. They still had to pay white pickers thirty-five cents per hour. All the others got thirty cents per hour.

Some farmers planted tomatoes, but that was a crop for which Otto had very little patience. He had a few acres of them planted on the ranch, but getting the crop off the field was backbreaking work. People hated to pick tomatoes, and Otto couldn't blame them. *"Who would want to spend all day—bending over to the ground, picking the squashy red fruit?"* Otto had no doubt—he would continue with his grapes.

In 1920, Henry Beckman decided he would plant beans. To ease the trouble of harvesting the crop, Henry bought a new harvester from Harris in Stockton. It was a gasoline-powered harvester made of wood, with an upper-level stacker. It cost $6,000.

ANNA HELPING WITH THE TOMATO HARVEST.

Henry also bought a Holt tail-seat tractor to pull the harvester. Beans were supposed to be a good crop that year, so Henry thought this would be a good investment. He sold 26,200 pounds of pinto beans and received a partial payment of one cent a pound! Henry hoped more money would be coming in later from the beans. At least Vera, Henry's daughter, had a grand time riding around on the deck and watching the machine in action.

HOLT TAIL-SEAT TRACTOR

THE HARRIS HARVESTER—JOE BECKMAN STANDING IN FRONT

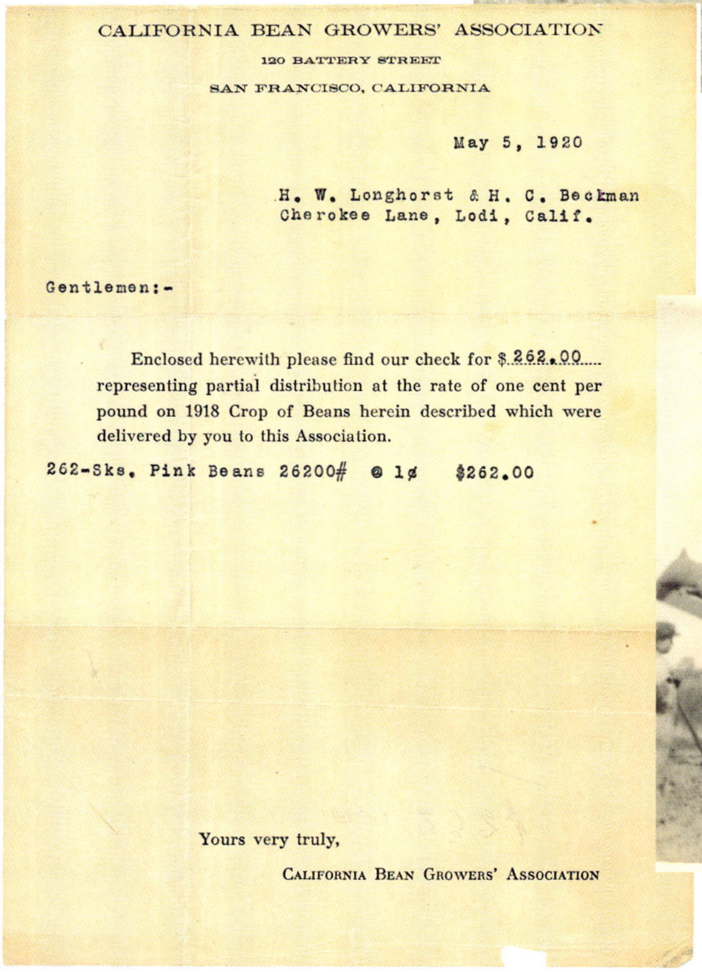

CALIFORNIA BEAN GROWERS' ASSOCIATION
120 BATTERY STREET
SAN FRANCISCO, CALIFORNIA

May 5, 1920

H. W. Longhorst & H. C. Beckman
Cherokee Lane, Lodi, Calif.

Gentlemen:-

Enclosed herewith please find our check for $262.00 representing partial distribution at the rate of one cent per pound on 1918 Crop of Beans herein described which were delivered by you to this Association.

262-Sks. Pink Beans 26200# @ 1¢ $262.00

Yours very truly,

California Bean Growers' Association

MAY 5, 1920, 26, 200 POUNDS OF PINTO BEANS WERE SOLD FOR A PARTIAL PAYMENT OF ONE CENT PER POUND.

VERA ON TOP OF THE HARVESTER

Otto saved a publication from the State Board of Viticultural Commissioners in Sacramento. Part of the report states:

"A great industry will be destroyed in this state by prohibition. An investment of many millions of dollars, safeguarded for years by state and government, will be wiped out overnight by state and federal legislation and the full realization is not yet upon us in viticulture California.... If there is a grower that does not know how to make unfermented grape juice of grape syrup we shall be glad to inform him; and if it is his desire to manufacture either or both of these articles in an extensive way we will be glad to refer him to sources that are prepared with plans to undertake the manufacture on some basis that may be mutually agreeable." [1]

They also stated in the same article: *"No new use has been discovered for wine grapes."*[1] Contrary to everyone's expectations, the demand for grapes actually increased. There were 8,071 carloads of grapes shipped from Lodi wineries, and dehydrators handled 18,000 tons, making the soon-to-be-famous grape concentrate. The wineries couldn't make wine, but any "head of household" could, using that allotment of 200 gallons. So the grape growers shipped the concentrated juice east, and everyone made their own wine. Of course, for the government's sake, people just celebrated the fact that everyone had plenty of grape juice to drink. *"Soon more 'non-intoxicating' wine was being made in America's basements each year than the commercial wineries had ever made before. Prohibition had brought the growers a bonanza."* [2]

The years 1920 through 1925 were in fact wonderful for the grape farmers. Grapes were being shipped east by thousands of carloads. In 1921, 9,133 carloads were shipped, and the next year even more. In 1924, Otto received $80.00 a ton for Zinfandel and $40.00 a ton for Tokays. By 1925 the railroads, reacting to the strong demand for grapes in the East, finally increased the number of cars available for the shipping of grapes. Farmers happily filled them all.

Everyone was planting grapes. As more and more came on the market, however, the market became flooded, and prices dropped. Grapes became harder and harder to sell. Prices were down on anything a farmer could grow, and the age old question—what to plant, seemed to have no answer. With grapes, you had invested years and major expenses. Changing from one crop to another, as they used to do in the old days of wheat and watermelons, was out of the question. The farming industry was once more starting to struggle, but it was in direct contrast to the rest of the economy. This became a time when many young men left the family farm and headed towards city life.

PACKING OUT TOKAYS ON THE SPENKER RANCH. THE HOUSE IS SEEN TO THE BACK.

1 State Board of Viticultural Commissioners, April 18, 1919.
2 Leon D. Adams, The Wines of America, 2nd ed., 1978 p. 26.

THE 1920S SEEMED TO HAVE NO PROBLEMS. EVERYONE WAS HAPPY, SINGING AND DANCING ALL NIGHT.

THE GOLDEN TWENTIES

THE BOOM TIMES OF THE GOLDEN TWENTIES seemed like a period when everyone's dreams could come true. Factories were using the new mass-production techniques perfected by Henry Ford to produce everything from radios to refrigerators. The Great War was over, and people were working and making money. They were out dancing all night and singing Irving Berlin songs.

The United States was experiencing tremendous economic growth, and now political growth as well. With the passage of the Nineteenth Amendment in 1920, women voted in a presidential election for the first time, and helped elect Warren G. Harding. *"Women's traditional roles were starting to change, both in the home and in society. The 1920s would see the emergence of the modern twentieth century woman."*[3]

Jessie was happy her girls were growing up in a time when women were finally treated as equal citizens. She felt this was long overdue and had agreed with Laura De Force Gordon that women are equal to men and could run any business as well as a man. Jessie certainly knew she could manage the ranches as well as Henry and Otto—if not better.

[3] Steve Von Berg

"THE NEW WOMAN" POSTCARD FROM JESSIE'S COLLECTION

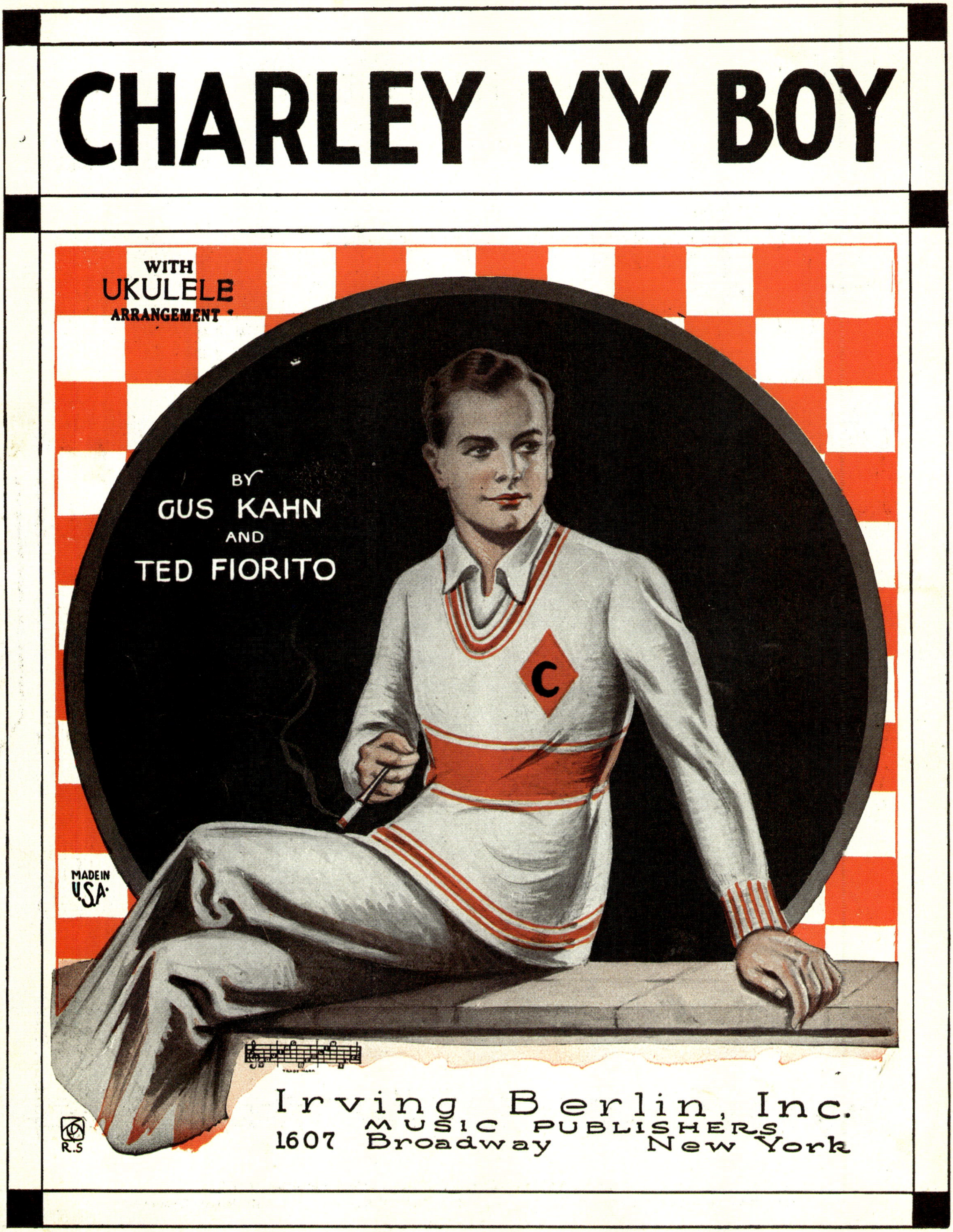

IRVING BERLIN WAS ONE OF THE MOST POPULAR COMPOSERS OF THE DAY AND HIS SONGS WERE EVERYWHERE.

The confidence and optimism of the time seemed to know no bounds. People were making money in the stock market and investing heavily. It seemed so easy! This made Jessie nervous, and she wouldn't let Henry invest in the market. However, Henry was convinced, along with Otto, that there had to be an easier and better way to make a living than farming. He had heard about the mining operations in De Beque, in western Colorado, and took a trip to look it over before investing in the company. He wrote to Jessie—still using his unique way of spelling.

June 4th 1921
Dear Wife,

Yesterday we went out in another direction to look at som more shale. There is surly enough hear and some of the best acres to be found. We are securing 480 acres hear besides all the other holdings the company has. Yesterday we road about 23 miles in auto, and then we took the horses and made about 15 miles ride, up som of the steepest trails I ever saw. In some places we would get off our horses and take hold of there tails and hang on and let them pull us up. The trip was surly a wonder to me—the sights are beyond belif! H.C.B.

Sunday morning, June 6, 6am

We stoped at the smallest place last night all ther is to it is a nice Hotel, and a few litle shacks, we leave hear at 8.15 for Watson 62 miles from the main line, and then we will take Autos again, and I expect it will be rough country. One night will haft to stop at a fram house and they say we will haft to sleep in the hay. I wish I had left my overcoat at home, for I have no use for it it is so warm hear. We expect to get back to Salt Lake next Saturday. I do not know when we will be home. I dot know that I am having a good time.
Yours as ever
H.C.B.

"THE SIGHTS ARE BEYOND BELIF."—HENRY BECKMAN

"SOME OF THE STEEPEST TRAILS I EVER SAW."
—HENRY BECKMAN

NOTE WHAT THE GENTLEMEN ARE WEARING ON THIS EXHAUSTING TRIP.

After Henry returned from this exhausting adventure, however, Henry decided not to invest in the company and stayed with farming.

The Golden Twenties seemed like a wonderful time to get married. On November 22, 1924, Anita and Herbert Woock exchanged their vows and the Lodi newspaper covered the event.

"St. Peter's Lutheran church was the setting for a beautiful and impressive wedding service at high noon last Saturday when Herbert John Woock and Anita Beckman exchanged nuptial vows and rings and were pronounced husband and wife. . . . Rev. Wessling delivered the wedding address, urging the bridal couple to preserve the happiness of the occasion by permitting the peace of God to rule in their hearts, the Word of Christ to dwell in their home and their daily actions to be guided by the will and name of Jesus."

Jessie was happy for her daughter. Herbert and his family were well known, and Herbert had become a close friend of Otto's and Henry's, and also a business partner.

"In 1919, Henry Beckman and Herbert Woock opened Superior Manufacturing Company in Lodi to make pumps. In 1925 Henry Beckman purchased the foundry and operated it under the name Atlas Iron Works, making manhole covers. Meanwhile, H. J. Woock, E. A. Glynn and G. O. Beckman, worked to revolutionize tire retread equipment. In 1927 they established Super Mould Company, developed a full circle retread "Lodi mold," and eventually obtained 28 patents."[4]

[4] Mickie Grove Museum where the Lodi Mold is on display.

HERBERT WOOCK AND ANITA ARE MARRIED.
VERA AND JOE ARE WALKING BEHIND THEM.

SUPER MOULD COMPANY—HERBERT WOOCK STANDING FIRST RIGHT NEXT TO THE DESK.

JESSIE'S GRANDSON, DELWIN HERBERT WOOCK

On September 23, 1927, Anita gave birth to a baby boy, Delwin Herbert Woock, and Jessie became a grandmother. After a hospital stay, Anita and her family moved to Jessie's home for her recuperation. They stayed until November. Anita returned to her home without the extra helping hands available at Jessie's, but she had a new appliance that should ease the workload—a washing machine. A company named Maytag had developed this machine a few years before. Jessie and Vera went over to Anita's to see the washing machine in action. The machine had a metal reversing agitator—the clothes swished back and forth, and then the water drained out. Of course, you still had to run them through the wringer and put them back into the tub with fresh water for the rinse, but it was an amazing improvement. Jessie planned to show this to Anna—what a change from her time!

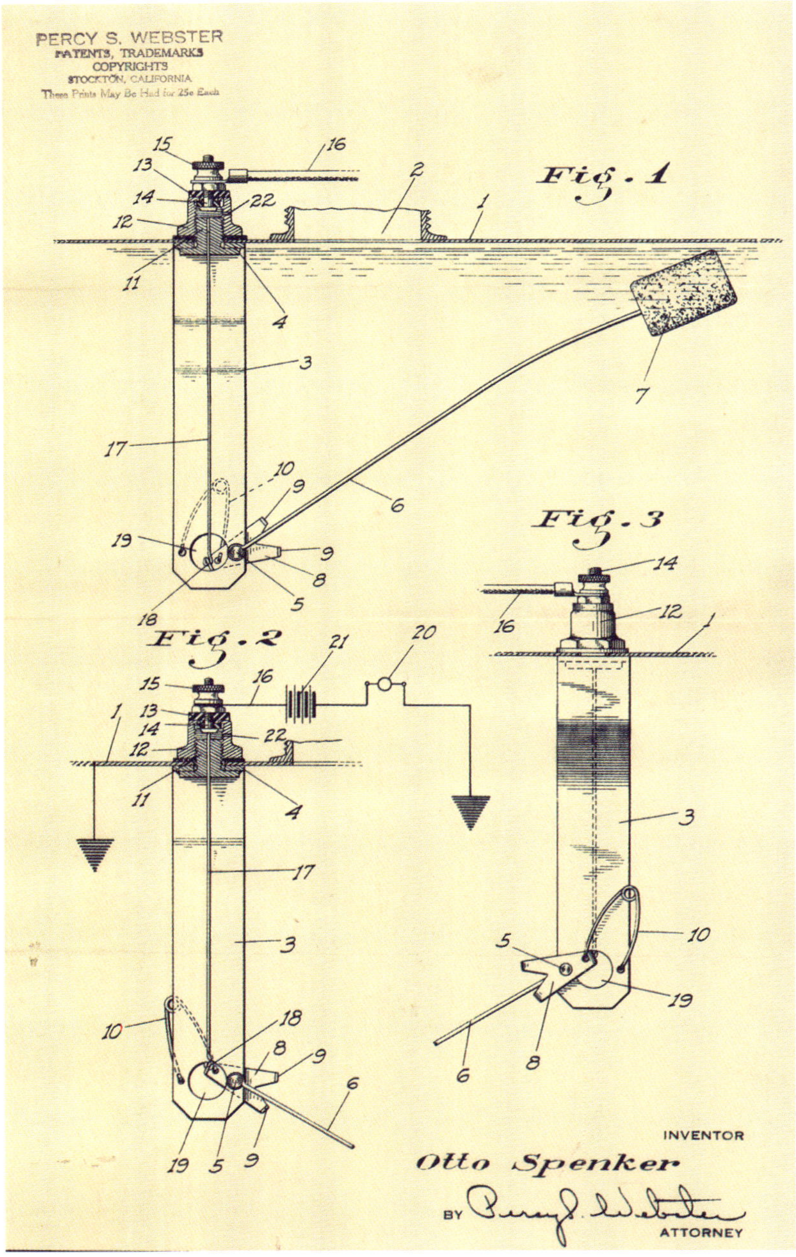

With the economy in high gear and appearing unstoppable, it appeared the inventiveness and know-how of Americans would inevitably push progress to new levels of achievement. It seemed as if people could reach their highest dreams. Otto had a dream. He had long wanted to develop an idea that industry could use—a new and different way to accomplish needed tasks. He had worked on ideas for farming equipment, for wiring in his house, and for photography. Now he had developed an idea for the automobile industry. He felt this idea would fulfill his dreams. He wrote:

"At this later stage of my life, I believe I have developed an idea for a mechanism for these new machines that is so necessary, no prudent driver should go without one. I have been working on this apparatus for nearly a year now and feel I have it working to full satisfaction. I have done all necessary preparation and will now submit it to the United States Patent Office. My idea, a fuel-level warning device for motor vehicles, should be required to be in every car on the road. Yes, I feel this is the idea I have diligently searched for all my life. This will find satisfaction and success. I will mark this day down as a turning point in my life. The patent has been submitted on Feb. 27th, 1925."

"THIS PATENT WILL SET MY FUTURE."—OTTO SPENKER

THE GREAT DEPRESSION

OTTO'S DREAMS WERE NOT TO COME TRUE, however, and the dreams of millions of others were crushed along with his. In late October 1929, the stock market wavered and then collapsed. This was the onset of the Great Depression.

In 1930 Otto wrote:

"How could so many years go by? My life seems to be going down equally fast. I had such great hopes for my fuel leveling device, but I have heard nothing encouraging from any source. It seems I will not have any success with this patent. The country is in a major depression and all the investments I have made are so many pieces of worthless paper. I am deeply in debt and have very little hope.

All my dreams are turning to dust."

Otto's dreams had turned to dust, along with the dreams of millions of Americans as the United States entered a decade long devastating depression. People in all avenues of life were affected—some 25 percent of the work force lost their jobs, while others took drastic cuts in pay. More than five thousand banks failed between the stock market crash and 1933, wiping out 7 billion dollars in depositors money.

The rural areas across the country were some of the most severely depressed, especially in the deep south and the mid-western states. In the Midwest—*"tractors had clawed the skin off the earth, scratching at it's fragile face to plant ever larger crops, more cotton and wheat to carry to market as prices steadily fell."*[5] This set the stage for the ecological and human catastrophe called The Dust Bowl. America, the country that had seemed unstoppable to the entire world, now had thousands of people destitute and some near starvation.

In the San Joaquin Valley, however, rural areas were less severely affected and extreme hardships were rare, largely due to the ideal soil that was readily available and equally ideal weather conditions. This was also a rural community with innovative farmers that could raise, grow, trade, and preserve food for later use. Everyone was having problems, of course, but they exchanged ideas about how to get by. People helped each other through the hard times. Here are a few memories of the Great Depression from people who survived it as children in Lodi.

"My father had this wine barrel that he stored Tokay grapes in for the winter months. He would select clean bunches of grapes and place them layer by layer in a barrel with sawdust in between each layer. They kept fine for months that way—one layer of grapes and one layer of sawdust." —ALBERT JAMES

"My mother had a barrel of salt water she would fill with string beans for the winter. When she wanted to cook some, she just grabbed a hand full, rinsed the salt water off, and they were fine." —CECIL McKINDLEY

"My earliest childhood recollection was being in a grape box, bumping along through a vineyard, watching my mother pick grapes. She had a rope tied to my box and as she would move along, she dragged my box with her. I felt a bump, bump and heard a scraping noise as I slid over the dirt. I was comfortable in my grape box, she had plenty of blankets for me to sit on, but we did this day after day. My mother was packing out Tokay grapes.

[5] *Freedom From Fear*, by David M. Kennedy, Oxford Press, page 194

Going to school was a happy occasion, especially the first day, when I wore my new shoes and new overalls. I had two of these overalls for the year, but only one pair of new shoes. As the year went on, I would wear a hole in my shoes. My mother would cut out a piece of cardboard and slip it into the shoe. Soon the other shoe had the same problem. Each night she checked my shoes and cut new cardboard. I remember she told me shoeboxes had the best cardboard for the job. This, of course, did not last the entire school year. When the shoes became hopeless, they were simply thrown away and I went barefoot. I did not feel bad, because many of the other kids in my class were having the same problems. When the weather got warm, everyone went barefoot.

My overalls were another problem. Being a boy, I was not careful with my clothes. I frequently tore a hole in my pants, or a major rip. Again this was checked each night by my mother and repairs were done as needed. My mother had saved my old pants and she made the patches from these so the fabric would match. Again, I did not feel embarrassed, because the pants of other friends of mine looked the same way.

We always had plenty to eat. My mother had a garden, and we had a milk cow. The only problem was when our only cow would go dry. Then my mother would trade other things for our milk supply. One of the things she traded were the fish I could catch in the slough. My uncle Fred was also a good shot with a gun, and we frequently had rabbit for dinner. Of course, we had chickens running all over the place. My mother usually knew where their nests were, so gathering eggs was no problem. When we needed a chicken for dinner, she had my uncle Fred shoot one or two. That was always a fun thing to watch."

—AL BECHTHOLD

AL BECHTHOLD ON THE FIRST DAY OF SCHOOL

Although most of the people in the rural areas of the San Joaquin Valley were getting along in these depressed times, in the towns of Lodi and Stockton, there were people who needed assistance. Jessie organized clothes drives and food drives through her church to help as many people as possible. The stories coming from other parts of the country were horrifying and it was unimaginable what was happening in the United States.

Many people Jessie and Henry knew had lost money in the stock market. Otto was a member of a very large group. Henry never invested in the market, but he did invest $85,000 in Herbert Woock's company in 1924 when they needed development money. That amount of money made Jessie nervous, and three years later, on June 11, 1927, Henry sold his shares back to the company. But the company did well, and they consolidated with the Super Mould Company in 1928 and were one of the few successful businesses during the Depression. People eagerly had their tires recapped instead of buying new ones. In 1930, the company went national. Jessie felt she had misplaced her concern. Sales continued to be strong, and in 1936, the name was changed a final time to the Super Mold Corporation.

On January 23, 1931, I was born. Jessie became a grandmother for the second and last time. I hope I added a little bit of cheer for this sad, depressed time. Anita and Herbert gave me the name of Wanda Anita Woock.

THE AUTHOR

SAN JOAQUIN COUNTY
FARM BUREAU MONTHLY

A Merry Christmas to All

Cups awarded by the California Farm Bureau Federation at the Annual Convention at Asilomar for largest center membership in the State.
Lafayette Center, San Joaquin County, (298 members) awarded first prize.
Garden Grove Center, Orange County, (291 members) awarded second prize.
J. W. Crill (left) President of Orange County. Otto Spenker (right) Chairman of Lafayette Center. See page 8 for details regarding these and other trophies.

December, 1930 | KEEP THIS AS A REFERENCE NUMBER. *See message on page 4.* | 10c per copy

AT LEAST SOME OF THE ORGANIZATIONS OTTO WAS INVOLVED WITH RECEIVED SPLENDID RECOGNITION IN THESE DEPRESSED TIMES. OTTO, CHAIRMAN OF THE FARM BUREAU'S LAFAYETTE CENTER, ACCEPTED THE AWARD FOR THE LARGEST INCREASE IN MEMBERSHIP.

Many Americans were living below the poverty line, as many as one-third. People wanted to get away from all the bad news, to escape into their own private worlds, so simple pleasures became popular. Gasoline sales, cigarette sales, and movie ticket sales increased. These industries actually made a profit during the Depression. This prompted Will Rogers to remark that *"America is the first nation in the history of the world to go to the poorhouse in an automobile."*

Of course, most of the world was suffering—not just the United States. In 1931, Jessie and Henry heard from their friend John Westphalen in Germany.

"You all know it is very bad in the old country and we all wish that the winter was over. Times are very hard at present, no work, all the young fellows too no work. My son in law has not worked for 3 years and he has four children. The eldest girl (11 years) is living with us. My eldest son with his wife (no children) came from India and lives with us—no work. The youngest also. Now I have to look after all of them. So I invested some money in good papers and thought to gain something so I could strengthen myself a bit. But I could not for-see that so bad times came. My papers went down to nearly nothing and I could not pay the difference, so nearly everything is lost and I am as poor as when I lived with you. When I were 10 years younger I would not care, but being 63 it is rather bad. I do not see a hole through it, for myself I don't care, but for the others—"

December, 1930 FARM BUREAU MONTHLY 19

Saving Your Time

Clear weather—soil just right for turning—lots of work crying to be done on the place—*a mechanical part needed!* No time to waste, getting word off to town. Every hour counts. *Telephone!*

But the telephone service should be dependable.

There should not be too many on the line, noise or interruptions from faulty transmission.

The wires should be properly strung.

The equipment should be kept in good working order.

THE PACIFIC TELEPHONE AND TELEGRAPH COMPANY

THE TELEPHONE COMPANY WAS FINALLY GETTING SUPPORT.

JESSIE'S CHALLENGE

HENRY'S FRAGILE HEALTH FINALLY GAVE OUT, and he had a fatal heart attack on March 27th, 1932, at the age of sixty five. Jessie was grief stricken. Her father was gone, and now her husband. The two deaths created a chasm in her life that would never diminish.

JESSIE AND HENRY IN 1930

Jessie knew she would have to supervise all operations on the Beckman Ranch, and she was prepared. Otto was having enough trouble with the Spenker holdings, so he certainly couldn't help her. In fact, she had major concerns about his management of the Spenker property and had planned to get involved before Henry's death. She had questioned many things Otto had done—his short marriage, the time he spent on his inventions, and the investments he had made. Jessie was glad she had so closely watched all the farming processes during the last ten years. She had kept detailed records through the years, and counted on this to help her now. Her son Joe would be a wonderful help, but at twenty-eight she had no intentions of him becoming the manager. Jessie stepped in and took charge of all the ranching operations.

Jessie was right to be concerned about Otto's management of the Spenker Ranch. With the onset of the Depression, her worries about Otto's speculative investments turned to alarm. Jessie confronted Otto and demanded to know the truth. The Spenker estate was in a precarious position, and Jessie felt she had to take control or all her father had built up would be lost.

It was a nightmare! Otto was devastated, but she had to take charge and save as much as she could. Property would have to be sold, which was one of many painful decisions she made. People heard about the change in command and several people came to her with suggestions, and it always included the oak grove. *"You could get more for that thirty-two acre oak grove than two hundred acres of bare ground. Why don't you just sell the grove and retain the rest of the land?"* Jessie's response was always the same: *"My father protected that grove all the days of his life, and I will also protect it now. It was his prize possession, and likewise mine."* The grove had been called Spenker's Grove in all the past years. Now Jessie took over the role of protector and the grove gradually assumed her name. The grove became known as "Jessie's Grove."

Jessie decided to sell the Adobe Ranch and the north half of the section adjacent to the Spenker Ranch, referred to as the Hart Ranch, and Otto agreed. The Woodbridge canal seemed to be a natural cutoff point, but when she sold the Hart Ranch, she retained seventy acres north of the canal and oak grove on Davis Road. These painful decisions removed all debts.

Otto did not look well. His main activities became working with the Boy Scouts and being a secretary for St. Peter's Lutheran Church. He also was a very devoted son and took Anna on many rides in his automobile.

OTTO TOOK ANNA TO OAKLAND TO SEE THE "SPLENDID" ZEPPELIN.

OTTO AND ANNA GO ON A TRIP
TO THE TOP OF MT. DIABLO

THEY GO TO LANDS END IN SAN FRANCISCO
TO WATCH THE FLEET COME IN.

ANNA'S COUSIN JULIA SPENKER CAME TO VISIT ANNA ON HER 86TH BIRTHDAY IN 1933. THEY HAD A GRAND TIME SHARING MEMORIES OF THEIR TRIP TO CALIFORNIA FROM GERMANY IN 1869. ANNA IS ON THE LEFT IN THE PHOTOGRAPH.

On December 5, 1933, the Twenty-First Amendment repealed Prohibition. In Lodi alone, there were five wineries ready to crush grapes and make wine. But the market was flooded—growers were offered $12.00 a ton, then $7.00 and then $5.00 a ton. Growers were angry and devastated. How strange, so many thought, that Prohibition had the exact opposite effect of what people thought would happen when it started and when it ended. The Woodbridge Vineyard Association, which had disbanded during Prohibition, reorganized. During the next few years, twelve farmer cooperative cellars opened and built wineries. Now farmers could crush their own grapes, share their proportionate expenses and receive a profit relative to the amount of grapes they brought to the winery. Joe, Jessie's son, was very much in favor of this idea and actively joined and supported the groups.

The price of grapes plummeted, but there was plenty of cheap labor with so many people looking for work. Then the Dust Bowl in the Midwest sent *"more than three hundred thousand from Oklahoma alone, and thousands more from Texas, Kansas and Colorado to California."*[6] Most of these people were destitute, and Jessie's heart went out to them. She brought two families to work on the Beckman Ranch and another family to work on the Spenker Ranch. Her mother could certainly use the help, and the family lived in the old house. Jessie wished she could make room for more families. A whole group had set up a camp on the Spenker Ranch on Turner Road by the canal. She told them they could stay there as long as they were careful of the property. They employed as many as possible to help with the grape crop.

The Depression continued on for ten years. Everyone was starting to be affected, from Wall Street to the small towns of America. Businesses were going bankrupt, people were losing their farms, some banks were failing, and there was massive unemployment. It was more devastating than any previous economic crisis. President Franklin D. Roosevelt attempted to stop the economic decline by having the government put money into creating jobs and improving the infrastructure of the country. After nearly ten years of these New Deal programs, however, the economy was still a long way away from the prosperity of the Twenties.

One thing that happened in 1937 that seemed to bring a little cheer to Otto was the passage of the Rural Electrification Act. Finally people living in the country could have electricity and all the wonderful appliances that city folk had begun to take for granted. The grange organizations were largely responsible for getting this act passed, and Otto and Jessie both felt they had a part in the success. Jessie planned to purchase a washing machine at the first opportunity. What a change from Anna's time! Otto said the act was long over due.

[6] David M. Kennedy, *Freedom From Fear*, Oxford Press, 1999, p. 195.

HITLER

In Germany, the response to the worldwide depression was leading in an ominous direction. Adolph Hitler was stimulating Germany's economy by building a war machine. *"Germany, like most of Europe, had been in an economic depression since the end of World War I. In the 1920's, Hitler had gained enough public support to be elected Chancellor of Germany. Within a year, after the death of president Von Hindenburg, Hitler seized total control of Germany. The swastika was now the symbol of German pride. Furthermore, Germany's economy began to boom as people went back to work, and ordinary citizens looked upon Hitler as the savior of Germany and German culture."*[7]

In 1937 Jessie received a letter from John Westphalen. He wrote:

"I think that I have told you already that I lost all my money with a bank, so that we have only 80 marks to live on a month. That is not much for 3 persons, but I thank the Lord that we have at least that. Our Hitler does all he can to help the poor, but I take nothing because we can't. We never had in our country a man like Hitler. I believe there is none like him in the world, and that means a lot. You would not know our land again, but there is a lot more to do. I saw our Hitler 5 times at Nuremberg. I was there with the politic corps. Of which I am a member. I enclose some little photos made there. It was a great day of the National Socialist Party. Millions were present in uniforms. Whole Germany stands after Hitler!"

"YOU WOULD NOT KNOW OUR LAND AGAIN."—JOHN WESTPHALEN

[7] Steve Von Berg

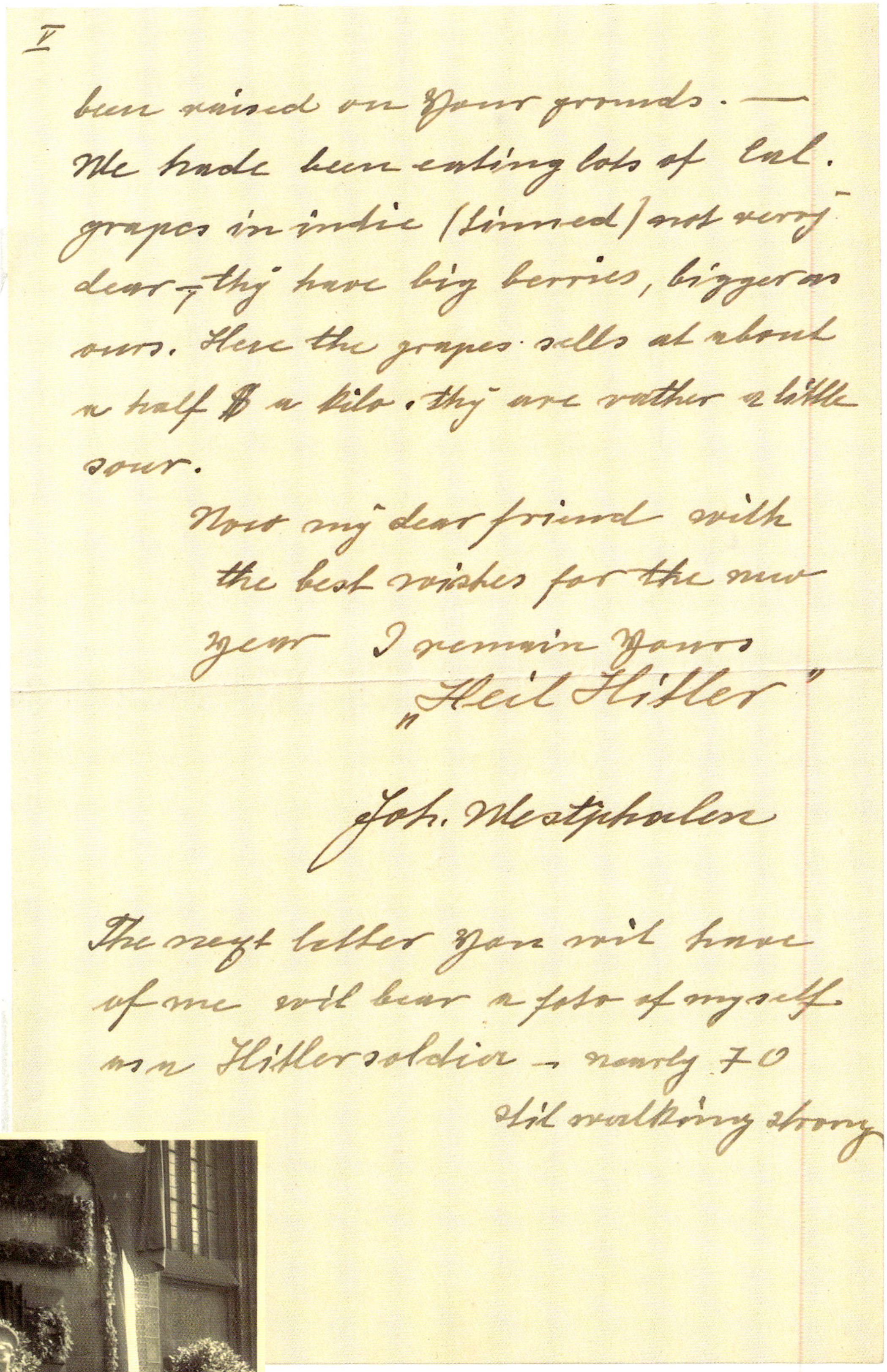

V

been raised on your grounds. —
We hade been eating lots of Cal.
grapes in indie (tinned) not very
dear,– they have big berries, bigger as
ours. Here the grapes sells at about
a half $ a kilo. they are rather a little
sour.

Now my dear friend with
the best wishes for the new
year I remain Yours
„Heil Hitler"

Joh. Westphalen

The next letter you wil have
of me wil bear a foto of myself
as a Hitlersoldier – nearly 70
stil walking strong

THE LETTER FROM JOHN WESTPHALEN

THE NEXT LETTER YOU WILL HAVE OF ME WILL BEAR A PHOTO OF MYSELF AS A HITLER SOLDIER—NEARLY 70 AND STILL WALKING STRONG!

In 1937, Jessie received another letter from John Westphalen. He wrote:

How are you getting along? Is the old mother still alive? We are getting old and the time runs too quick! I am 68 in March and have much trouble with rheumatism, but it has to be born. Before we lost all our money, I had made up my mind to pay you a visit some day. I should like to see the old place once more. I guess I would not know it. There is no hope for that anymore. Is the marshland still in existence where we used to shoot ducks? I can't remember the estate in detail. Where are all the alfalfa fields? Here lots has changed too. Our country sits like a rock in the front of New Europe, stronger than ever before. All this we owe to our ingenious Führer Hitler. But you will see all this one day for yourself, or do you not think of seeing the old Fatherland once more?

We have a special organization with the ones to lead and help our countrymen in foreign countries. N.S.G.S.G.—it means National Socialist German Workman's Association. I have a charge also in this association as political leader. I have to do my work in a couple of streets. I've read the newspapers you had sent, but I found nothing in them of this type. Have you not there an organization of Germans of this kind? The purpose of this organization is not so much to get people up against their lawful government, no—only to keep them as fine Germans together in touch with the old country.

Now my dear friend with the best wishes for the new year.

I remain yours — "Heil Hitler"

John Westphalen

WESTPHALIA ENCLOSED THIS PICTURE IN ONE OF HIS LETTERS. THE SCENE WAS IN 1932 WHEN CHANCELLOR BISMARK, "IRON CHANCELLOR," WALKED OUT OF THE FELDHERRENHALLE WHERE HE HAD JUST SIGNED OVER THE LEADERSHIP OF THE GERMAN GOVERNMENT TO ADOLPH HITLER. NOTICE SOME OF THE MEN ARE SALUTING THE OUT-GOING CHANCELLOR. THE HITLER SALUTE CAME ALONG WITH THE SWASTIKA, WHICH REPRESENTS A CROSS WITH HOOKS.

STORM CLOUDS

THE *LODI NEWS-SENTINEL*, February 10, 1938 recorded the onset of a major storm.

"A gale of near-hurricane intensity that lashed the entire California coast yesterday ripped its way through the Lodi district and left in its twisting path property damage conservatively estimated at $500,000.

The wind, believed to be the strongest and most damaging ever to hit this district, began blowing with dangerous force yesterday morning and shortly after noon reached a destructive climax that tore roofs from residential and commercial buildings, uprooted whole orchards piling the trees in heaps along fences and sending ornamental trees along city streets crashing into homes with terrible force. Giant sycamores were twisted from the ground at Hale Park.

Orchards and farmland suffered the largest damage. Mrs. M. T. Bailey's almond orchard, consisting of nearly 10 acres, was swept clean by the gale. On the Acampo road, olive trees lining the highway for more than a mile were plucked from the ground and swept down the thoroughfare like matchsticks."

Otto wrote in his diary on February 9: *"Biggest storm ever—about 11 to 1 hardest storm ever known here—buildings, trees, power lines—everything laid flat. No electricity for a day or so. South side of grove and barnyard looks like it was hit by a cyclone. All the old live oak trees laid down, broken off—most of them uprooted. Terrible to look at!"*

The storm could have been read as an omen. Once again, war clouds were gathering over Europe, and in September 1939, war broke out. The whole world waited and watched and most of all wondered *why*? It was now apparent that Hitler was not satisfied with just strengthening Germany's economy, he had designs on controlling all of eastern and western Europe. In the fall of 1939, Germany attacked Poland, and the war began.

What would America's role be? Would she join in the conflict? People watched with fear and horror. Germany—Anna's and Joseph's birth nation, Hartwig's, Westphalen's, and her aunt's Germany, was again causing a major war. Jessie was devastated. She knew the people in Germany were going through a major economic depression, along with most of the world, but surely war was not the answer. How could an educated Christian nation that was the birthplace of some of the world's greatest composers—Bach, Beethoven, and Wagner, to name only a few, along with scientists who made major breakthroughs in chemistry, medicine, physics, and Martin Luther who started the Protestant religion, start two major wars in twenty-two years? Jessie knew her world would never be the same.

Life did continue on in the United States. It was a familiar feeling—the war in Europe was so far away. It was far away, but the world seemed to be getting smaller. People were more connected than they had been in the past, even if an ocean separated them. The war became a major concern in everyone's daily thoughts.

But at home, the economy finally started reviving. Grape prices were soaring. This was a surprise, but the war in Europe stopped all their grape production and so the United States filled in the gap. Jessie thought with this terrible news, prices would be shattered again, but just the reverse happened.

Since Jessie was now in charge of the Spenker Ranch, she made the decision to increase the vineyards. In 1939, she planted 12 acres of Carignane and 15 acres of a new variety called Burger. The next year she added an additional eight acres of Zinfandel to the Spenker vineyards.[8]

A friend of Anita and Herbert, Ed Kurtz, owned over 600 acres of Tokay grapes at this time. He rode the wave of increased demand all through the war.

The government passed a minimum wage law, setting the pay at $.25 an hour. Jessie was glad to hear that, because so many were desperate for a job that some people took advantage of them. This minimum wage still seemed terribly low to her and she always paid workers a higher wage. This developed a loyal group of laborers.

The war escalated in Europe. France fell in June 1940. The United States passed the Lend-Lease Act in 1940 and thus openly supported any nation willing to stop Hitler. The news reaching the United States was filled with one horror story after another. Only England stood between the United States and Hitler. Hitler, the man Westphalen had so admired and thought would do great things for Germany, turned out to be one of the most evil geniuses the world had ever seen. "We must support England at any cost" many Americans declared. Jessie had seen some of Hitler's speeches in the newsreels at the Lodi movie theater and wrote about the spellbinding power he appeared to have over people. Germany was attempting to take over Europe! Hitler's evil, hypnotic power was unmatched in history.

[8] Recorded in the Department of Agriculture in Sacramento, 1220 N. street, by Marion Dameran.

OTTO AND ANNA

NEITHER OTTO NOR HIS MOTHER, Anna Spenker, were forced to witness the years of world war that followed. Otto's health deteriorated at an alarming rate, and he went to a hospital. Two weeks later, on August 9, 1940, Otto Spenker died at the age of sixty nine.

I have attempted to research the cause of Otto's death. The hospital where he was a patient for the last two weeks of his life informed me all hospital records prior to 1950 were destroyed in 1980. The cause of his death remains a mystery.

Dead was the man who had so many dreams, a beautiful gift for words, an inventive spirit, a tender, loving heart, and a creative imagination that always gave him hope his dreams could yet be realized. Otto was a very special man.

Jessie was deeply saddened by Otto's death. She did not write down the cause of death, she only wrote that for the last ten years he had appeared to be more and more despondent and inactive. Anna was ninety-three years old and still lived in her own home. With Otto gone, Jessie hired a lady to live with her. She would do the cooking and see to the daily chores. Anna was devastated by her son's death. Jessie did all she could to help her mother.

Anna passed away on February 5, 1941 at the age of ninety-four, only six months after the death of her son. Anna, the pioneer woman that cared about her past and wanted to pass it on to future generations, was gone. Anna knew in her heart she had lived through a historic part of the history of this country, and she related it in vivid detail so it could be preserved. Jessie was made heartsick by her mother's death, but celebrated the long, rich life she had lived. Anna was and always would be an inspiration to Jessie—a pioneer lady, strong morally and spiritually. The details of her life's story would be treasured for generations to come.

OTTO AND ANNA ON THE FRONT STEPS OF THEIR HOME

OTTO AND ANNA SPENKER

WORLD WAR II

ON DECEMBER 7, 1941, the Japanese bombed Pearl Harbor and the United States was instantly plunged into the war. This attack was not caused by political maneuvering, as so many wars have been in the past, this was a major assault that electrified the entire nation. Every citizen, regardless of sex or age, was outraged and fully accepted the need to go to war. Everyone wanted to know what they could do. Men volunteered for the service. Women went to work in factories, manufacturing the weapons of war, and the name "Rosie the Riveter" was born.

Americans were terrified of another Japanese attack, but attention was focused on England and Europe. Immediately after President Roosevelt asked Congress to declare war on Japan, Japan's "Axis" allies, Germany and Italy, declared war on the United States and World War II had begun for the United States.

Herbert Woock, Anita's husband, was a veteran of World War I and commander of the American Legion post in Lodi. Beginning on December 8, he worked with the community leaders organizing air raid practices and blackout procedures. The siren could go off at any time, and everyone had their instructions. In schools, all children were to climb under their desks while the teacher turned off the lights and shut the door. They were to remain this way until the all-clear siren sounded. If you were out in a car, you were to pull over to the side of the road, stop, and turn off your lights. At home, you were to turn off all power sources, shut all doors and windows, go to the most interior room of the house and close the door.

After the passage of Presidents Roosevelt's Executive Order #9066 on February 19, 1942, Herbert worked with the FBI on plans for the removal of approximately one hundred and ten thousand Japanese-Americans living on the Pacific coast. Nearly two thirds of them were American citizens. The evacuation was set to begin on May 18, with 2,980 coming from northern San Joaquin county who were taken to temporary accommodations at the Stockton Fair grounds. Four months later they were relocated in permanent camps at Tule Lake and in the Mojave desert in California, and to locations in Colorado, Utah, Arkansas, and other interior states.

War on two fronts galvanized the country into action. All the men of required age were called into service, and other people went into the war plants. The people who had been so destitute in the Dust Bowl found work, and at wages they had only dreamed. To ease the labor shortage, the government initiated the Bracero program to bring Mexican nationals to agricultural areas. Farmers were required to provide housing while the workers were on their ranch. During the war, the federal government ordered all major distilleries to convert to the manufacture of commercial alcohol for munitions and all Thompson seedless grapes to be made into raisins for the armed forces and allies.

Jessie's son Joseph was thirty-eight years old in 1941. His age and his work as a farmer exempted him from the draft. Anita hoped that her son, Delwin, who was fourteen, would avoid the war.

VERA'S HUSBAND ED PERRIN, A GRADUATE OF ANNAPOLIS, BECAME THE CHIEF INSTRUCTOR IN THE RADIO-RADAR DEPARTMENT AT MCCLELLAN AIR FIELD IN SACRAMENTO. THE TRAINING WAS FOCUSED ON THE REPAIR OF FIGHTER PLANES.

ED, SECOND FROM THE RIGHT, INSTRUCTING HIS STUDENTS. THE PLANE IN THIS PHOTOGRAPH IS A P39 AIRACOBRA.

IMPORTANT INSTRUCTIONS

1. Coupons can be used only in connection with the vehicle described on the front cover. Detached coupons are VOID.
2. If you stop using your car, this book and all unused coupons must be surrendered to your Board within 5 days.
3. If you sell your car, this book and all unused coupons must be surrendered to your Board. The purchaser will not be issued a gasoline ration unless he presents the receipt which you receive at the time of such surrender.

☆ GPO

FOLD HERE

A BASIC MILEAGE RATION

UNITED STATES OF AMERICA
OFFICE OF PRICE ADMINISTRATION

NAME OF REGISTERED OWNER
Jessie S. Beckman
ADDRESS—NUMBER AND STREET
923 S. Pleasant
CITY AND STATE
Lodi 7 Calif.
LICENSE No. AND STATE | YEAR MODEL AND MAKE
25C592 Cal. | 1941 Pontiac Sed.

Holder must fill in any blank spaces above before the first purchase of gasoline.

318647

OPA FORM R-525 C
A17
MILEAGE
318647
(License No.) (State)

OPA FORM R-525 C
A16
MILEAGE
318647
(License No.) (State)

RATION COUPONS FOR GASOLINE

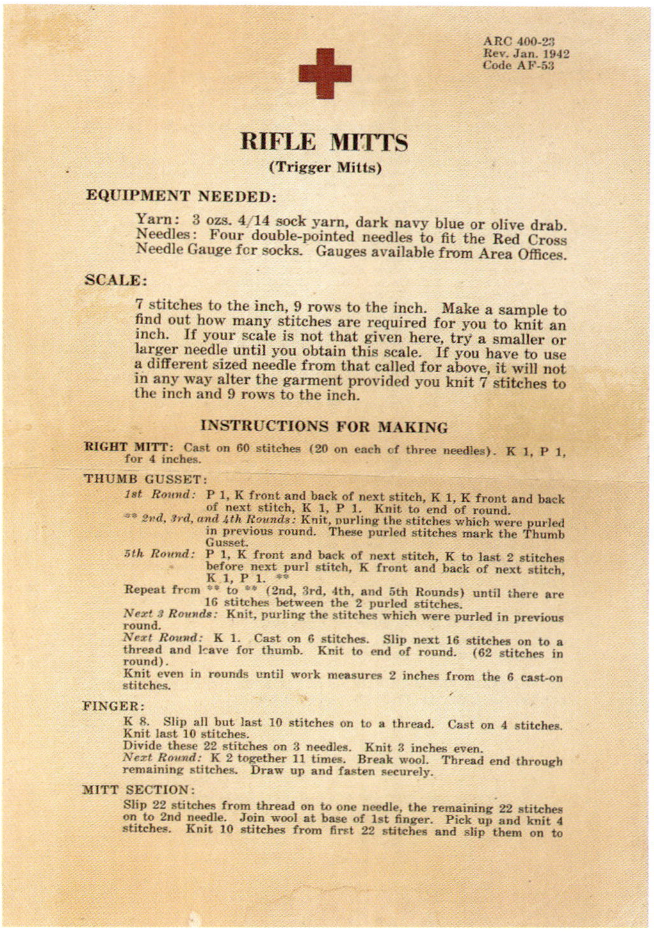

ARC 400-23
Rev. Jan. 1942
Code AF-53

RIFLE MITTS

(Trigger Mitts)

EQUIPMENT NEEDED:

Yarn: 3 ozs. 4/14 sock yarn, dark navy blue or olive drab.
Needles: Four double-pointed needles to fit the Red Cross Needle Gauge for socks. Gauges available from Area Offices.

SCALE:

7 stitches to the inch, 9 rows to the inch. Make a sample to find out how many stitches are required for you to knit an inch. If your scale is not that given here, try a smaller or larger needle until you obtain this scale. If you have to use a different sized needle from that called for above, it will not in any way alter the garment provided you knit 7 stitches to the inch and 9 rows to the inch.

INSTRUCTIONS FOR MAKING

RIGHT MITT: Cast on 60 stitches (20 on each of three needles). K 1, P 1, for 4 inches.

THUMB GUSSET:

1st Round: P 1, K front and back of next stitch, K 1, K front and back of next stitch, K 1, P 1. Knit to end of round.
** *2nd, 3rd, and 4th Rounds:* Knit, purling the stitches which were purled in previous round. These purled stitches mark the Thumb Gusset.
5th Round: P 1, K front and back of next stitch, K to last 2 stitches before next purl stitch, K front and back of next stitch, K 1, P 1. **
Repeat from ** to ** (2nd, 3rd, 4th, and 5th Rounds) until there are 16 stitches between the 2 purled stitches.
Next 3 Rounds: Knit, purling the stitches which were purled in previous round.
Next Round: K 1. Cast on 6 stitches. Slip next 16 stitches on to a thread and leave for thumb. Knit to end of round. (62 stitches in round).
Knit even in rounds until work measures 2 inches from the 6 cast-on stitches.

FINGER:

K 8. Slip all but last 10 stitches on to a thread. Cast on 4 stitches. Knit last 10 stitches.
Divide these 22 stitches on 3 needles. Knit 3 inches even.
Next Round: K 2 together 11 times. Break wool. Thread end through remaining stitches. Draw up and fasten securely.

MITT SECTION:

Slip 22 stitches from thread on to one needle, the remaining 22 stitches on to 2nd needle. Join wool at base of 1st finger. Pick up and knit 4 stitches. Knit 10 stitches from first 22 stitches and slip them on to

Gasoline rationing was strictly enforced, and some items—such as meat, butter, and even shoes were rationed. Sugar was under the strictest rationing because the United States was importing 62 percent of the sugar it used, and large amounts of sugar were needed in the manufacturing of alcohol for explosives.

Jessie was eager to help in any way possible. She again joined the Red Cross and spent countless hours doing the different assignments they had for housewives. Vera and Jessie spent every spare moment knitting sweaters, socks, or rifle mitts.

JESSIE AND VERA KNITTING RIFLE MITTS

Horrifying news started arriving from the war front. Hitler's plans to take over Europe were now open and obvious. No country was too large or remote to stop his forces, and it appeared he was confident of the success of his goal. With his blitzkrieg strategy, using fast-moving tanks in division size units with infantry supported by Luftwaffe fighter planes, Hitler appeared undefeatable. By the end of 1941, Nazi Germany dominated the European continent.

In the summer of 1941, the confident Hitler led his forces into Russia—deep into Russia, to attack Leningrad, and then winter started. Winter was Russia's strongest defense with the massive, vast frozen plains. German troops marched into the frigid land. Supplies ran out, men froze, and the battle was smothered in snow and ice. Leningrad did not fall to German forces. Germany's losses were staggering. *"For the first time in more than two years of unbroken military victories, the armies of Hitler were retreating before a superior force. December 6, 1941, is another turning point in the short history of the Third Reich and one of the most fateful ones. Hitler's power had reached its zenith; from now on it was to decline, sapped by the growing counterblows of the nations against which he had chosen to make aggressive war."*[9]

By the second half of 1943, the Allies had defeated the German U-boat submarine threat. Now supplies and troops could be successfully transported to Europe. In 1944, the Allies effectively established air superiority over western Europe and United States troops, along with British and Canadian troops, landed on the beaches of Normandy. This massive invasion started to drive Hitler's troops out of France. Russia started attacking German forces at the same time in their country. They drove Hitler's army out of Russia and continued on into Poland, Czechoslovakia, Hungary, and Romania.

In 1945, the German regime started to collapse. Russia occupied the eastern third of Germany, and the other allies moved into the north, south, and west of Berlin. On April 30, Adolph Hitler committed suicide, and Germany surrendered on May 8, 1945. One of the most evil men in history had finally come to his death by his own hand amid the destruction of his country. His name will be vilified for generations to come throughout the world.

On September 2, 1945, Japan surrendered, and the world was finally at peace.

[9] William L. Shirer, *The Rise and Fall of the Third Reich*, Fawcett Books, 1959, p. 1132.

PEACE

AT THE END OF THE WAR, Jessie and her family, along with the entire country, felt an overwhelming relief. People were eager to make up for the lost years. Industries were in high gear to meet the demands of a populace that had made money during the war. Cars were rolling off the assembly lines, and television sets were appearing in more and more homes.

After the war, grape prices skyrocketed, with prices going to $100.00 per ton. This same historic year, 1946, saw the largest shipment of grapes from Lodi Vineyard Association go to eastern markets. The demand for the Flame Tokay continued strong, and Ed Kurtz, one of the largest shippers in the Lodi district, was farming 1,100 acres of the popular grape.

In 1946, Jessie finally started hearing from Westphalen again. His letters were heartbreaking, and she could well imagine even he was better off than many people in Europe after this terrible war. She never heard from her aunt, even after numerous attempts to contact her. Jessie feared she had not survived.

August 9th, 1946
Dear Jessie,

Our house is still intact by some miracle. Most of our neighbors are living in the cellar. We almost have no intact window panes left in the whole house. Glass is hard to get, so we have to nail the windows shut with boards. You have to do what you can. Not much hope left at the age of 78. Before the war I weighed 210 pounds and now I weigh 140. Who would have thought that we would have to go through this misery at our age. I used to make good money in India, had my own home. Now the old people are emaciated, stooped over from lack of food—all because of the horrible War. Crippled people wherever you look. If only we had a United States of Europe already, then there would be no more war.

October 14th, 1946

Dear Jessie, I am so happy whenever a letter comes from you. The last one took four weeks to arrive. One wonders how many hands it went through.

It is horrible to think what the coming winter will bring us. If you would see the old people walking along the street, pale and hungry, your heart would melt. The young folks don't feel it so hard, they get used to it. We have very little bread and for a whole month only one fifth of a kilo of fat. So we eat vegetables without. There are people here which have relations or friends in the states. They had several times got parcels from them, lard or corned beef. Then I said to my better half I would write to you, perhaps you could help us over the coming winter by sending us a little box with some smoked lard (bacon) we would be so thankful. I don't like to beg, I never did—but for my poor wife I would do anything. I would send you something nice for it. That is what we need some fat. You can believe me that I would not ask you if it was not out of bitter need. If you see that the wife is getting everyday thinner and weak, anybody will try to alter it. I was a little ashamed first, so I wrote a second and third letter to you, the last one in German. Finally I am sending this one to you with deepest thanks.

We have to wash without soap. The soap we get here breaks apart like dust. You can imagine how everything smells, when we have worn things over and over for 8 years and no soap to wash.

Please let me know what language you prefer that I write. The paper is coming to an end, and it's difficult to get too.

Best wishes, Westphalen

October 28, 1946

We were and are having a horrible time, believe me. What can a little person do against such things? Just sit still. Our country tumbled back at least 58 years, and that's how long it'll take to repair the damage. By then, we'll watch from above. What I saw today in Bonn would break your heart. This once beautiful city is in total ruin, and thousands of people are buried under the rubble. This awful war has brought so much suffering to the world—you can't imagine. And all the broken people are not the ones to blame. The others who are responsible can never justify it to God.

September 28, 1946

My grandson (the one who lost his arm) was with us. We three, was one week going to the woods, 1? hours from here. We sought the little fruits from the beech trees. They are little three-cornered fruits and it takes eight hours to gather one pound and a half. But still we will have pressed oil out of them at the mill. They are not good to gather with my heavy hands—they are so little. You need 12 pounds to give one liter of oil, and the woods are swarmed with people to gather them. People are desperate for fat. It's been missing for five years. Try to eat potatoes or green vegetables without some fat.

December 13, 1946

I want to take the opportunity to thank you for all your efforts. Yes, we have been through very bad times. When one doesn't have enough to live it is truly horrible. Lately we have hardly felt the hunger pains, it's very bad. Just due to your generosity and love of humanity have we finally had a good meal again. We therefore had a wonderful day today, joyous for both of us. I hope to God he will reward you and again thank you so much for everything. I wish you a Merry Christmas and a very Happy New Year.

Your family, Westphalen

On May 14, 1947 Westphalen wrote:

Things are worse than before. We can only get a little corn flour, and it tastes like sawdust. No more meat, even though I waited in line for 2 hours. We have to accept it. On the black market you have to pay $300 for a sack of wheat! You can imagine how happy we are when we receive one of the packages from across the "big pond." We are becoming more & more indebted to you. I am sending you a very special ring in gratitude for all you have done. I hope it arrives safely.

Jessie's heart ached for them. She read Westphalen's letters to the ladies at St. Peter's Lutheran church and to the people at the Red Cross. She organized drives to collect items to send to the devastated people of Europe. She took contributions and bought the food needed so desperately. She had been warned to send more little parcels than one big one, because many times some never arrived at their destination. Jessie continued her dedicated helping of these people, and encouraged many others to help the people in need in war-ravaged Europe, for many years after peace had been declared. Unfortunately the "very special ring" did not make it through the mail to Jessie.

JESSIE

IN 1949, JESSIE WAS SEVENTY-FOUR YEARS OLD. Vera's husband Ed had passed away, and she and Jessie lived together in the house on Pleasant Avenue in Lodi. Jessie continued her close supervision of all the ranch property and her son, Joe, came over every morning for a conference about the ranches and how they would be managed.

The late forty's and early fifty's brought many different opportunities to Jessie to develop the oak grove. It was considered to be prime property and an ideal location for exclusive home sites. Jessie emphatically rejected all and any ideas to change the grove.

Jessie, the grand Christian lady who experienced two world wars, saw women gain the right to vote, held out a helping hand to countless people in this country and in Europe, and successfully managed three large ranches until shortly before her death, died in 1952. Jessie was seventy seven years old. Jessie patterned her life to follow in her father's noble footsteps, and succeeded in every step of the way.

Jessie was a true pioneer lady of the San Joaquin Valley.

JESSIE

SAN JOAQUIN VALLEY

THE YEARS AFTER WORLD WAR II were prosperous ones in the San Joaquin Valley. Farm prices remained high, and the grape industry continued to be strong with the Tokays leading the way. Approximately twenty-two thousand acres of Tokays were planted in the Lodi area. They remained a very popular eating grape and made excellent brandy, port and sherry wine, which were sweet and often had an alcohol content of 17 to 21 percent. More wineries started opening in Lodi, and the emphasis remained on the fortified wines.

At the same time, Napa and Sonoma Counties were also developing a group of wineries. In contrast to Lodi, they were concentrating on the increasingly popular California table wines, using such grapes as Zinfandel, Chardonnay, and Chenin Blanc. These produced a "lighter" wine with less sugar and alcohol.

In the late 1950s, it was apparent the market was in transition, and a group of farmers and winemakers, under the encouragement of the San Joaquin County farm advisor, Jim Kissler, started growing grapes for the table wine market. Varieties such as Zinfandel, French Colombard, Chardonnay, Chenin Blanc, and Barbara were suggested and the once famous Tokay grape gradually lost its sovereignty. Lodi, the district that Leon D. Adams described as "viticulturally unique,"[10] entered the market of fine wine. As in the past, Lodi's incomparable climate produced exceptional products of superior quality and the new varieties of grapes flourished.

The cycle was once again changing, as it had so many times over the past hundred years in the San Joaquin Valley. The same valley that raised the largest wheat crop in the world, watermelons and Tokay grapes that could not be equaled anywhere else, was now embarking on an impressive future in the world of fine wine. The vines planted by Joseph and Jessie are treasured for their age, outstanding quality and flavor. Joseph would have been proud of the Lodi area where he decided to settle after his long voyage over a hundred and fifty years ago.

[10] Leon D. Adams, "The Wines of America," 2nd Edition, 1978, p. 410.

PICKING THE ZINFANDEL GRAPES JOSEPH PLANTED IN 1889. PHOTOGRAPH BY NICK SIKEOTIS.

Epilogue

THIS HUNDRED YEAR STORY OF LIFE in the San Joaquin Valley has come to an end, but the valley continues to grow and change. At this time there are an estimated 783,000 acres of grapes planted in San Joaquin County. In Joseph's time the valley was a moving sea of grain stalks, now the scene has changed to rows upon rows of grapes vines.

Lodi, the small area in the San Joaquin Valley with the unique climate of warm sunny days and cool delta breezes in the evenings, along with deep sandy loam soil, is now growing grapes for the wine market. The quality of these grapes is gaining recognition throughout the industry, and has encouraged the development of a winery on Joseph's ranch, named in honor of his daughter, Jessie.

The winery follows in the family tradition with Jessie's great-grandson, Greg Burns, working as the managing partner in the vineyards and making the wine under the guidance and direction of our consulting winemaker Barry Gnekow for Jessie's Grove Winery. Jessie's great-granddaughter, Joline Meyer, has joined the work force by keeping the books for the ranch and winery. Joline has increased the authenticity of the ranch's antiquity with her beautiful horses. Horses were always an important part of the ranch, and thanks to Joline and her son, Dylan, they are back.

The Zinfandel vineyards, planted by Joseph, Otto and Jessie, have been carefully protected and preserved. Another old variety, planted by Joseph and Otto, is the Carignane. These grapes are also protected and valued for their age, and distinctive flavor. With careful pruning, monitoring of moisture, and thinning of the crops under Greg's supervision, along with the excellent soil found on this ranch, varieties can reach their maximum potential and produce outstanding wine.

Jessie's Grove Winery has won many awards in recent years. In 2002, they won the 20th Annual Atlantic International Wine Summit competition with Royal-Tee, made from the Zinfandel grapes Joseph planted in 1889. On October 3, 2003, they won first place in a contest in New York City sponsored by The Wall Street Journal for Zinfandel wine with their Vintner's Choice. In April of 2004, Vintner's Choice won "Best Pacific Rim Red Wine" in the Pacific Rim International Wine Competition held in San Bernardino, California. The same month their Carignane won "Gold Medal and Best of Class" from the 2004 West Coast Wine Competition. In May of 2004, their West Wind Zinfandel won "Best of Show" in the New Orleans Food and Wine Extravaganza. Joseph would be proud of the grapes he planted so many years ago.

Nick Sikeotis has joined the group, and is the winery president and sales manager for Jessie's Grove Winery. He has introduced our wines to many restaurants and to popular markets across the United States. Nick has also revived Saturday events in the oak grove which feature popular musical groups and dramatic productions. These events bring back the time when Otto managed picnics in the oak grove.

The wine-tasting room is housed in one of the oldest buildings on the ranch—dating back to 1874. A small museum is included in this room, and there is a collection of prized photographs on the walls to help the visitor imagine what the early days were like. Improvements on the ranch have been developed with careful emphasis placed on retaining the original integrity of the old buildings and grounds. Artifacts are placed with care so they can be appreciated by the visiting public.

You are Invited

Come—step back in time,
walk through Joseph's ranch,
Anna's house,
the oak grove Joseph and Jessie saved.

Come—visit Jessie's Grove Winery,
walk through our museum,
taste our award-winning wines.

Sip the wine and imagine what it was like to live

Way
Back
Then

in

The San Joaquin Valley.

PHOTOGRAPH BY JON BJORK

Chronology

1854	Joseph arrives in America
1859	Joseph joins a covered wagon train and goes to California
1861	Start of the Civil War
1863	Start of construction of transcontinental railroad
1865	End of the Civil War
1869	Completion of transcontinental railroad
1869	Anna arrives in California
1870	Anna marries Joseph
1871	Otto is born
1875	Jessie is born
1879	First grapes shipped east from Lodi
1888	Thomas Edison starts to manufacture phonographs
1890	San Joaquin County raises largest wheat crop in the world
1896	Henry Ford builds his first car
1901	The Pan-American Exposition
1906	San Francisco earthquake
1906	Benjamin Holt develops the caterpillar tractor
1908	Ford produces the Model T
1911	Jessie votes in a state election
1916	Joseph Spenker passed away
1917	"Great War" starts
1918	Peace
1919	Eighteenth Amendment passes—Prohibition
1920	Nineteenth Amendment passes—women's right to vote in national elections
1929	Stock market crash—start of the Great Depression
1930	Dust Bowl
1933	Twenty-First Amendment ends Prohibition
1937	Rural Electrification Act passed
1939	World War II starts in Europe
1940	Otto passed away
1941	Anna passed away
1941	Japan bombs Pearl Harbor—United States enters World War II
1945	World War II ends
1952	Jessie passed away

Family Tree

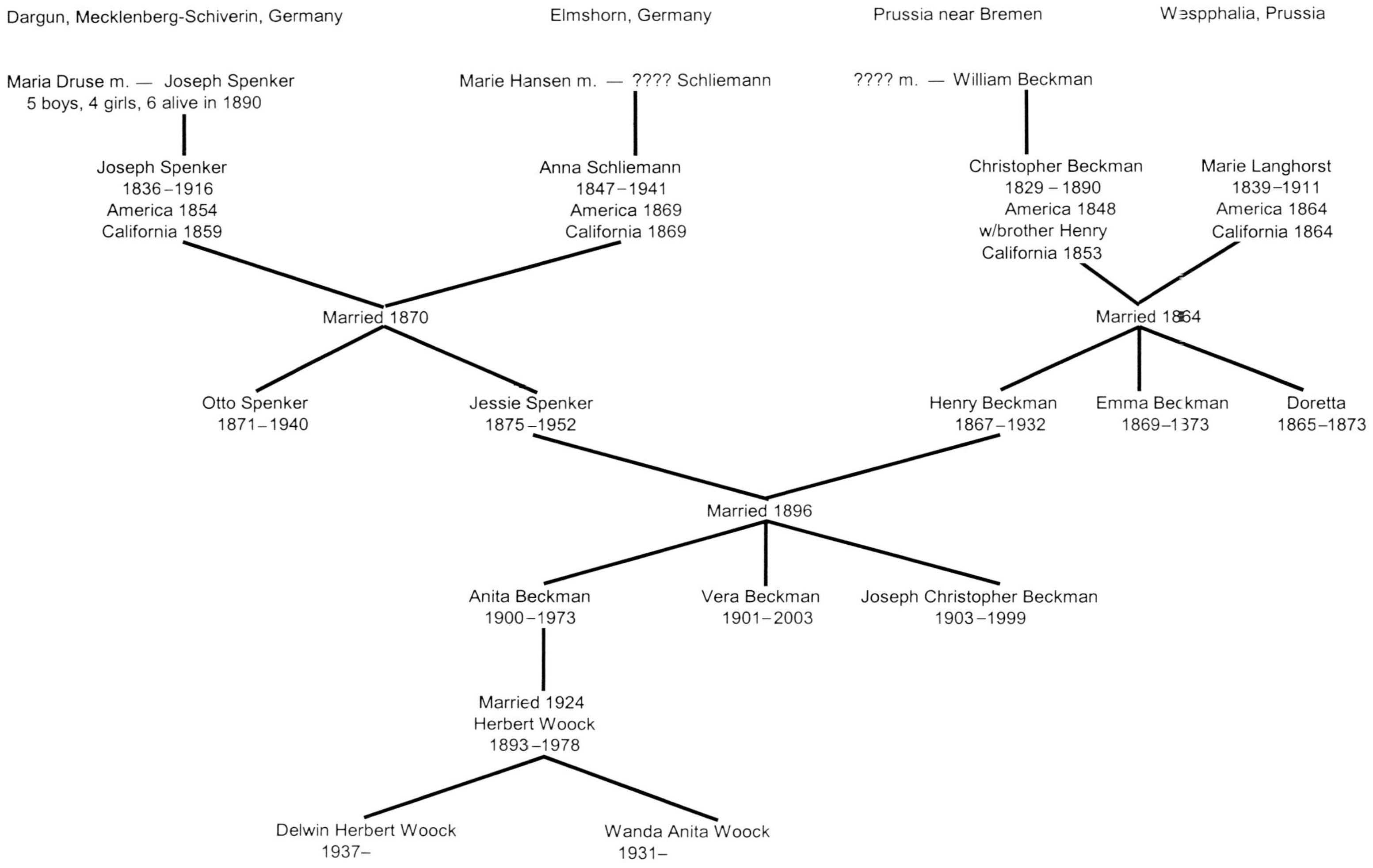
Dargun, Mecklenberg-Schiverin, Germany
Elmshorn, Germany
Prussia near Bremen
Wespphalia, Prussia
Maria Druse m. — Joseph Spenker
5 boys, 4 girls, 6 alive in 1890
Marie Hansen m. — ???? Schliemann
???? m. — William Beckman
Joseph Spenker
1836–1916
America 1854
California 1859
Anna Schliemann
1847–1941
America 1869
California 1869
Christopher Beckman
1829 – 1890
America 1848
w/brother Henry
California 1853
Marie Langhorst
1839–1911
America 1864
California 1864
Married 1870
Married 1864
Otto Spenker
1871–1940
Jessie Spenker
1875–1952
Henry Beckman
1867–1932
Emma Beckman
1869–1373
Doretta
1865–1873
Married 1896
Anita Beckman
1900–1973
Vera Beckman
1901–2003
Joseph Christopher Beckman
1903–1999
Married 1924
Herbert Woock
1893–1978
Delwin Herbert Woock
1937–
Wanda Anita Woock
1931–

Index